Ardis Reitan

ROOM OUTSIDE

A New Approach to Garden Design

John Brookes

PENGUIN BOOKS

PREFACE

The subject of landscape design is always a difficult one to locate in the categories of libraries and bookshops. Is it architecture, horticulture or the arts? I would like to suggest that it is certainly the last, and falls somewhere between the first two, so perhaps it should go on all three shelves! With this in mind I have tried to explain and illustrate the process of designing a garden which will not be merely a collection of plants but a usable extension of the home into the outdoor world.

I have tried to present the more obvious factors in the order in which they should be taken when working out the design and where detailed technical information is missing it should be sought from the hundreds of specialist books on the subject. The book is designed to be as basic and international as possible. Where specific plants or materials mentioned are not available locally, nearby nurseries and other specialists should be consulted for substitutions. Naturally, the instructions given by the grower or manufacturer on all plants and materials you buy should be followed closely.

Photographs and plans which are not credited to another landscape designer or architect are of my own work.

First published in 1969, this is a new paperback edition of the original. In the meantime, like everything else, the cost of printing has leapt up. So for this paperback the colour plates that appeared in the original have been dropped and other small alterations (and corrections) have been made.

Over the last ten years, the range of some of the materials – pots, seating and paving for instance – has increased. But the role that the garden can play as an extension of the home has not changed, and I believe the book is just as relevant now as when it was first written.

Penguin Books Ltd, Harmondsworth,
Middlesex, England
Penguin Books, 625 Madison Avenue,
New York, New York 10022, U.S.A.
Penguin Books Australia Ltd, Ringwood,
Victoria, Australia
Penguin Books Canada Limited, 2801 John Street,
Markham, Ontario, Canada L3R 1B4
Penguin Books (N.Z.) Ltd, 182–190 Wairau Road,
Auckland 10, New Zealand

First published in Great Britain by Thames and Hudson Ltd 1969
First published in the United States of America by The Viking Press 1970
Published in Penguin Books 1979

LIBRARY OF CONGRESS CATALOGING IN PUBLICATION DATA
Brookes, John, 1933–
Room outside.
Includes index.
1. Landscape gardening. I. Title.
SB473.B73 1979 712'.6 78-15387
ISBN 0 14 00.5077 9

Printed in Great Britain by
Jarrold and Sons Ltd, Norwich
Set in Monophoto Univers Medium 689

CONTENTS

INTRODUCTION

As working life becomes more and more hectic and communal pleasures more varied, it seems more than ever essential that the individual and his family should have some place into which they can retreat; somewhere quiet where they have time to think, and can enjoy and refresh themselves by re-establishing contact with nature.

If one looks at the garden throughout history this rôle as a place of escape has always been important. Nevertheless, this is only one of its uses, for a garden is fundamentally *a place for use by people*. It is not a static picture created in plants – the reason so many of our gardens fail is that we tend to follow a plan, in a nurseryman's catalogue or garden layout sheet, which perpetuates this picture-book ideal. Plants provide the props, colour and texture, but the garden is the stage, and its design should be determined by the uses it is intended to fulfil.

Until one has considered what one wants to do in a garden, how can a plan be provided for it? No two people are alike; their ages and interests will differ, as will their senses of scale, colour and form. How many kitchens and living rooms are alike? Many might have the same furniture and fittings in them but, despite twentieth-century standardization, they will all have been adapted by an individual personality and the end products will vary.

We have allowed ourselves to be conned into believing that the garden is only a set-piece for showing off plants, to be admired for perhaps two or three months of the summer, and not even looked at during the winter.

In whatever part of the world, and in whatever period of history, the garden has always adapted itself to the needs of the owner, whether providing a shelter from nature, or a retreat from the heat; a place for entertaining, for household use or, latterly, a place for parking the car. Plants are important, of course, but the first consideration should be the fitness of the garden for family use.

1 THE EVOLUTION OF GARDEN DESIGN AND USE

When Man first ceased to be a nomad and settled in one place, his instinct was to surround himself with a protective wall. Wild animals were obviously his foe, so he created a circular barrier round his dwelling, probably of thorn or scrub. Within this protection he was safe, his family and later his cattle were safe, and Man, or more probably Woman, first started to grow food. Over a period of centuries cultivation improved, probably with the organization of plants into rows. A crude form of irrigation was worked out and, through the linear requirements of these two, the garden eventually developed in square or rectangular form.

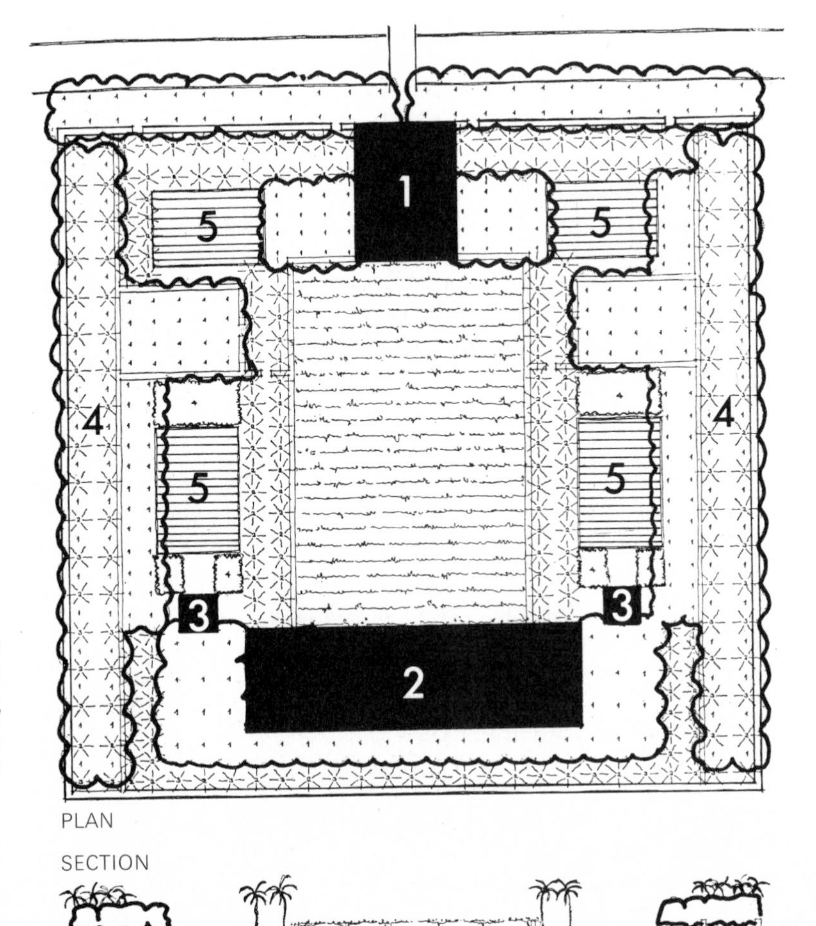

1 Plan and section of a garden at Thebes in Egypt (c. 1400 B.C.), showing the early dominance of rectilinear design. The enclosed garden is approached through a massive gateway opposite the house and contains walks, pools, and a central area covered with vines

1 *gateway*
2 *house*
3 *pavilions*
4 *vine-covered trellises or arbours*
5 *pools*

Egypt

Some of the earliest recorded gardens of which representations have come down to us were in Egypt. The scrub or thorn enclosure of primitive man had been replaced by a mud wall but, in the illustrations we possess, the house, or rather the palace, was still within the enclosure. The garden, with its shady palms and vine pergolas and its large tanks of water, was now a retreat not from wild beasts but from the overpowering heat of the Nile Valley. It was a private oasis, taking on a religious significance as the embodiment of coolness and beauty, food and water – a place offering peace and escape, shelter from cold winds and shade from the sun; a place where plants could grow and man could rest.

Persia

The private oasis or paradise garden reached the height of its development in the design of the Persian glorieta, and from this the Indian and later the Moorish garden evolved. The glorieta developed thousands of years after the Egyptian garden; man was now more concerned with aesthetics and wrote and sang of the qualities and beauties of his garden. The peak of the growing season in that region is in spring, before the dusty, all-absorbing heat of summer, and in the glorieta the fresh greenness of the new year was captured. The jewel-like conception of this private world appears in Persian art again and again. Its formal design is repeatedly recorded in the layout of Persian carpets – the cruciform shape represents the water canal in the centre with areas of planting around it. In this cool, sweetly scented atmosphere, life was lived outdoors, one sat, ate or made love on carpets laid on the ground, and it is easy to see how earth and water, sun and rain came to take on an overpowering mystic significance.

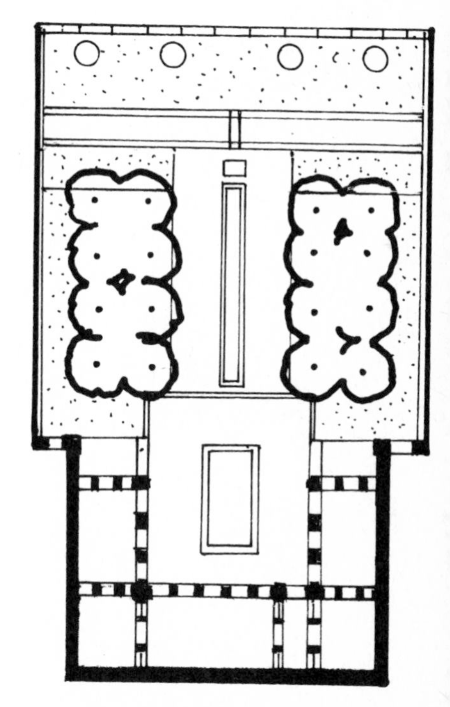

2 A reconstruction of a Persian courtyard garden. Pools of water run from the house down to a canal at the bottom of the garden. Shade is provided by blocks of trees

China

Further east successive Chinese dynasties had also endowed garden art with a high degree of mysticism. The garden was used to re-create on a small scale the 'awfulness' of untamed nature. It was a place in which to walk, sit, contemplate and draw refreshment from the realization of one's place in nature. The essence of the Chinese garden was transferred to Japan, where the style of the traditional garden layout is basically the same.

The Roman Empire

If the Chinese prayed or contemplated in their gardens, and the Persians sat in and wrote about theirs, it was the Romans who really used the garden in a more practical and domestic manner, bringing it into the centre of their houses. (The Greeks, incidentally, were not private or garden-minded – they lived more in public.) The Roman urban house developed round a central garden court called the atrium and a cloister or peristyle, which is the direct antecedent of our monastic cloister and court. The walls of the peristyle were painted with garden scenes, so that the whole became a sort of inside/outside room from which all the other rooms led off. The house presented a blank wall to the street and looked inwards to the quiet garden court which became the focal point and main living area where everything took place, including prayer – the family's god or gods being enshrined in a small formal layout at the centre. Still water or a well was probably also included in the layout, with perhaps a fig tree or a vine to give added shade.

The Roman country garden as described by the younger Pliny was larger and comparatively sophisticated, with sheltered areas for sitting and under-floor heating.

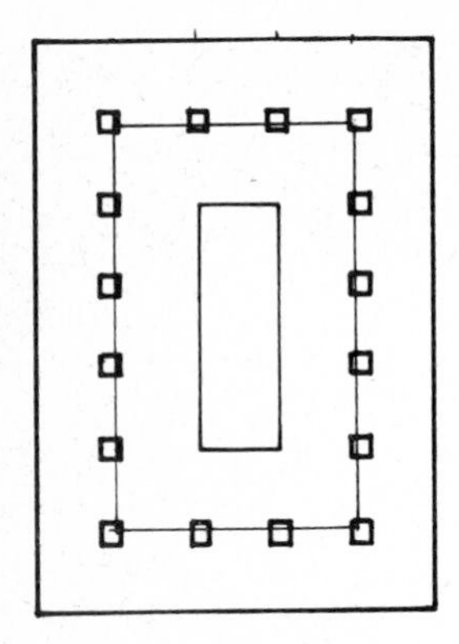

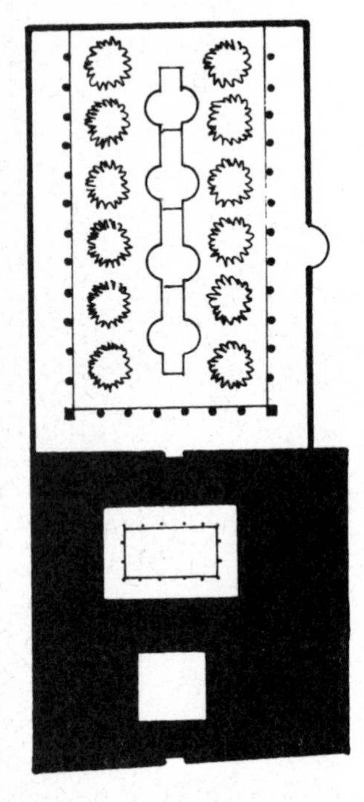

3, 4 Top: Plan of a garden at Pompeii. The house looks inwards on to a colonnaded peristyle, with the garden and pool in the centre. The surrounding walls may have been painted with trompe l'œil *garden scenes.*
The larger Roman houses (centre) had an outside garden, or xystus, as well. This was an axial layout with a central pool running out from the house

5 Right: The Alhambra, Granada. Elements of both the Roman and Persian garden can be seen in the courtyard complexes. The Court of Myrtles is in the centre

Spain

Areas of Spain were occupied by both Roman and Moorish invaders for considerable lengths of time, and the principles of the atrium garden and Persian glorieta were fused in the Moorish court. The best examples of this still exist at the Alhambra and Generalife in Granada, where we find not just one outside room, but a whole series of courts percolating through the complex of buildings, so that one is never sure whether one is inside or out. This is planning on a sumptuous scale with water providing the cooling element as in Persia, but used more adventurously to link each successive area, while the sound of its movement is exploited to enliven the deadening heat of summer. Canals, brimming and clear,

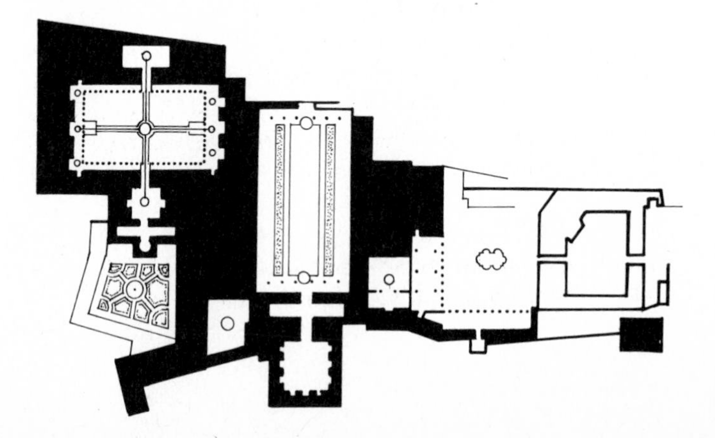

6 *Water canal and jets in the gardens of the Generalife, Granada*

produce superb reflections which are seen in their entirety only when sitting on the ground. The whole area forms a garden complex, perhaps more architectural than horticultural in design, for use by a court living outside in summer. It is scaled for communal living, but in such a way that both the individual and the assembly feel equally comfortable within it.

In these gardens the view is first used as an element in design, and nature is allowed to creep back into the private enclosure, though still held at a distance.

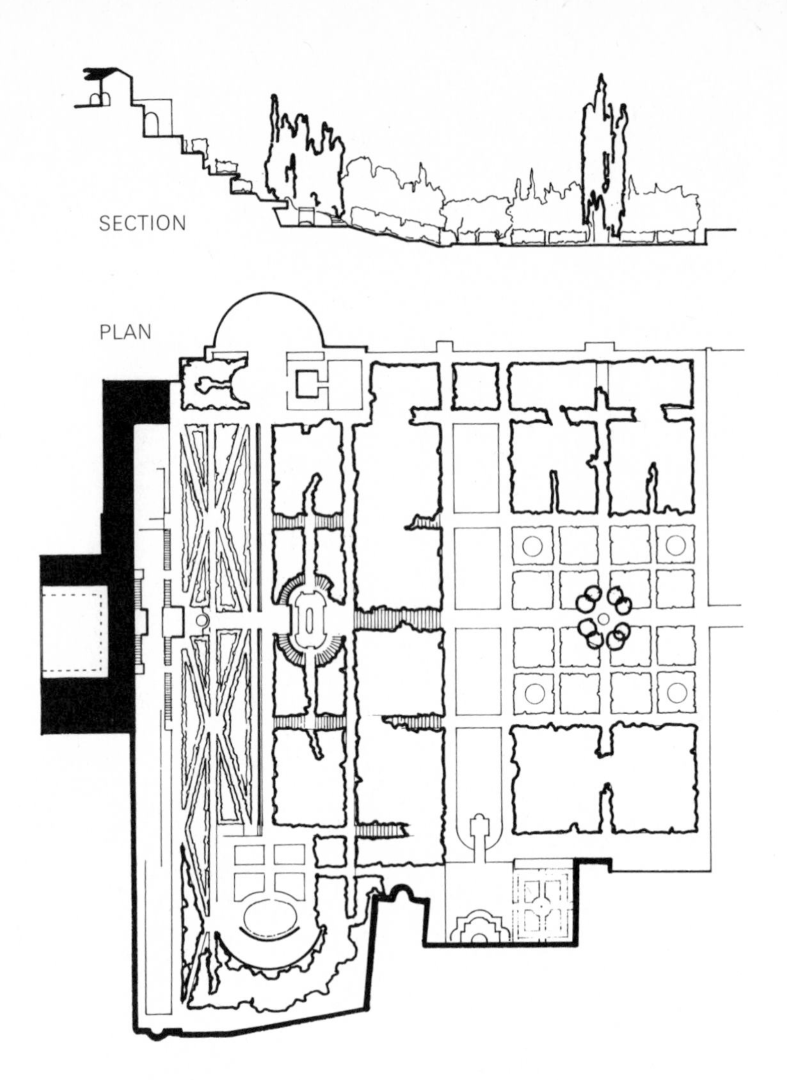

7 The gardens of Renaissance Italy owed much to Roman models. At the Villa d'Este the axial plan has been enlarged to give views running down the hill, but the garden is still enclosed. Water is a great feature and is used in many ways: still and running, in falls and fountains

Renaissance Italy

The formal gardens of the Italian Renaissance, although strongly architectural, were the first to make greater use of decorative plant material. Much of it, in the form of hedging, provided the architectural link between the house and the garden which is the distinguishing feature of the villas of the period. Planting formed the framework for these layouts, which were often carved out of a hillside, and it was also used to create effects within the composition – that of moving under trees from shade into light and back again, for instance, was a favourite in a climate where the light is strong and bright. In this setting, always accompanied by the cooling sound of rippling, playing or cascading water, the great of the day entertained and displayed their collections of statuary – often pirated from Roman ruins.

Seventeenth-century France

If the Italian Renaissance garden had a certain flamboyance about it, the French formal garden was decidedly for show. Laid out on similar lines, though on flat ground and in a temperate climate, it was designed primarily for court life, to be seen and used, often by several thousands. The French court and also lesser households tended to keep open house – in fact, Louis XIV insisted that his courtiers stayed at Versailles so that he could keep an eye on them. Thus the garden came to be used for theatrical productions, firework displays, mock water battles, or just as a promenading ground in which the members of the court could show off their finery.

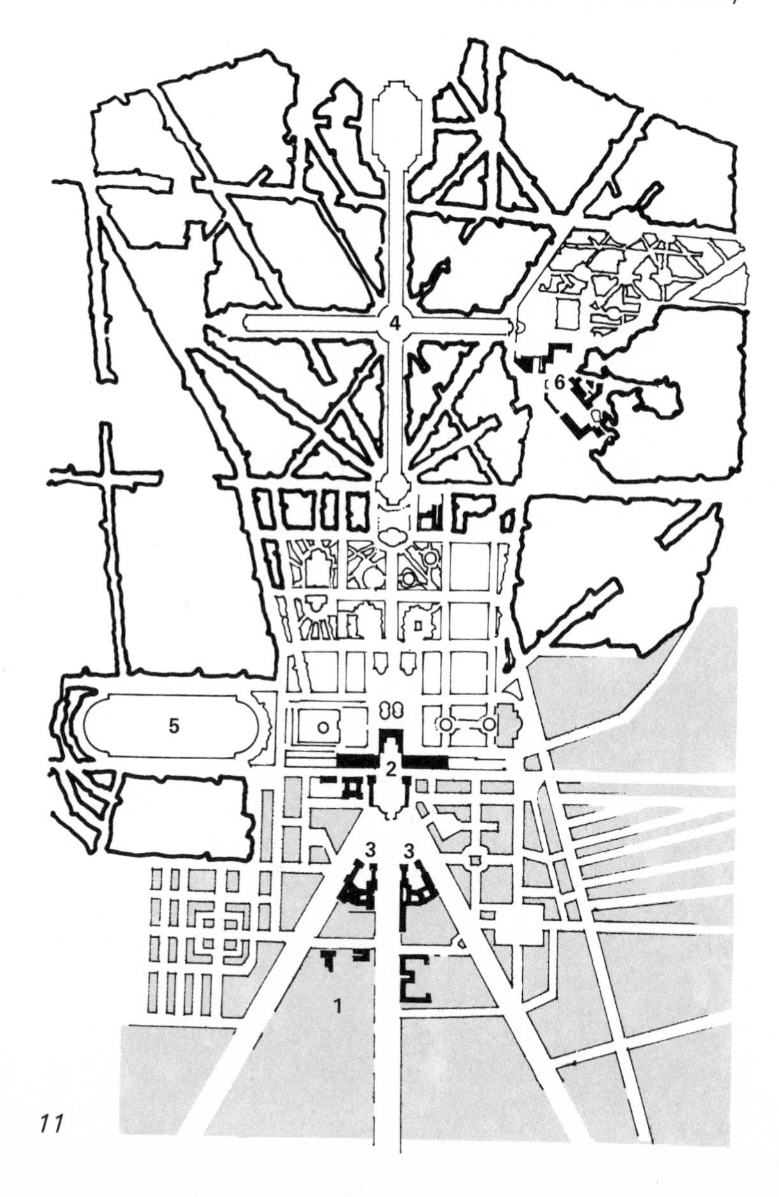

8 French Renaissance gardens, developed from the Italian garden, reached the ultimate in geometric layout at Versailles. Water is used in great canals and vast pools. Boundaries have disappeared and the garden pattern runs on into the surrounding town. Flat areas are developed as formal parterre gardens

1 *town*
2 *palace*
3 *stables*
4 *Grand Canal*
5 *Pièce d'Eau des Suisses*
6 *Grand Trianon and Petit Trianon*

It is little wonder, therefore, that floral display was unheard of, since sufficient colour was provided by the users. The French garden was probably the ultimate in design for use and display, although it is probably true that the domestic garden of today can take just as heavy wear in proportion to its smaller area.

Despite the need for public areas in both Italian and French gardens, the individual himself still often wished to withdraw into his own small green world to relax and refresh himself. Both types of garden therefore included a 'giardino segreto', a secret garden, hidden away for this purpose and walled about with greenery.

England

Before the development of the Renaissance gardens of France and Italy there had been a medieval type of formal walled garden, and in England this lasted until the fifteenth and sixteenth centuries.

9 The cloister of Lincoln Cathedral

After the fall of the Roman Empire the monasteries were the repositories of such culture as remained, and their buildings were laid out on the court and cloister plan after the Roman style. The monks used the courts for growing medicinal and culinary herbs and the pools to breed fish for eating.

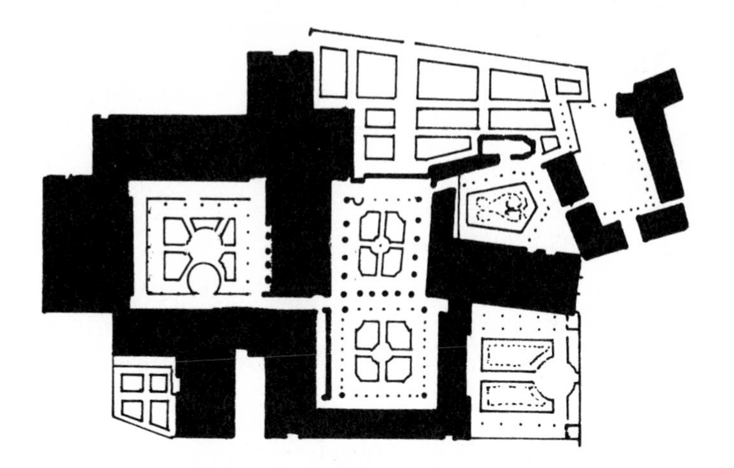

10, 11 During the Middle Ages the formal parterre layout was preserved on a smaller scale in the cloistered courtyards of monasteries and seats of learning, where it provided privacy and isolation from the outside world. Left: The Abbey of Citeaux, France. Above: The central part of Oxford showing the interlocking pattern of college buildings and courtyards

The great secular buildings of the Dark and Middle Ages were fortified houses and castles which had only a limited amount of garden space inside the walls. If anyone went beyond the walls it was probably only to hunt or fight, so the garden space was very much a place to be used. It was cultivated by the ladies of the household and provided them with a place to wander, bathe and take the air.

As times grew more peaceful, however, the encircling walls grew lower, the garden areas grew larger, and a simple formal pattern of garden design developed. This reached its culmination in the seventeenth century, though on a smaller scale than in France, for the English have never been so fond of show as the French and their gardens have always been places for family use; for sitting, strolling and meditating.

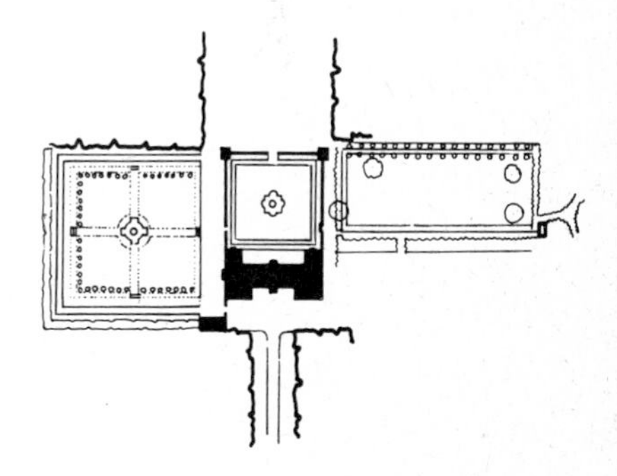

12 Medieval enclosure gradually relaxed as the necessity for it lessened, and views were opened up. At Montacute House in Somerset, the seventeenth-century garden has become an extension of the house, with relics of an earlier fortified enclosure still visible in the two gazebos at the corners of the wall. The pattern is still formal and axial

Eighteenth-century England

Not until the eighteenth century did garden design become a definite art form in England. It has been said that the landscape school developed in this period was our only truly indigenous export. The layout of the gentleman's park became a highly sophisticated aesthetic exercise, appreciated only by an upper class which was well travelled and versed in all the arts. This was a time when gardens were perhaps more talked about than used. The scale of the settings designed by Kent and Brown was not related to the individual and left

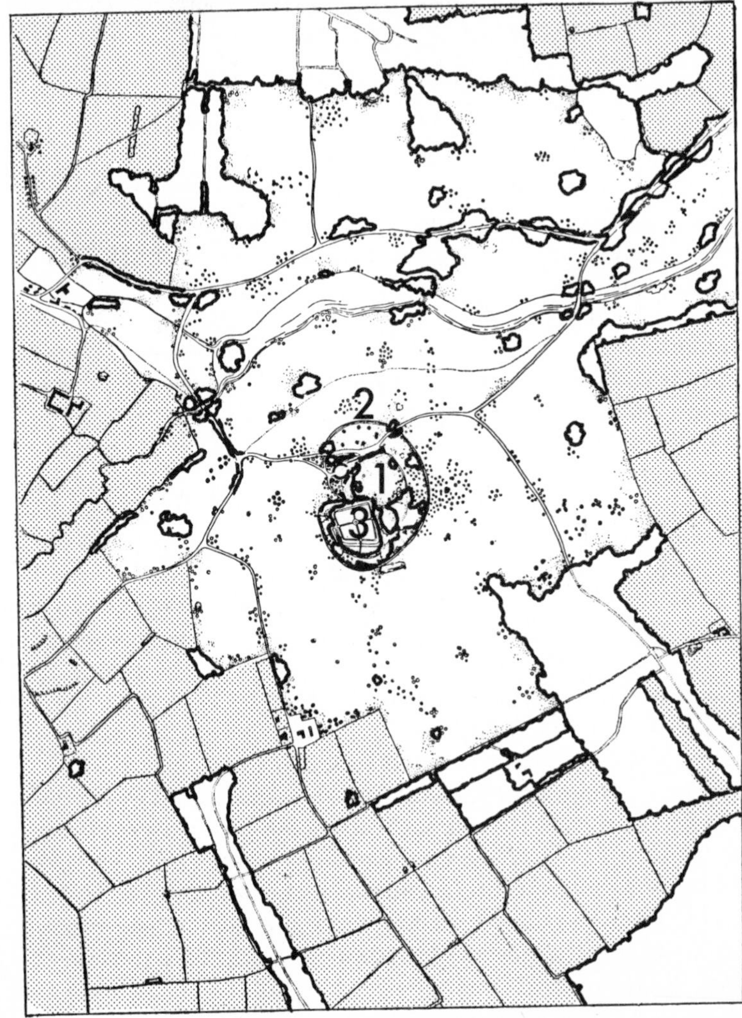

13, 14 Previous garden forms, on whatever scale, had always provided a garden for use, with enclosures and cultivated plants. The English informal garden of the eighteenth century, by contrast, was a picture – an idealized re-creation of natural landscape. Kent, Brown and Repton sought to do away with boundaries and let nature run right up to the house. Above: Shardeloes Park, Buckinghamshire, by Repton. Right: Heveningham, Suffolk, by Lancelot Brown

1 *house*
2 *ha-ha*
3 *vegetable garden*

no place for him, though there was a place for his deer, his strange sheep or highland cattle, as amusing decorations in an otherwise sublimely pastoral (some would say sublimely boring) landscape.

Nineteenth-century England

The new merchant classes of the early nineteenth century reacted against this with an intense desire to manipulate the garden. Though their villas and grounds were smaller they crammed as much as possible into them with the enthusiasm and heavy-handedness of the novice. The increasing use of iron brought metal furniture, statuary, urns, busts and conservatories, while reaction against the apparent austerity of the previous century and against the blackness of the Industrial Revolution created an insatiable craving for colour which brought exotic plants from China, India and the west of the United States. Repton, who succeeded Brown as the leading designer of his day, was faced with the dictums of the eighteenth century, the demands of the nineteenth, and the need to find a way of combining the two. Since he was not, however, a horticulturist, he probably found the increasing range of plant material on the market an embarrassment.

The nineteenth-century garden had now become a showground, in which one was allowed to stroll, but not at any cost to walk on the grass. It was as far from relaxed as the Victorians themselves, doubtless providing little profound pleasure to the owner, and even less to the gardeners who tended the tortured plants.

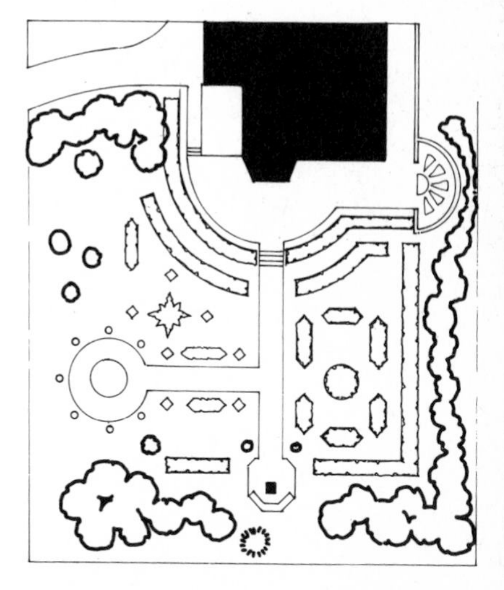

15 The nineteenth century produced a new gardening public, with smaller gardens. The essence of the eighteenth-century park was scaled down and natural plantings were replaced by recently-imported specimens. There was also a revival of interest in formal Italian garden layout. The result was a mess. A drawing from Hughes' Garden Architecture *(1866)*

William Robinson & Gertrude Jekyll

Towards the end of the nineteenth century people were beginning to tire of the harsh, contrived forms of the typical Victorian garden and an element of romanticism began to creep in. This coincided with the idea of the writer and gardener William Robinson of placing plants in a more natural setting as he had seen them growing in Alpine meadows. His contemporary, Gertrude Jekyll, called attention to the attractions of plants other than colour: leaf shape, texture, etc. She did not, however, neglect colour. Being much influenced by the Impressionists, she graded it carefully and worked her plants into superb groupings or borders, which were not entirely herbaceous but included a certain amount of shrub material.

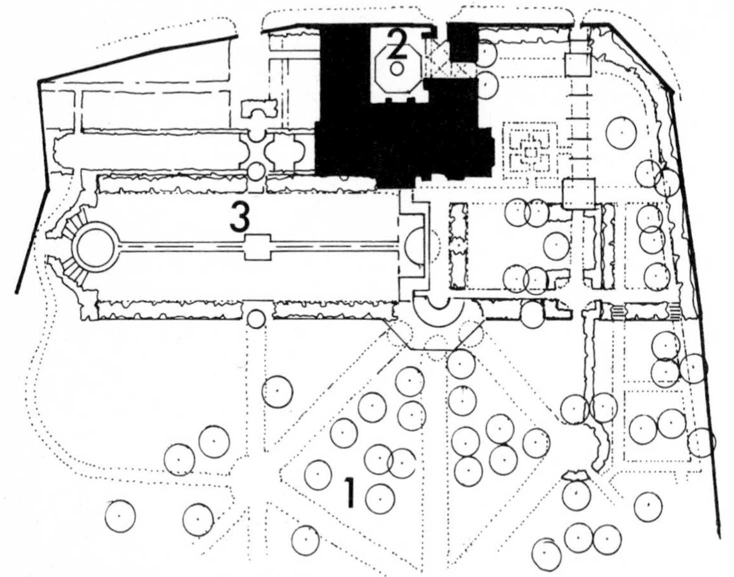

16 The architect Edwin Lutyens, whose garden designs were planted by Gertrude Jekyll, established a new type of formal layout. His garden has a succession of rooms contained in strong axial patterns running out from the house. The Deanery, Sonning

1 *wild garden*
2 *courtyard*
3 *canal garden*

17 The Colonial American garden was a utilitarian one in which bloom was incidental. It provided herbs used for medicine, food and dyes. Always enclosed, it lay just outside the doorway. At Old Sturbridge Village, Massachusetts.

Such gardens were created for country-house owners, whose considerable staff of gardeners staked, tied and cut down the plants throughout the year in addition to maintaining the kitchen garden. The owners were knowledgeable plantsmen, who walked round at weekends, perhaps with house parties, to admire the subtle effects. The garden was still a thing of show – a horticultural exercise – intended only for partial use on summer days: for croquet on the lawn, swimming, or perhaps tennis. The pattern was changing, however. Gardens were becoming smaller as labour grew less skilled and eventually all but unobtainable.

America

Meanwhile the American yard was evolving. The Spanish courtyard or patio had crossed the Atlantic to Mexico, South America and California, differing slightly in form due to climatic variations, and with added plants, but always in association with the house. From this a new twentieth-century style had developed – a style in which the garden was accepted as an additional room to the house, to be used by the family both by day and by night. The house was not planted dogmatically in the centre of the site, thus inevitably breaking up the garden into small unrelated areas at the back, front and sides, but was sited to take account of the sun, view and prevailing wind, while also leaving more open and usable garden space. For the first time the automobile had to be considered, its parking, access and garage. The swimming pool, the barbecue, outside seating: all were features to be incorporated, and the designs which evolved to encompass these amenities were no longer axial but took freer shapes and patterns from modern painting and sculpture.

From now on, a style of garden could be produced to suit the site, whatever its shape, without the restrictions of a formal geometric style. Once again the garden was an outside room designed to meet the needs of the people who owned it. After a hundred years garden design was becoming an art form again and plants were being relegated to their proper subsidiary rôle.

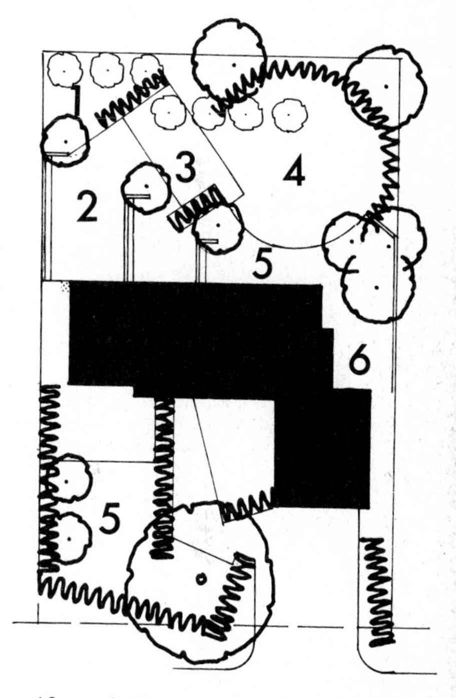

18 California garden-designers took all the previous elements of garden design and adapted them to the small lot surrounding the average house. Working within a formal but asymmetric design, they incorporated all the features needed for twentieth-century outside living. Garden designed by Garret Eckbo, 1945

1 *play area*
2 *children's yard*
3 *flower area*
4 *grass*
5 *terrace areas*
6 *service area*

Japan

The influence of Japanese garden design at its best led, not to the copying of the details of a style with deep religious significance which had been highly developed over hundreds of years, but to the appreciation of the joy of texture and

19 A Japanese garden: a flowing and restful pattern is built up by the controlled use of planting, rocks and water

shape not only in stone or water but in plants as well. Hand in hand with this love of individual shape the idea of the asymmetric or free-shaped garden was developed, in line with similar developments in art, architecture and sculpture.

Scandinavia

In Scandinavia the growing season is short. The winter is long, dark and very cold. Probably as a reaction to this comes the determination to get the most out of nature in a far shorter span of summer time, and to use all space to the full. Many Scandinavian summer houses are sited by lakes in heavily wooded areas of birch and pine, and this is the accepted flora of the garden surrounding the house. The garden-minded person may manipulate this type of vegetation and introduce more floral colour close to the house but he doesn't 'garden' it. In this way a more peaceful, less contrived, and certainly less demanding type of garden has evolved.

Scandinavian influence is also responsible for increased interest in the growing of house plants, and particularly the appreciation of their form and leaf shape. The English had always grown pot plants for colour, but this was a new approach – similar to that which Miss Jekyll had advocated, but applied to the indoor scene.

20 The decking and fencing of a garden by Lawrence Halprin pick up the timber structure of the house, creating an effect of serenity

During the earlier part of the twentieth century, the larger English gardens slowly declined as a result of labour difficulties. With the rise of a new affluent middle class, developers started building small suburban houses with the now typical front and back gardens and inevitable side passage. Any design contemplated was a scaling down of the Edwardian country garden. What had been a wide, sweeping path, suitable for a rural setting, was reduced to a mean, pseudo-rustic wriggle in the suburb. A pleasant formal garden on a large scale, with a pool and a summerhouse looking out over the fields beyond, when telescoped to suburban scale, became a pointless mess.
At the same time responsibility for plant breeding passed from the garden staff of the country house to the tradesman. The market was flooded with larger blooms, in more garish colours, with frills, stripes and doubles galore. Scent, foliage and stamina declined, and competitive horticultural shows encouraged this degeneration. So the small garden was not only ill-designed but ill-planted as well, and became a master to be served each weekend, by clipping, staking, mowing and weeding.
However, a new form of garden thinking started to emerge with the new architecture after the Second World War, particularly in America and in Scandinavia. Garden thinking in these countries had arrived at very similar conclusions through completely differing circumstances.

21 *A courtyard by Robert Zion*

2 WHAT DO YOU WANT?

What, one might ask, has all this history got to do with me and my plot? The answer is that one can draw two conclusions.

The first is a negative one. If, by studying gardens of the past, we can see that each evolved to meet the needs of people of a particular class, in a particular place, at a particular time in history, then we shall not be trapped into wholesale copying of these styles today. Too often the style of a house contrasts not only with the style of its interior but with that of the garden as well. The incongruity of a between-the-wars 'semi', with Regency furniture and a cottage-type garden must be obvious.

The positive conclusion to be drawn is that these historical gardens did meet the needs of their users, whether consciously designed to do so or not. The garden, whether large or small, was an extension of the house and the activities of the people in it. Just as the walls of the house gave privacy, so the enclosures of the garden acted as a screen from adverse elements. If these old gardens had not worked, there would not still be so many of them in an excellent state of preservation today.

To many the garden they have is still a time-consuming chore, offering no pleasure, privacy or shelter, and a constant burden which restricts other activities. This, then, is not a bad point at which to start when considering what one wants from a garden today.

What are your other activities besides the enjoyment of your garden? How much time can you afford, or do you want to spend in it? It is no good, when faced with an acre, saying that you will simply grass it all over for ease of maintenance since, over a period of time, this involves a lot of mowing – motor machine or not!

A fair assumption for an average family is that father works normal hours, 8 or 9 a.m. till 5 or 6 p.m. On summer evenings he might have two or three hours after eating which he could spend in the garden and possibly one day at the weekend, but this is generous, not allowing for normal social life and other activities. A normal housewife cannot usually spend much time outside (although she might more pleasantly do much of her housework in a well-designed garden when the weather is fine – sewing, shelling peas, ironing) and children usually do no work there, but make a lot of additional labour for those who do.

24 Small – the enclosed garden of a house at Halun Siedlung, Berne, Switzerland (right)

22

23

25 Large – part of a garden by Taylor and Green

Outside help is sometimes forthcoming for heavy cultivation in the winter, but usually only for unskilled work.

Consider how many weekends you spend away from home – not necessarily on holiday, but sailing or on business – and bear this in mind when thinking of a greenhouse or frame. Think of the summer holidays – do you go away for a fortnight or for six weeks? Consider not only how much time can be spent in the garden, but how much money as well. Do not overreach yourself and attempt too grand a layout, however suitable it might be, if the quality of the basic work will have to suffer through shortage of funds. All these broad issues will affect later planning.

Different age groups have different behaviour patterns and will accordingly need different features in the garden. If these are not considered from the start improvisations will have to be found which may wreck other features for other people. For instance, it is not unusual for two small boys to kick a ball about on a piece of grass or to play games, but if the piece of grass is surrounded by a herbaceous border, its chances of staying in prime condition for any length of time are remarkably small. This should be planned for. Thus it is worth considering what features various ages will require in their outside room.

Starting with the youngest: a warm sheltered corner with a hard dry surface, readily accessible and visible from the house, will be needed for a baby's pram. The same sort of area, only larger and with some light overhead structure for partial shade, will suit toddlers. A sand-pit, from which cats can be excluded and which will drain easily, would also be a good idea, as would some shallow water in which to splash about. This should be easy to empty in order to prevent birds bathing in it and depositing oil from their wings – starlings particularly do this. A deeper pool, raised to a child's shoulder height, might be an alternative and will serve to sail boats on or dabble fingers in.

As a child grows larger so does its collection of toys, and a store adjacent to the terrace is a good idea, so that things can be popped away when visitors arrive or when it rains. Space for a tricycle is often needed and if there is a hard, easily negotiable circuit to pedal round, so much the better. Care should be taken, however, to ensure that no harm can come to a child if it runs off the circuit, and some form of curb will prevent this.

Small personal plots are sometimes wanted for the children if they can be guided and encouraged in what to grow. The desire for a private little 'garden', preferably in a secret

26

27

28

corner, is fairly common. That the ensuing vegetation is probably nine-tenths weed is incidental.

The need to climb and explore seems to be inherent in all children at a particular stage, and the provision of some tree or structure will distract their attention from low roof-tops. It will be seen from any of the adventure playgrounds, of which there is now a large number, that children of this age seem to have no fear of heights and are full of ingenuity. No serious accidents have ever occurred on such playgrounds, so this form of play is less dangerous than it looks.

An area in which no damage can be done when playing with a ball is useful, although an area which is too small is worse than none at all, since the scale of the site must inhibit the scale of the activities.

In many households there tends, at a certain stage, to be a need for pets: rabbits, guinea pigs, etc. In my own home, in addition to the family dog, we seem to have had, in quick succession, a magpie, rabbits, white mice, and a mallard hatched by a bantam hen! Unless very well organized, pets' housing does not make an attractive feature and should be screened, although it would also be as well to locate it near the house, out of full sun and under cover.

29

The teenager will probably wish to sunbathe with friends, again on a sheltered terrace, and to swim if possible. A boy at the tinkering stage might require a toolshed, and hard standing for a boat, motor-bike or old car, and this too will need screening.

Some of these requirements will obviously overlap with those of the older generation. Quick-drying, hard terracing for sun, shelter and privacy is one; an area by the house is convenient for meals outside, and an area near the living room for evening entertaining is ideal.

30

31

32

33

A conservatory is often a useful halfway stage with inside-outside living and should be sited on the warm side of the house.
Special features for the old generation would probably include a lawn for practising golf shots or fly casting and, obviously, for playing tennis or croquet. There is something very evocative about the sound of croquet mallet and ball. Old people look for privacy in the garden with a sense of peace and tranquillity, and a warm corner for them to sit in is essential (though perhaps it should not be in direct sun). Beds which are easy to reach will be a help to them if they are gardeners, since they are often fond of the individual specimen and have time to appreciate the growth of plants.
There is a difference between hard manual labour, which should be kept to a minimum, and pottering. Pottering is to be recommended for anybody suffering from any form of nervous tension. It is one of the few pastimes which is completely relaxing and utterly absorbing. The love and attention lavished on house plants in the city flat proves, I think, the inherent need most of us feel to indulge in this activity. Pottering can often be made easier if beds are raised with a brick or stone wall which prevents stooping and serves as a useful seat as well. There are various gadgets on the market to help you get down to the garden, but it would seem to me far easier to bring it up to you!
Gardens which can incorporate some if not all of these features will automatically become gardens for people – outside spaces which are used – and, like French gardens,

34

although on a much smaller scale, they will not need so much horticultural effort in proportion to the pleasure they give. Plants provide the setting for the scene, but they should not be the sole star performers unless this is particularly required.

Over and above broad leisure uses to which a garden may be put are the fundamental domestic needs of many households, which should also fit into the pattern. Storage for toys has been mentioned, but storage is also necessary for the thousand and one tools and gadgets which any household seems to collect. If this can be built into the house, or adjacent to it where it cannot be seen and linked by a covered way, this is ideal, but too often the structure seems to take up the best position in the garden and become the focal point, unfortunately. Household rubbish receptacles must also have a place and again a corner is often now built into the house. Bear in mind, though, that in summer the bins may attract flies and they should not therefore be sited near a sitting area. If convenience dictates a position which is too prominent, it is a simple matter to build a timber structure in which to hide them. In another part of the garden it would probably be useful to have a place to tip garden rubbish and – if one chooses – to make compost of it. Sources of organic manure get harder and harder to track down, and any organic bulk to add to the garden improves it.

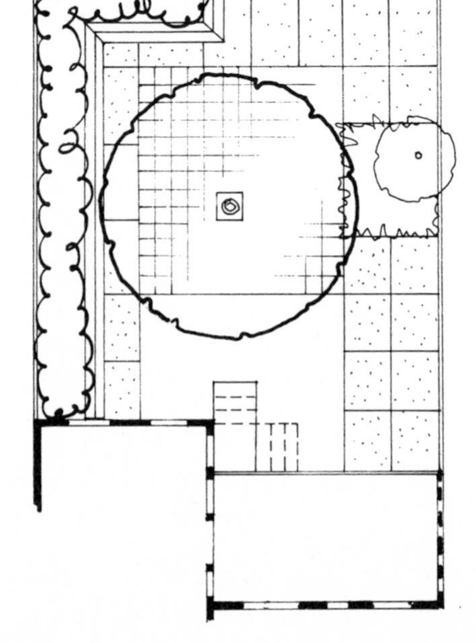

35, 36 Complete simplicity need not exclude character. Plan and picture, right: A garden in California designed by Lawrence Halprin to require the minimum of maintenance. Note the bench seat round the left-hand side

If vegetables are to be grown they should have an easy, clean access from the house and be as near as possible to it. A vegetable garden, if well managed, with herbs edging the beds as in the old walled kitchen gardens of country houses, can look very attractive. The average household, however, likes it to be screened, and fruit bushes – which are wasteful of space – can often be used for this. It is probably no longer economic to grow large areas of potatoes or cabbages, but smaller amounts of more choice vegetables are well worth the trouble. Many small areas with easy access are, therefore, probably better than two or three large beds. It should be possible at all times of the year to pop out and cut a lettuce or pick some sprouts without climbing into gumboots.

It goes without saying that when herbs are grown they should be as near the kitchen as possible. A herb area can be most attractive and can well be worked in with herbaceous plants or small shrubs, to make a decorative bed.

The designers of greenhouses seem to be curiously backward. It ought to be possible to produce a structure which is fairly inconspicuous but efficient. The pitched-roof types impose themselves too strongly upon a small garden and are difficult to work into the site, as obviously they should not be surrounded by large trees or shrubs. The lean-to is perhaps a more sympathetic shape, but not everyone has an outbuilding or wall for it to lean against, and some laws now require that it should not lean against the house. Siting must obviously be for optimum light, and the planning of the surrounding area should take this into account.

It is surprising how so small a thing as a washing line, even when out of use, can wreck a garden pattern under it. For many, happily, its days are numbered, thanks to the washing machine and the strict rules imposed by housing associations on hours of hanging, but those who need one should site it carefully with a hard, dry path underneath.

Lastly, we should consider the family cat or dog. It is quite useless to try to develop an area of planting which is constantly walked on, and strict training from an early age is the only way to stop a dog from doing this. Cats are more difficult to train, but I have found that by planting to create a dense mass one can at least deter them.

Unless one has either a vast area of grass, some of which can be left rough, or a very well-trained dog, it is better to give up the idea of a perfect lawn. An alternative might be a loose gravelled area which can be raked over after use by the offending animal. Perhaps a combination of lawn and gravel area would work with a well-trained pet.

37

3 WHAT HAVE YOU GOT?

38 Old, twisted privet stems, revealed during the thinning out of an overgrown shrubbery and retained as a feature

39–42 Below: Various methods of creating a point of interest

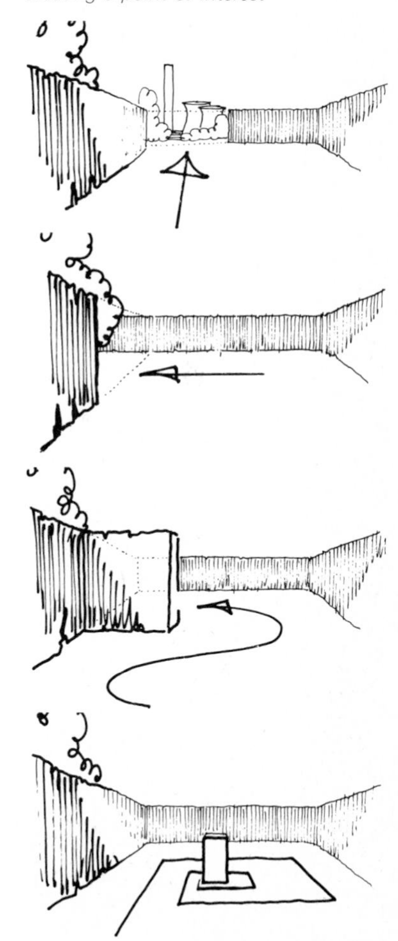

When evolving a design for a garden, one should consider not only what is wanted but also what is there already. Perhaps the most fortunate are those trying to develop an existing old garden with, say, the odd gnarled apple tree. However, on closer inspection of an apparently featureless new plot, there is usually something worth developing if one has an idea of what one is looking for. Perhaps it is a view; not a grand panoramic sweep, but a church tower for instance or a fine tree in an adjacent garden. Simply by screening round the area and leaving an opening to take in this view one can make a feature of it. Conversely it is often possible in the older, more established garden to open up a view by cutting down a strip of privet which has been screening it and, at the same time, to increase the apparent size of the area immeasurably.

When a site has nothing of note outside it, the design must turn inwards to create its own internal point of attraction.

In the initial eagerness of the layman to start from scratch, the site is often cleared completely and levelled – a particular crime of builders if they are not watched. This destroys any intrinsic feature of the site which could perhaps have been emphasized. Any change of level is to be welcomed and is a characteristic which can be exploited in several ways, without resorting to the all too frequent creation of a bastard rockery by sticking rocks into a bank. In fact it is often worth while introducing changes of level by altering the area on a cut-and-fill principle. A formal terraced effect can be achieved or a rolling, free enclosure created. The use of earth banks, subsequently planted or grassed over, as a means of both screening sound and breaking up the site generally, is not exploited enough in large gardens.

Care must always be taken, however, when excavating ground to keep the topsoil and subsoil separate. Whether excavating by hand or by machine, the procedure is to remove and stack the topsoil, adjust the level of the subsoil and then return the topsoil, raking to a finished gradient.

If a structure is being erected on the site, the excavated soil – or spoil – can often be put to good use; ensure, however, that the subsoil and topsoil are kept in separate heaps. It is worth digressing to explain the difference between these two and their fundamental importance.

43 The cut-and-fill method which can be used to create level areas and formal or contoured banks

SOIL

The depths of soil and subsoil layers vary in different parts of the country according to the hardness of the underlying rock and the amount of erosion it has suffered. Usually, the thicker the soil layer the more fertile it is, being richer in humus and the mineral elements essential for the nutrition of plants.

The formation of all topsoil depends on the process of surface weathering – rain, sun and frost all play their part in breaking up the parent rock. Chemical weathering also takes place along with biological decomposition; earthworms, for instance, are effective in bringing up soil particles from the lower layers to the surface, thus turning the soil as in digging and ploughing.

In some places the topsoil is not related to the parent rock and has been transported by some natural agency from another locality; glaciers, for instance, carry drift material forming a soil type known as boulder clay and this material bears no relation to the rocks beneath. Alluvial deposit washed down by a river is another example of transported soil.

Subsoil

There is no hard and fast line between subsoil, topsoil and rock, the first two being formed from the last. However, between the real topsoil or growing soil and the rocks beneath there is usually a fairly definite layer of stones or larger boulders and much smaller soil particles. This is the subsoil.

Topsoil

The basic mineral structure of the soil is worked on over a period of time by myriads of bacteria, fungi and algae, while the micro-fauna and micro-flora work upon fallen leaves and dead roots to decay them. From the ensuing organic debris humus is produced. This process is of the utmost importance in the formation of a soil to support vigorous plant life. It has been estimated that it takes about two thousand years for one inch of topsoil to accumulate and its delicately balanced structure can be quickly destroyed by misuse. Over-compacting or stacking too deeply for long periods will halt the perpetual processing and the topsoil will revert to subsoil.

From this it can be seen that the value of good topsoil is inestimable – the loss of it through misuse on building sites should be a criminal offence. It is the medium in which all our food is grown, and from which all plants and grass draw their food. Being friable it also acts as a drainage medium. When moving earth round in the garden for whatever purpose, always bear in mind its value to any future development.

Soil types

Plants cannot live in subsoil, and water will stand on it. Similarly clay soil, which is sticky or 'colloidal', holds the water and is therefore badly aerated, heavy and cold. The reverse happens in a sandy soil. Having coarser particles, it is well aerated, well drained, and is consequently a dry soil and a light one.

Both these soil types will benefit by an application of organic matter, humus or compost. The organic particles will help to break up the sticky structure of clay, thus aerating the soil and allowing further weathering action to take place, while in a sandy soil the added organic matter will hold the coarser particles together and help them to retain moisture.

An ideal soil for growing is loam, which contains a percentage of both sand and clay particles with the correct amount of organic matter. Other soil types might be chalky (usually a hungry soil) or peat (strongly acid). Generally speaking, the darker a soil the richer it is, and the warmer also, since it will absorb more heat from the sun's rays.

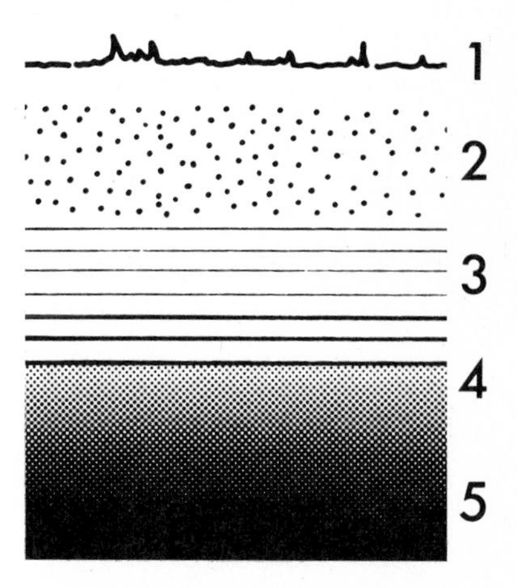

44 SOIL STRUCTURE IN SECTION
1 *vegetable topsoil*
2 *subsoil*
3 *gravel*
4 *stones*
5 *rock (sedimentary or igneous)*

Acid and alkaline soils

Another factor influencing plant growth is the acidity or alkalinity of the soil. This is simple to diagnose, and one can get a fair indication of the state of one's soil from its type.

The presence of limestone in a soil will obviously create some alkalinity, and a chalk soil is obviously the extreme case of an alkaline soil. An acid soil indicates the absence of limestone – this might be a peaty or sandy soil. There are other factors which can affect the other soil types and here the various home outfits for testing the soil type are helpful. Chemically these measure the hydrogen ion concentration of a suspension of soil in distilled water. This concentration is expressed as a number known as the pH value. A pH value of 7 in the soil indicates an even, or neutral, balance (an ideal garden soil has a pH value of 6·5). Lower figures indicate the degree of acidity, and higher ones the degree of alkalinity. There are some soil testers on the market which register pH values in terms of colour variations.

Natural plant association

It is not so much soil testing as the subsequent selection of plants for a particular soil type that seems to baffle people. In this connection it is worth looking at some of the natural plant associations, or groups, growing on any particular soil, because they must have a liking for the particular degree of acidity or alkalinity present. The later selection of garden varieties can be based on these associations.

On a chalk or alkaline soil one can expect, from the smallest to the largest, thymes, sun roses, dogwoods, yew, box and beech, with wild clematis, or traveller's joy festooning the hedgerows; on an acid soil, various fine grasses, heather, rhododendrons and birch trees. Other groups, such as marram grass, buckthorn and pine, grow in coastal areas where the plants have to withstand the heavy saline content in the air and the strong wind. The riverside has another distinct plant association: flag iris, rushes and reeds, osiers and alders, while poorly drained land often has rushes and buttercups on it.

45, 46 Protecting tree roots when the surrounding gradient is changed: By means of a retaining wall (top) By banking

EXISTING TREES

A large tree will have taken many years to develop and it can give great character to an otherwise dreary site – not only to one garden but, in a development, to many. Think very carefully before you decide to remove it. If it creates too much shade, it can be pruned to open up the crown, while still allowing a balanced head to remain, but not mutilated to a stump as is far too often done.

When moving earth about or digging foundations, tree roots need protection. It is amazing what disturbance a large tree can put up with, but the results of disturbance to the root system can often take a year or two to show before part or all of the tree dies. The roots of a tree not only feed it, but anchor it as well and by cutting the main guy roots one severely weakens the tree on that particular side.

WATER TABLE

A tree can be harmed not only by tampering with its roots, but also by the removal of water from them. Under the top or subsoil (depending on the height of one's land) there is a line called the water table to which water standing in the earth's surface rises. Where one gets standing water on low ground, the water table has risen above ground level. It has been found recently that a large building development involving major excavations can change the water table and lead to the deprivation of plants dependent on it. Again this phenomenon might take some time to show itself.

47, 48
UNDRAINED SOIL High water table Plant roots near surface Stunted growth
DRAINED SOIL Plant roots grow down Healthy growth

49 *An old tree and its shadow give character and depth to a garden by Roland Weber*

To recognize the built-in potential of one's site – its levels, its soil and existing vegetation – is one thing; the preservation and extension of that potential is another. In creating a garden, the built-in character of the site should be developed not only topographically but ecologically as well; that is, by encouraging plants which are right for the soil and the climate. The reason the Scandinavian garden *looks* so right is that the plants in it are natural. It *is* possible to play a trick on nature and produce your own alien environment, but holding back what wants to grow naturally involves a great deal of money and constant maintenance. Decide then at this stage to follow the general character of your site, allowing the garden to develop almost as it would naturally, since this will reduce subsequent work enormously.

From this, I hope, can be seen the falsity of growing rhododendrons or mountain laurel on chalky soil or importing Westmorland water-worn limestone into a sandy garden. No matter how beautiful these items are in themselves, they are bound to look incongruous and conflict with their surroundings.

4 STARTING FROM SCRATCH

House types

For those lucky enough to be building on a new site the foregoing considerations could well determine the type of house they build and should certainly dictate its orientation whether for sun or view or both.

For those with no view to look at, the atrium type of house is worth considering since, being built round an internal courtyard, it cuts out the surrounding world. As the chaos and noise of twentieth-century living grow, this has much to be said for it. The Romans appreciated the internal peace it afforded, even though its outer walls abutted the street – so did the monks and the builders of colleges. Such a house would have the benefit of an enclosed draught-free garden, ideal as an outside room to sit and eat in, and ideal for young children, being in full view of the house. The creation of such a garden would, however, be more a matter of outside decoration than horticulture.

This type of building also lends itself to restaurants, schools and indeed to housing *en masse*, where the basic plan is juxtapositional and the side of one house provides the garden wall of the next.

50 Above: The peaceful internal garden of an office

51 Below: Carefully positioned features and specimen plants in a courtyard garden. The house of architect Ruprecht Dröge

52 A model for courtyard housing

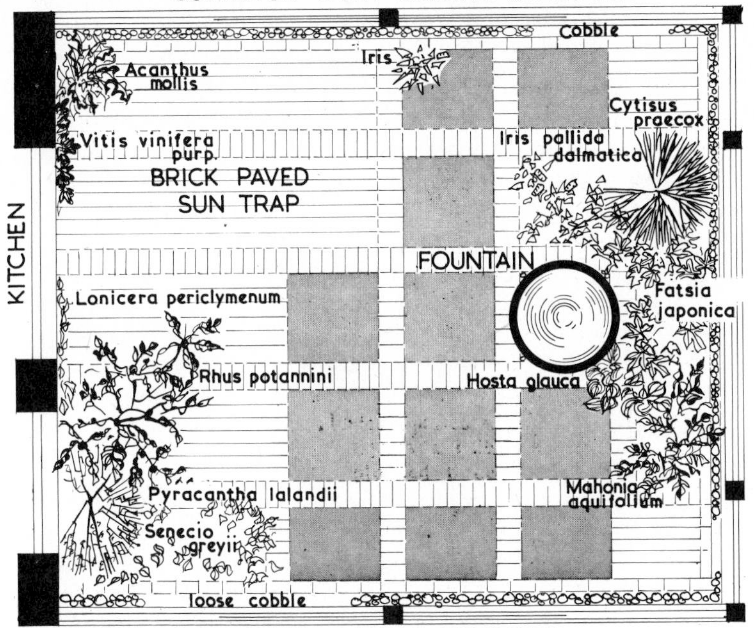

53, 54 The courtyard garden of the architect Michael Manser's house (left and below). A brick pattern runs off the building module and is partly infilled to provide a sitting area. The rest of the pattern is infilled with grass or planting and a small fountain is included to bring life and interest to the area

55, 56 Below: Two views of the enclosed garden of a canteen. Concrete blocks on the terrace serve as occasional benches or tables

A variation on the atrium theme is the U-shaped building looking into a three-sided courtyard with a view beyond. This is often seen in older houses and farms where the fourth side would originally have been a wall, so that the whole made a shelter from a prevailing wind, or perhaps even a fortified enclosure.

It is this enclosed or partly enclosed area which becomes the true outside room, the potential of which has always been most fully seen and developed in countries with warm climates. As soon as the house type becomes more formal the problem of back and front – or public and private – presents itself. Builders and developers in Europe tend to position houses squarely in the middle of a plot, so that the opportunity to combine the two is slight. The American builder, on the other hand, tends to orientate his structure more carefully, making better use of the levels and the site potential, so that the garden can wrap itself around the house instead of being divided up. When done *en masse*, however, such a solution needs careful handling, with well-positioned blocks of trees so that the overall pattern of housing does not become haphazard.

57 Sheltered by trees, a Swiss farm nestles into the hillside

When siting a new house it is as well to remember that, while a hilltop position can give a fine view, it is usually exposed to winds and driving rain. The older hilltop houses one sees usually sit in the arm of hills or are backed and silhouetted by large trees. They sit within the contours of the site and appear to belong to it because the shape of the land has been used and the structure built of indigenous materials.

58 Right: A mosque in Tunisia. The structure belongs to the flat, hot desert and sits halfway between it and the sky

59 A mill house in Cambodia blending with the surrounding jungle

60 A concrete roof-line echoes the rocky crags beyond. A house at Campione d'Italia, Switzerland, by Dolf Schnebli

This air of belonging to the site, not only in the positioning of the house but also in the materials used, is fundamentally important and a sense of fitness for location should be carried on into the garden, not only in the use of hard materials, but soft, that is planting – as well.
I am not advocating a traditional approach to the development of a site. The design of the house and garden upon it can both be as modern as you like, provided they still retain their congruity to each other and to their setting. It is this congruity, so immediately appealing, which is so difficult to achieve in new buildings, though it is always admired in old ones, when the walls have mellowed and background planting grown up to hold the structure in its midst. The

61 Strict, man-made forms combine with natural scenery to make a superb pattern

instant appeal of house and site can very occasionally be achieved by contrasting strict man-made forms with flowing natural ones – but it is not a solution to be attempted lightly.

Broad garden planning

At this stage garden planning is very broad, combining what one has on the site with what one is about to put on it, and subsequent detailed design must fit into this initial conception. The blocks of planting and areas of grass, for instance, can be positioned as a painter might position his slabs of colour, to make up a composition.

62 *The flowing line of hills*

Broadly speaking, the fewer individual eye-catchers included in the layout the better, in order to avoid the fussed look of Victorian gardens where 'objects of interest' were introduced like currants in a plum duff. We tend to use such objects as a substitute for good design, but if the pattern is pleasing and inviting to walk around it does not need to be studded with punctuation marks.

A lesson can be taken from natural scenery and the way in which it flows with no discordant details. It is this visual peace and restfulness which preservationists strive to maintain and which one should try to re-create on a smaller scale in the garden. Add colour as well if you like, but on the same broad flowing simple lines.

Perhaps at this stage it is worth a moment to consider the Japanese garden. It is basically a simple garden, with little or no variety of colour but full of interest. The underlying tone is green, which unifies all the different areas of planting and all the trained specimens. The whole layout is not visible at one glance so that one wanders around the area discovering things, and the house and garden are fused together into a whole. The Japanese garden coheres in the same organic way and has the same restful appeal as the flowing pattern of the countryside.

63 *The gentle meandering line of a river*

Because this type of garden was created for the Japanese way of thought and for Japanese living, it cannot succeed in detail elsewhere. When we in the west try to re-create such a garden we tend to pick out only the superficial decorations and probably scatter them about in an ill-conceived rockery. Nevertheless, whether our garden is old or new, in town or country, and whatever its size, we can learn from the underlying discipline and coherence of the Japanese garden. The same principle will also apply in a back yard. Simplicity and the subordination of objects to the basic pattern of the garden will combine man-made structures, natural characteristics and site function in one overall conception.

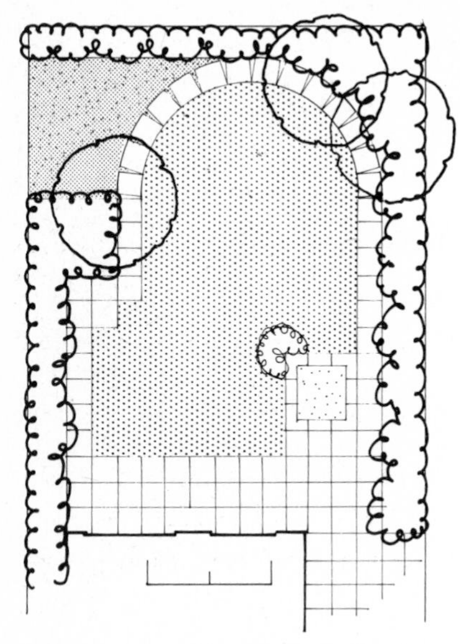

64 A basically regular formal design

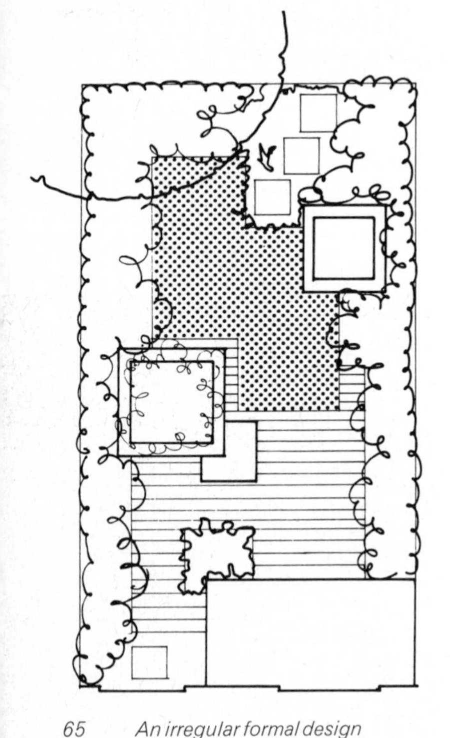

65 An irregular formal design

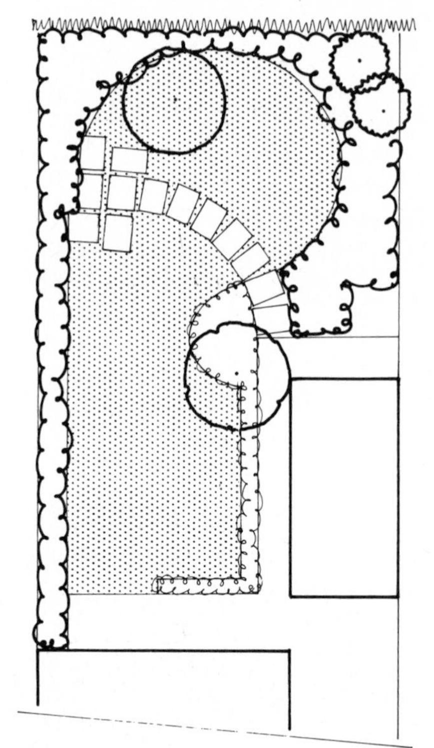

66 A geometrical, curving layout

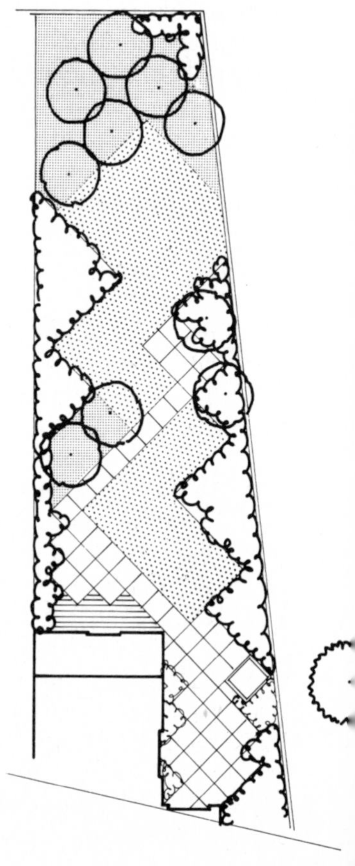

67 Right: The pattern at an angle to the house

5 BASIC PATTERN

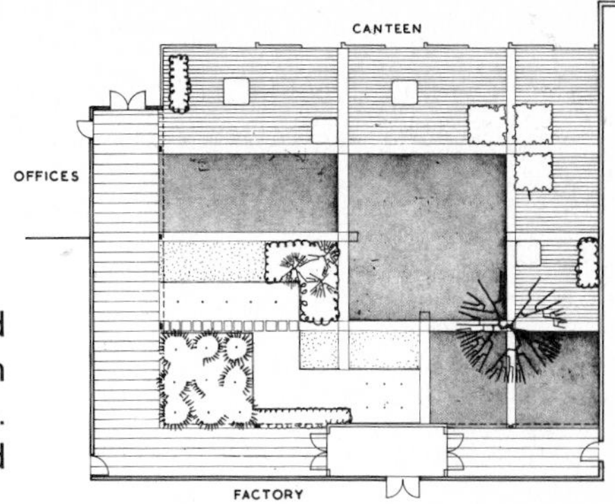

68, 69 *An abstract design uniting building and garden. A canteen garden in a commercial building*

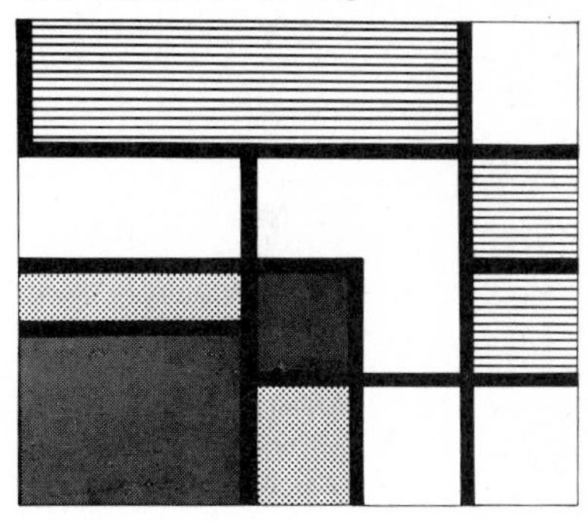

There is no book of rules for design. It is a personal thing and different people's solutions to a problem will differ as much as their reactions to any other visual or physical stimulus. There are, however, one or two guidelines on shapes and patterns generally.

We have seen that it is the simplicity and harmonious detail of the countryside which appeals – the sweep of a hill or the curve of a river. Look at any piece of good man-made design, from an airplane or car to a good suit, and the same principles apply: classic simplicity, and lack of trimmings or superfluous decoration. A novice will always over-decorate, substituting trimmings for basic pattern, but simplicity is all – though this does not preclude subtlety.

One of the failings of the average garden designer is his inability to consider the ground plan first of all purely as a pattern. Art students get over this by working with collage, that is, making patterns and shapes with coloured papers. Looking at modern paintings can also help one to see how areas of colour and texture can be counter-positioned to form a balanced whole.

The pattern which one wants to produce has to tie together all the functions of the garden. Initially one is not thinking in terms of paving or planting and the line of the pattern

70 *Below: Part of a small garden designed by Roland Weber. The strong ground pattern, of stone infilled with wooden blocks, is softened by lush green planting so that a satisfying balance is achieved*

can subsequently be the edge of a lawn, a planted area, or a path – it doesn't matter at this stage.

Start by getting the established facts of a site – its shape and existing features – down on paper in plan form. Use a simple scale, say $\frac{1}{8}$ in., $\frac{1}{4}$ in. or $\frac{1}{2}$ in. to 1 ft according to the size of the garden; or using graph paper, which is in tenths, might be easier. Plot the boundary; if it is irregular take guidelines at 90° to an established point, preferably the house, and mark the boundary points on these. In the same way mark any particular specimens or features that are worth keeping. (If any of these are trees, mark not only the diameter of the trunk but the spread of the overhanging branches, as this may affect what you can grow underneath.) Put in arrows indicating views you wish to keep or emphasize.

1 tree
2 dustbins
3 view
4 neighbouring trees
5 screen planting

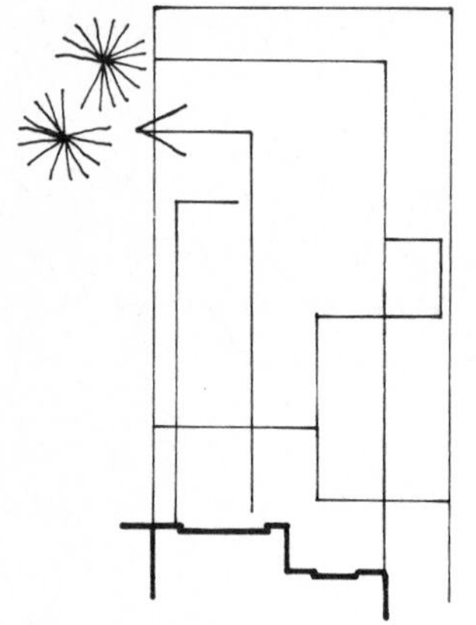

71–73 Building up the garden plan
Mark in what is on the site already and position roughly the features you want to include
Work out a rough pattern
Translate the pattern into a garden plan

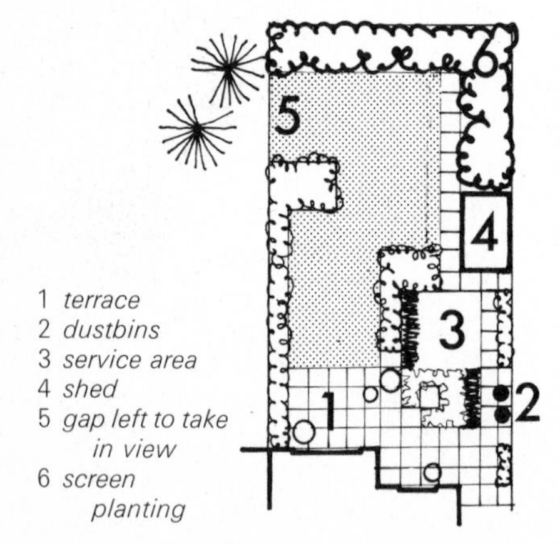

74 Above: Part of a garden designed as a series of rooms or areas for different uses: incidental seating for children in the foreground and a place beyond to catch the evening sun. When covered with vegetation the overhead beams will give a greater feeling of enclosure

75 In this garden by Roland Weber the planting draws one onwards and invites one to see what is round the next corner

Next mark roughly the areas you wish to designate to your family's various requirements – greenhouse, compost heaps, vegetable garden, garage, terrace, etc. – positioning them according to the need for privacy, easy access, evening sun and the other factors mentioned in Chapter 2.

Now start to evolve a satisfactory pattern on tracing paper laid over the plan. Such a pattern will often present itself straight away from the features marked on the plan or from the fall of the ground. A garden should be interesting and inviting when viewed from the house, for if it can all be seen at one glance the casual observer is not going to go out and explore it. The area can be open plan, or a series of rooms; its levels can be changed with steps or interest can be created by gentle mounds. A rough starting guide is that anything sited near the house will tend to follow the same fairly regular pattern and it is often a help, to start with, to extend some of the lines of the house outwards – from a window, for instance, or some jutting corner. These lines can run into the remainder of the site to join up the other features. The regular-shaped area abutting the house may need to be hard surfaced.

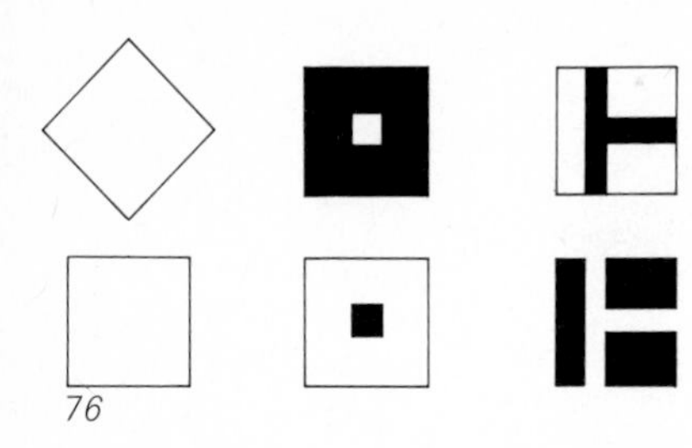

76

77, 78 *Below: One pattern created inside another and backed up by planting*

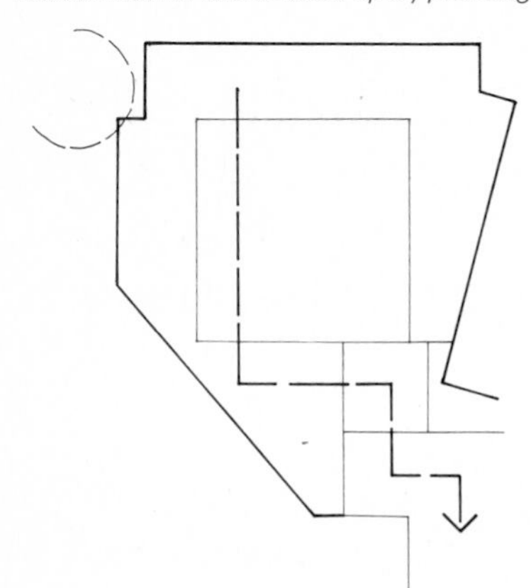

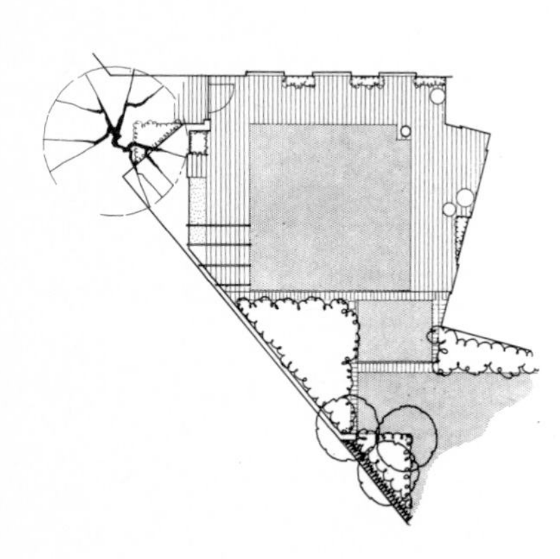

79 *Above right: The ground plan set at an angle to the house. The paving is precast concrete slabs with an infill of concrete brushed to expose the aggregate*

80 *Right: The ground plan following the line of the house with the area round the boundary planted out*

As the pattern develops, one realizes that it is the shapes left over between the guidelines which are important and not the lines themselves. Too often gardens are designed round the paths, which, though of vital importance, in fact cover only a small area. The leftovers then become unrelated pieces of a jigsaw.

A formal pattern near the house does not necessarily have to be square to it. By turning the pattern at an angle of 45° to the house, and evolving the remainder of the garden on these lines, one can get away from the box-like shape of the ordinary house plot.

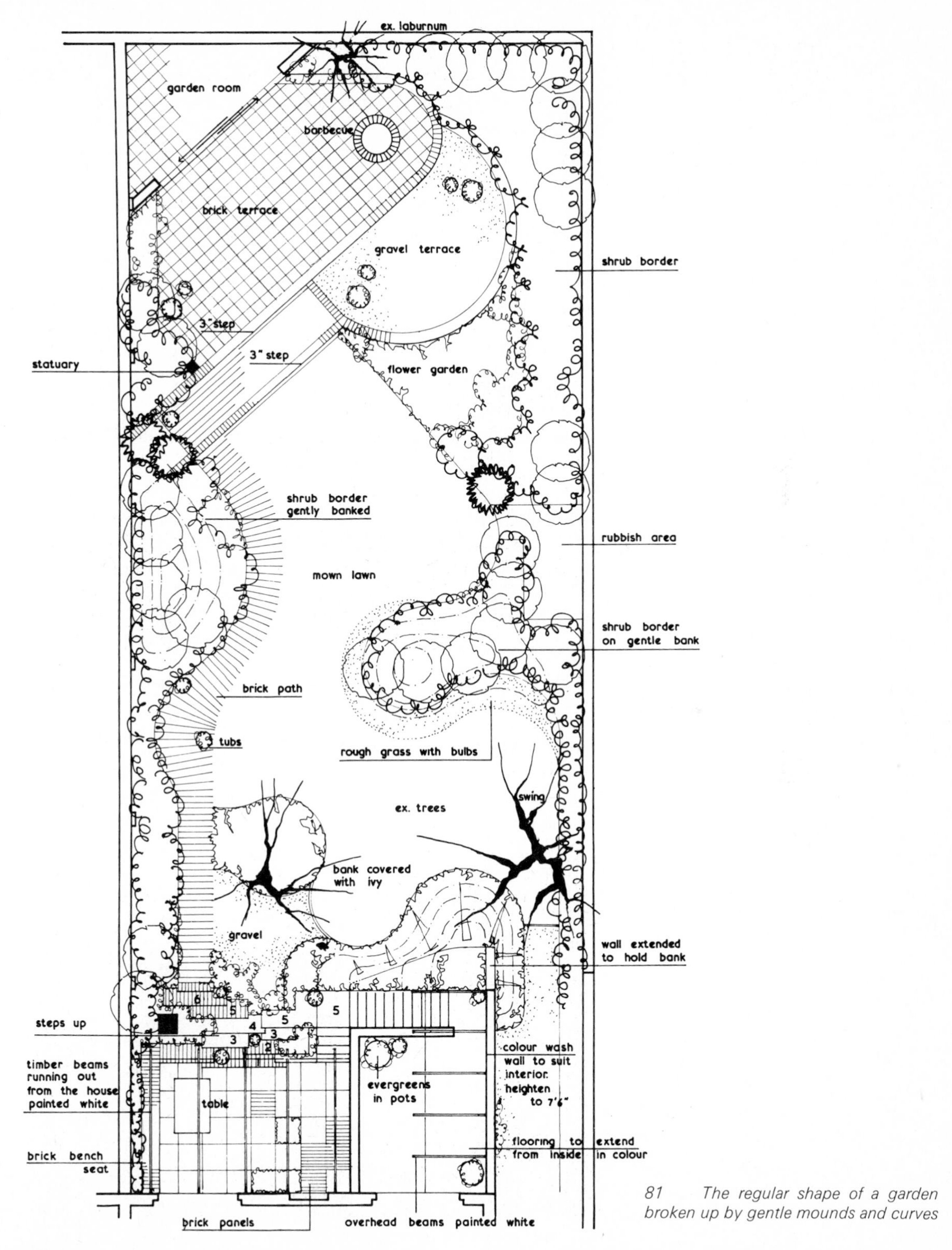

81 *The regular shape of a garden broken up by gentle mounds and curves*

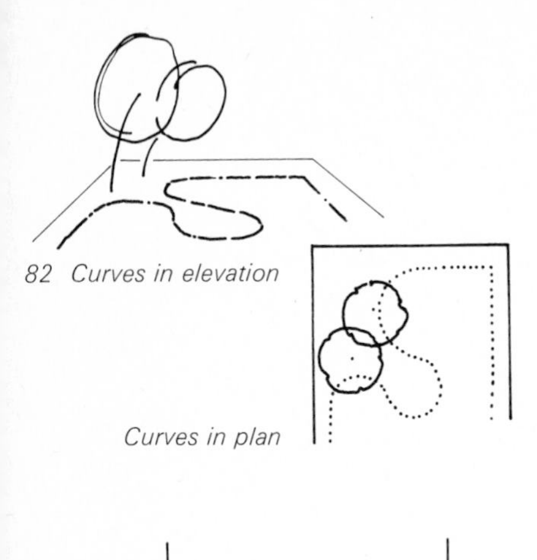

82 Curves in elevation

Curves in plan

83 Symmetry and asymmetry – but both balance

As the pattern moves away from the house, it can become looser, more flowing and more informal. On a small, confined site complete informality is generally difficult to achieve, as it is essential to hide the boundaries of the area and create another shape inside them; the best compromise is to produce a curving pattern with flowing lines but still with a regular or geometric basis. Too often pointless curls and scallops are used: a flowing pattern which is basically geometric will 'read' and embrace the whole garden, whereas serpentine meanderings will not. When using sweeps and curves think of natural curves and copy these. They are always fairly gentle – the wanderings of a river estuary when seen from the air, or the shape of a shell or leaf – and, from a practical point of view, the gentler the curve the easier it is to maintain subsequently. Moreover, in practice an angle becomes much sharper when seen from eye-level than it appeared on the plan.

The accompanying diagram shows that balanced design need not necessarily be regular. The layout of the average garden is too much inhibited by straight lines. If the design can be loosened up, the ensuing garden will be much more interesting – hedges, for instance, don't have to be straight, and paving and paths need not be at right angles to the house or boundary.

A fat woman will not decrease her embarrassment by wearing a horizontally-striped dress, and it is not wise to heighten further an already high and narrow hall by the use of vertically-striped wallpaper. The same principle applies to the lines of a garden: if the area is long and thin, a path straight down the middle will only emphasize this by dividing the area into two pieces. A side-to-side pattern will increase the apparent width of the area. If the pattern breaks up the shape so that when planted the whole is not visible at one glance, the area will appear larger still besides offering an element of surprise as one walks through it.

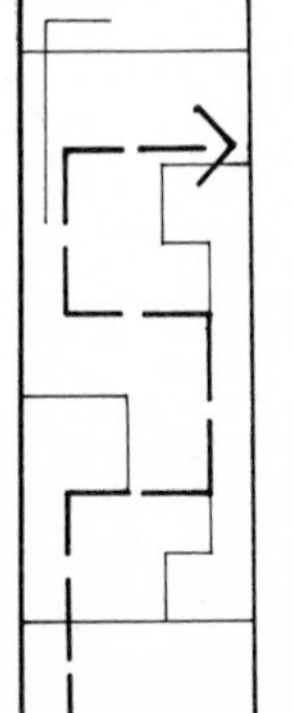

84–86 A side-to-side pattern of stone slabs gives an appearance of greater width to a narrow garden

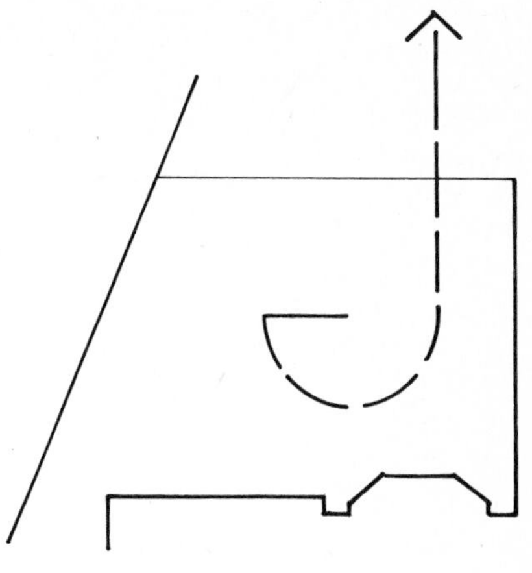

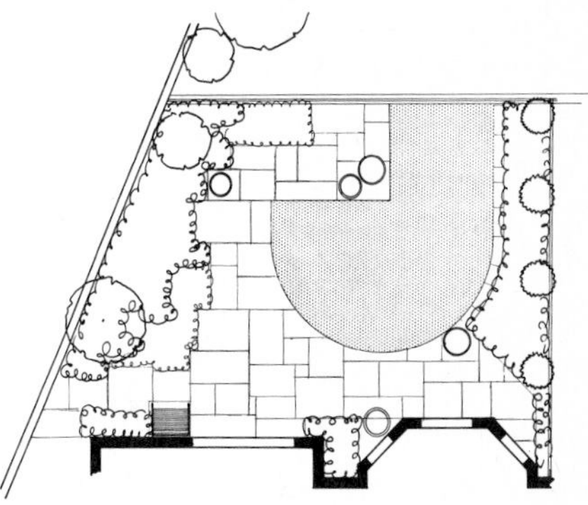

87–89 *A garden designed to embrace a view (left and above). The pergola helps to frame and focus the view*

If there is a view worth keeping, the pattern should turn towards it, perhaps distracting the eye from any unsightly features in neighbouring gardens. If there is no view outside the garden, the pattern should turn in on itself and some internal focal point should be provided. Similarly, if one has an irregularly shaped boundary with which no internal pattern

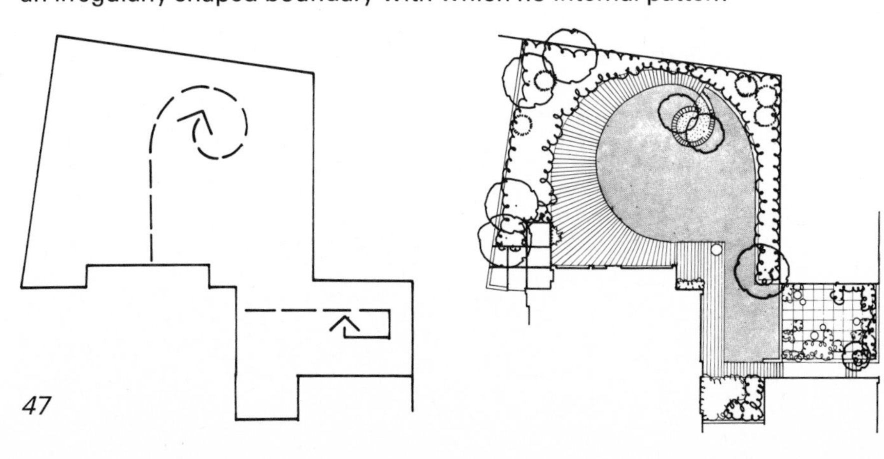

90, 91 *A design providing an internal point of interest (see photographs 92 and 93)*

92, 93 Above: A brick path turns in on itself and rises to form a wall round two specimen trees at the focal point of the garden. Right: Two years later the planting round the edge of the garden has grown up to blend with the trees outside the site and conceal the boundary wall

94 The quickest way from A to B is a straight line but a zig-zag path with a regular outline is visually wrong and irritating to walk over besides making mowing more difficult. The path need not in fact always follow the line a person walking over it would take

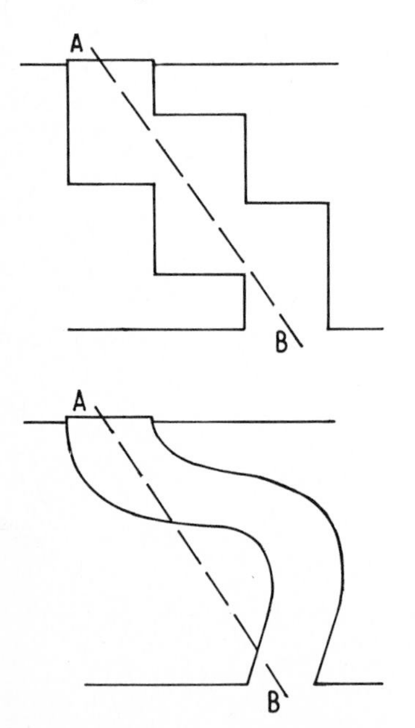

will work, it is best to re-create another shape inside it and plant out the intervening space.

All these factors can work on differing scales, and on any size of site.

A pattern should now be evolving, though it may not at this stage be very practical. The next step is to make it so. For example, the shape of a terrace should suit the type of surfacing to be used, as it is expensive and not always possible to cut square slabs to make a curved edge. Paths should link up relevant points – the kitchen door and the vegetable garden, or the terrace and the living room. The shape of the lawns should be easily manageable for your mower, and the corners of planting beds not too sharp for anything to grow in them, or too easy for the milkman to jump over – some day he is bound to land short!

Try now to build up the plan into the third dimension by siting your areas of planting. These masses will strengthen the lines of your scheme and help to direct the eye or screen an eyesore. It sometimes helps to put the eye to the level of the paper and try to visualize the pattern as it would be seen when completed.

Put in the points of interest as well – a clump of trees or a thin, pointed specimen. The actual types of trees, shrubs and plants have still not been decided, but you should by this time know that, say, a dense six-foot high screen is wanted at point A, or a standard tree to give some shade on the terrace at point B.

The final working plan can only be decided in the light of thorough knowledge of your type of soil and weather conditions. You will have to decide on your levels, which will be based on those of the house and those surrounding the site – if it is a new site, it might mean a considerable saving on cartage to use any spoil available from the foundations of the house for altering the levels. In the light of these decisions you will have to see if any drainage is necessary.

The different types of surfacing must be considered – what they will do aesthetically and what they will cost practically – and this covers not only pavings and pathways, but gravel, lawn or ground plantings as well. The same goes for the types of structure you want – a shed or greenhouse, a barbecue, fish pond or swimming pool.

Plant varieties come last of all and should be considered in two ways: those to be used structurally in the composition of the design and those which are to provide horticultural interest. The purely horticultural aspect tends to be very much over-emphasized as a result of the never-ending stream of plant catalogues and garden books available. Little wonder that the novice, after being seduced into buying a collection of ill-assorted varieties, cannot make the design of his garden visually coherent – he has been conned into putting the cart before the horse!

These elements making up the final plan will be examined in detail in subsequent chapters.

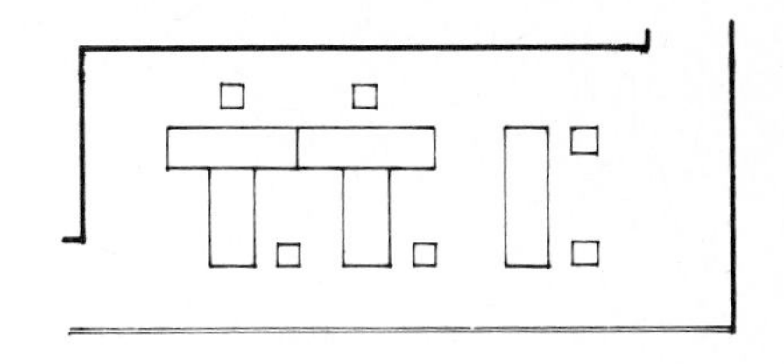

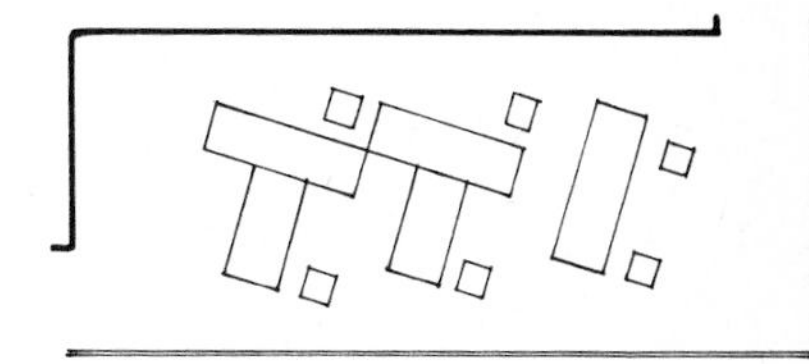

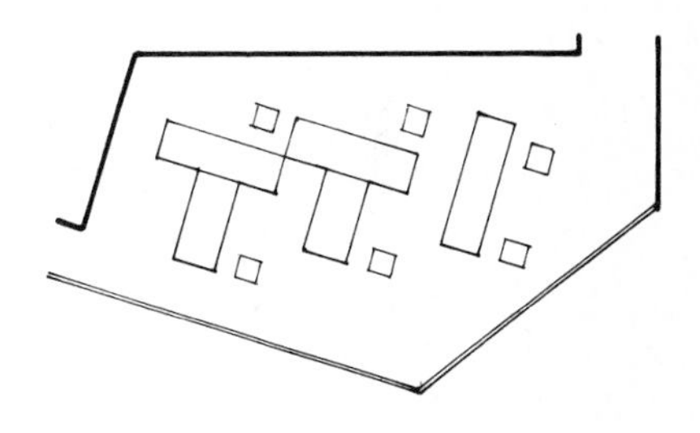

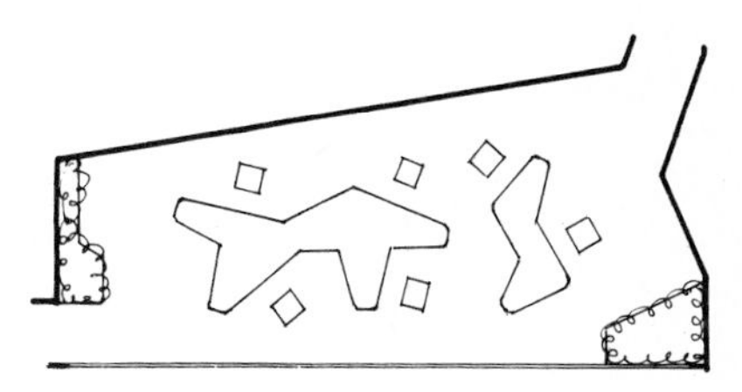

95–98 Above: Sketches showing alternative ways of arranging basic elements within a framework – in this case desks in an office

99 In the courtyard of a school: boulders strategically placed in the corner of a bed to discourage children from cutting corners

6 GROUND SHAPING AND DRAINAGE

100 The eighteenth-century park at West Wycombe, Buckinghamshire, laid out by Brown and altered by Repton. No boundary is visible: the lake flows on and into the countryside without interruption

Several basic principles can be learned from the English eighteenth-century landscape school and the use its great practitioners, Kent, Brown, and Repton made of ground-shaping. They used earth as a sculptor uses his material, moulding it to form a gentle valley or hill, the one providing soil for the other; and by damming an inconspicuous stream they formed a lake which nestled in the folds of the hillocks. The whole, when planted with large groups of indigenous trees, formed a rolling parkland, a softened or idealized form of natural landscape. One of the subtleties of the moulding was that it was often used to screen the boundaries of the park or the walled vegetable garden. Any building in the way of a view was either demolished or ornamented to become a feature. Tree groups were planted to emphasize the shape of the hillocks.

A favourite trick of Capability Brown was to provide a view of the house, sitting in its parkland, from the entrance to the drive at the edge of the property. The way then wound through trees and mounds, often making quite a long journey of what was actually only a small distance, to present the visitor suddenly at the front door of the house. From the windows of the receiving rooms he saw the whole idyllic landscape laid before him, with the grass of the meadow sometimes running right up to the house.

The park was often stocked with deer or highland cattle, to add interest and movement, and a boundary was necessary to keep them away from the house. Such a boundary had to be invisible, as a fence would have destroyed the illusion of the unity of the park, and so a ha-ha or ditch was used. Where a visible boundary was necessary, a standard, very simple, three-bar metal fence was employed, and many examples of this can still be seen.

Whatever scale we are working on, we can learn much from the parks of the eighteenth century and from the way ground-shaping was used in them. This subject was covered by Repton in his copious writings on gardening and the points he makes are as apt today as they were then. But whereas he worked with men and barrows taking months to complete the work, we today can employ a bulldozer to do the work for us at comparatively little cost. (They usually work on a per-day rate.)

101 The ha-ha: an eighteenth-century device for doing away with fences. A ditch provides a barrier but the eye can travel on uninterrupted. This idea can easily be adapted to smaller sites

1 *retaining wall*
2 *ditch*
3 *original level*
4 *sight line*

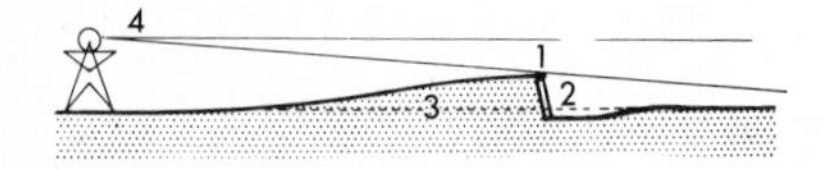

102 Petworth House, Sussex. Brown's pastoral landscape flows right up to the windows

For those who want an informal feeling, the moulding of earth gives depth and mystery to a site. On a larger scale moulding can be used to screen unsightly buildings, and divide up areas of housing. Modern landscape architects are using the hidden boundary technique to integrate power stations, dams and motorways into our already overburdened countryside.

Wherever and whenever there is any excavating on site it is always important to keep the topsoil and subsoil separate. The topsoil should be stripped, stacked, and the necessary shaping done with the subsoil. Only when this is complete and consolidated should the topsoil be reintroduced and spread, working it as little as possible to avoid breaking up its vital structure. The depth of topsoil necessary depends on what one intends to grow. Grass needs a minimum of 2 in., coarse shrubs a minimum of 9 in., if the subsoil is not solid. If spoil from a building site is to be used, decide where to make the piles of topsoil and subsoil to avoid later double handling which will lead to the expenditure of extra time and money.

103 In this spacious garden the line of the terrace embraces the view beyond. The landscape architect, J. St Bodfan Gruffydd, removed a line of trees and built a ha-ha just beyond the edge of the terrace to unify the garden and the surrounding country in one harmonious composition

Earth can be moulded into shape in one of two ways. It can be sculpted or chiselled, making no concessions whatever to the topography around it, or it can be moulded to appear as natural as possible. The former technique is pure sculpture, and its aptness in small-scale work is limited, but the moulding of earth could be used far more to give interest and variety to even the smallest site. Its effectiveness depends on the manner in which it is done. The finished mound should look as if it had always been there as part of the earth and should not appear to have been dumped. Because a natural gradient is comparatively shallow, not more than about 30° from the horizontal, a mound covering only a small area cannot be very

104 On a small scale a quite gentle grass mound can add enormous interest. Note the flowing line of the hillock

high, although it is possible to retain one side with a wall provided the support is not normally visible. The cross-section is important in order to make the mound look natural, and few machine operators are alive to this. Constant supervision on site is therefore necessary, as well as final careful hand raking.

Contours and sections

Sections and contour drawings often make little difference to the average machine operator, but it is necessary to produce them for estimating the amount of soil needed and, if the work is to be done by a contractor, the cost. Contour drawings are very simple and the accompanying diagram explains the method.

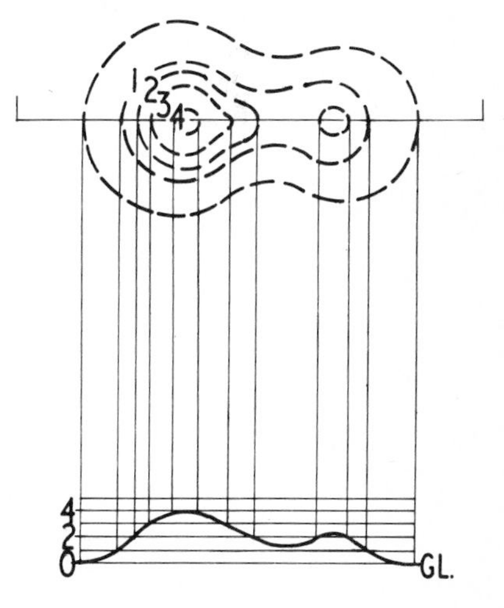

105 A contour drawing. Plan (top) and section

Protection of existing features

When machinery is working in the vicinity of trees or shrubs it is advisable to erect some sort of temporary fencing which will protect your specimens, or at least let the operator know that you want them preserved. For some reason, whenever a site is being partly cleared, or earth moved with large machinery, the operator develops megalomania and nothing is safe from destruction. If the site allows, fencing should be erected round any trees at the width of their branch spread to prevent workmen from lighting bonfires underneath. (This applies more often to builders than landscape contractors.) If a tree has already been damaged, the wound should be

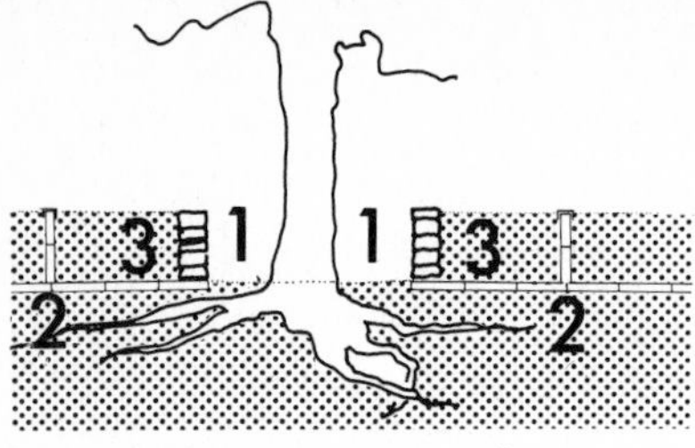

106 Section of a dry well (above)

1 dry well
2 vertical and horizontal tile drains
3 material added to raise the ground level (a layer of topsoil on loose stones)

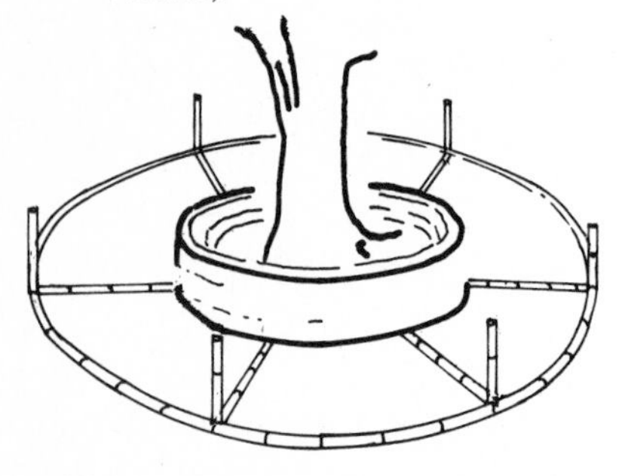

107 Above: The preliminary spacing of tile drains before backfilling round the dry well

108 Below: The tile drains should be laid in a protective arch of brickwork to avoid breakage

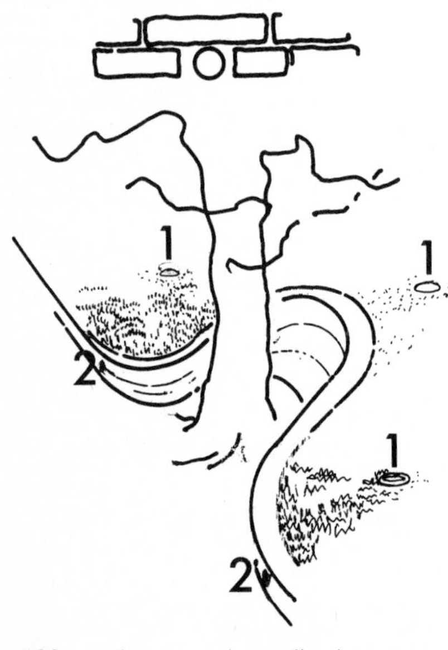

109 An open dry well where tree roots are only partially covered by additional earth

1 vertical tile drain outlets
2 horizontal tile drain outlets

pared with a sharp knife to facilitate healing and painted over with a preservative.

When shaping the ground it is sometimes necessary to raise the level around an existing tree. In this case a dry well should be constructed around the tree to ensure that the earth added above the old ground level does not touch the trunk. It goes without saying that any damage or unnecessarily heavy weight inflicted on the roots will cause the death of the tree; moreover, excessive compacting or additional soil lying on the surface for any length of time (particularly if it is water-retaining clay) will prevent the roots getting sufficient oxygen.

The dry well is made by building a wall around the tree trunk some 12 to 18 in. away and banking it up with earth on the outside. The space between the wall and the trunk should be kept clear of rubbish. If the fill is particularly heavy or deep, agricultural land drains can be placed round the tree and connected to the main drain to take off excess water. The inclusion of the occasional bell tile, or land drain set on end will allow more air to get to the roots. This technique can also be used to partially surround a tree if it stands halfway up an incline.

The reverse of this procedure is sometimes necessary in order to protect a tree's roots when it is sited on an incline, and the general grade is lowered.

Earth moving on quite a small scale can be done by hand if there is no access for a machine. This might be on the simple cut-and-fill principle (see diagram 43). The same basic rule about not mixing topsoil and subsoil still applies. Time and again on new sites one sees exposed subsoil banks of far too steep a gradient left by developers. The action of rain washes the clay or chalk away and herbage never has time to take root and arrest the process. A simple method of stabilizing such a bank on a small scale is to lay bracken on it, plant rampant trailers in pockets of earth and peg wire netting over the top. Turfing, when the individual sods need pegging, is another solution although the subsequent maintenance is difficult.

DRAINAGE

Where ground contouring has been carried out on an uneven site, or on a flat one with non-porous soil, some form of drainage might be necessary if water is standing (as a result of the earth's becoming compacted during the operation). This can be alleviated by tilling, or by spiking and brushing in fine grit to break the compacted crust.

Drainage is not always essential if the soil and subsoil are porous, but if it cannot be felt underfoot, the state of the land can usually be judged from what is growing on it. Much that is written about drainage makes it seem excessively complicated, but for everyday purposes it is quite simple.

Dry well or soakaway

An isolated patch of dampness can be relieved simply by digging a dry well. This is a hole under the damp spot, approximately 3 ft square and 3 to 4 ft deep. Fill it with coarse rubble, top with ash, backfill the surface layer with topsoil and replace the turf.

Water will not percolate through if impermeable or too heavily compacted soil is placed on top of a soakaway.

French drain

This is a ditch backfilled with rubble and ash only, which acts as a water-conducting channel. A French drain can often meet the need for a temporary drain, but will become blocked comparatively quickly as silt and soil leach through from above.

Tile drainage

Where a more extensive drainage system is necessary, clay tile drains can be laid underground with an outlet to a ditch or watercourse. These can be laid in a single line, or a network laid in herring-bone fashion will provide more thorough drainage.

The gradient of the laterals in a herring-bone pattern should not be greater than 1 in 250, with the main drain similarly graded to the outfall. The drain trench should be excavated to the required depth and the base rounded to fit the tile pipe. Backfill with excavated material with either the surface sod laid over the drain, or a layer of hard core or ash first.

Where the outfall flows into an open ditch or watercourse, make sure the flow breaks on to a hard surface to avoid erosion, and put a grid over the outlet to keep vermin out.

The depth at which tile drains are laid will depend on the type of soil – as will the density of pipe runs in a herring-bone pattern.

TILE DRAINAGE SPACING

Soil Type	Spacing (yd.)	Depth (ft.)
Clay	4–7	2–2½
Loam	8–12	2½–3
Sand	12–8	3–4

110 *Small door yard garden with picket fence*

7 ENCLOSURE

Having decided on the basic form of the garden and its levels, the next move must be to plan the type of enclosure and boundary demarcation.

Much will depend on the type of house and site and the position, whether in town or country. Broadly speaking, the simpler the boundary enclosure the more suitable it will be, not only for the site it surrounds but for the community as a whole – since other people will have to look at the outer side of your fence.

If the character of the site and its position can be adhered to, so much the better. Local walling or fencing materials, where applicable, are best, since they blend with the area and with neighbouring boundaries whether of fields or other properties.

Where a boundary abuts a house, a greater feeling of unity will be achieved if it can be constructed in the same brick or timber as that used in the house construction. The fewer types of material used in the structure of a house and the area surrounding it the more a link between the two will be apparent.

The actual positioning of the house and its integration with the site have been discussed, but it is equally important to integrate the boundary and all the other objects to be placed upon the site. The aim should be to blend them into the area, not to use them as decoration. This applies to suburban sites in particular. The visual unrest of many developments built between the wars must be obvious – neighbouring houses in different styles, with differing boundary fences and gates, rivalling each other in their ugliness, while the higgledy-piggledy nature of the planting behind each fence compounds the unhappy effect. There is much to be said against the open-front development on the grounds of lack of privacy, but there is also much to be said *for* it in terms of visual serenity.

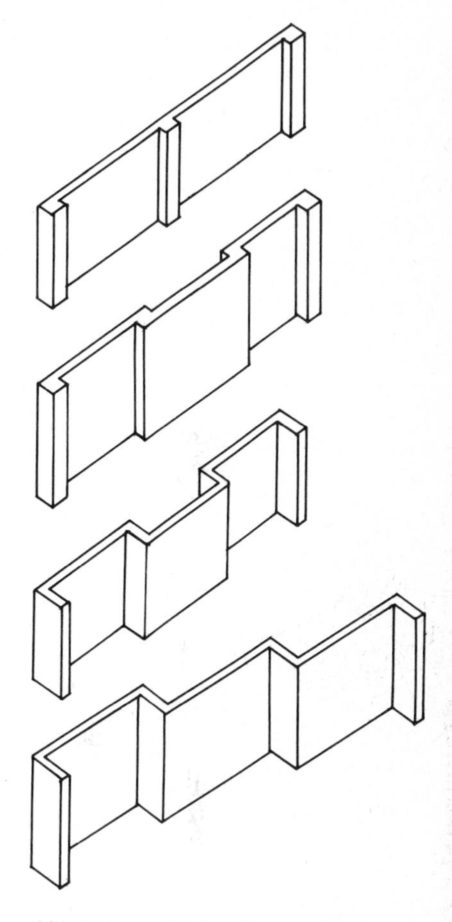

111–114 Brick walls
A $4\frac{1}{2}$ in. wall with 9×9 in. piers
Castellated $4\frac{1}{2}$ in. wall with 9×9 in. piers and dummy piers provided by the setback
A $4\frac{1}{2}$ in. or 9 in. castellated wall
A variation on the castellated wall

WALLING

Garden walls, very common in England and Europe, are much less so in America, except in cities or rural areas where field-stone is easily available. But there are those who do like sheltered privacy. For use in a built-up area, walls should be brick, or, possibly, concrete – either in blocks or cast *in situ*. The height should be above eye-level, that is not less than

115–117 Brick walls

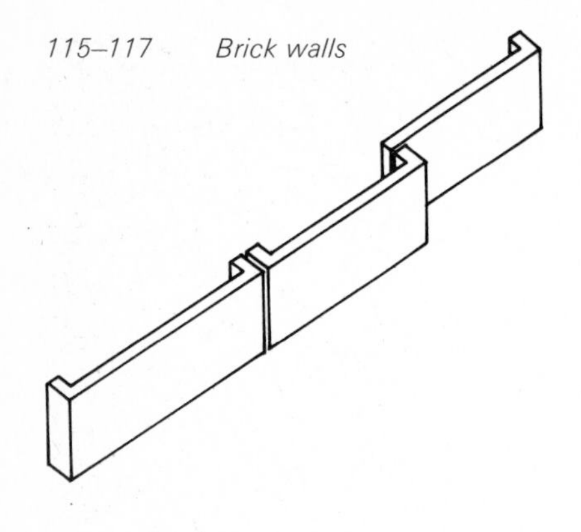

Breaks and double piers in a castellated wall

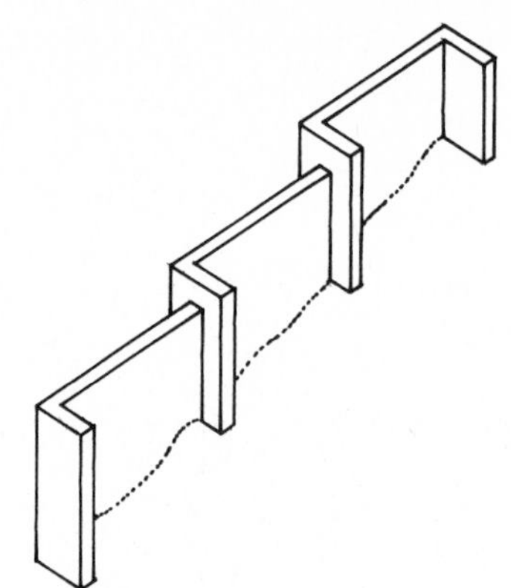

Breaks incorporated at the castellations on a sloping site

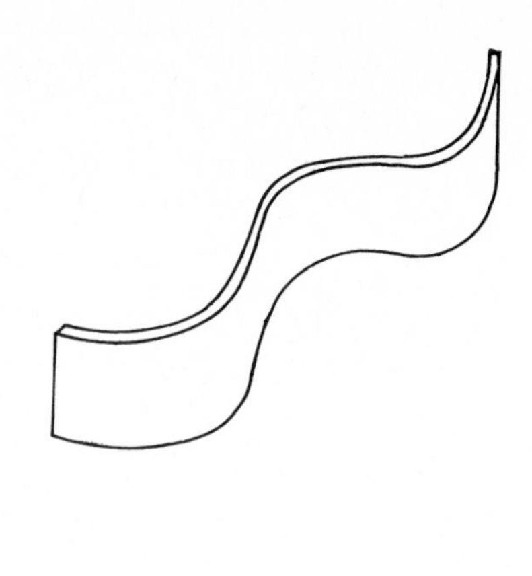

The curved or serpentine wall

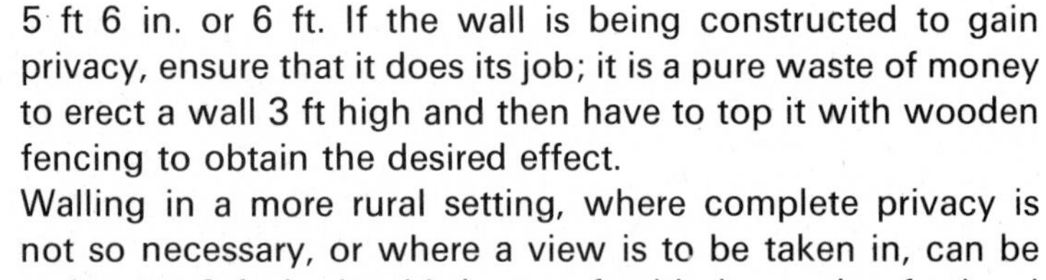

5 ft 6 in. or 6 ft. If the wall is being constructed to gain privacy, ensure that it does its job; it is a pure waste of money to erect a wall 3 ft high and then have to top it with wooden fencing to obtain the desired effect.

Walling in a more rural setting, where complete privacy is not so necessary, or where a view is to be taken in, can be as low as 3 ft. It should then preferably be made of a local material – flint in chalky country, dry stone in a limestone district, or random walling in a granite or slate area.

Hollow screen walling and the more ornate types of walling with cladding or decoration applied should be reserved for inside the garden. Your particular choice might be your neighbour's aversion – and this can work both ways!

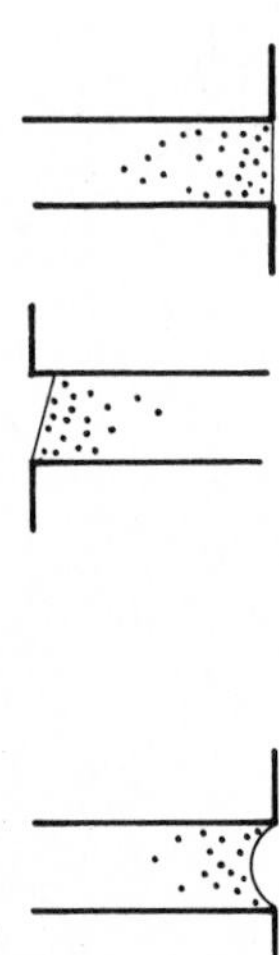

118–119 Jointing
Flush joint (top) and struck weather joint
Keyed joint (bottom)

Brick

Bricks for outside use should be hard in nature, frost-resistant and able to withstand the elements for, while a wall used in house construction has only one side exposed, an outside wall has two.

A brick wall should ideally be at least two bricks thick. A wall which is only one course thick, besides being less strong and needing buttressing at regular intervals, also looks very thin and unsatisfactory. This can be overcome to a certain extent by staggering the wall, with panels stepped forward and back, or by building it in a serpentine shape; but both these treatments are perhaps too decorative for a boundary.

120 *Brick garden wall and flagstone paving*

The two-brick wall

A wall two bricks thick should, of course, have a concrete foundation. It can be bonded in several ways, according to the pattern preferred. Provided the height does not exceed 6 ft, it should not need buttressing unless exposed to particularly strong winds.

Damp-proof course

For normal garden use a damp-proof course should not be necessary. For the meticulous – and their wall will last longer, since a dry brick wall will not be so readily attacked by frost – a damp-proof course 6 in. above ground level can be inserted during construction. This should be made of hard brick, slate, mastic asphalt or else, most economically, bituminous sheet (of which there are many types on the market).

121 *Concrete strip wall foundation suitable for most soils. The width of the strip should be three times the thickness of the wall*

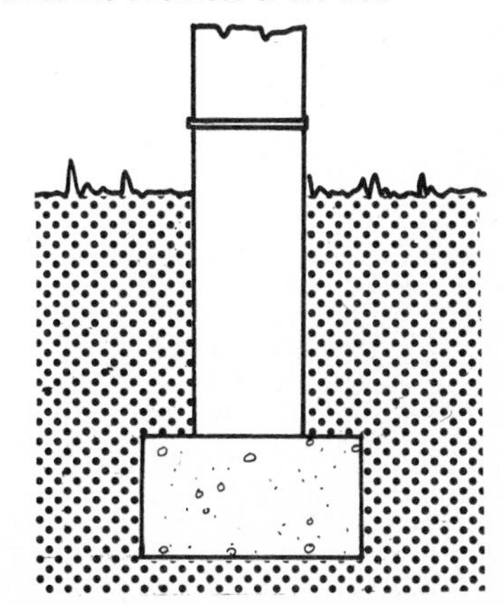

122–125 Brick bonding and coping

Left: English garden wall
Right: English bond

Left: Stretcher bond
Right: Flemish bond

126–128 Below: Retaining walls
Left: Mass concrete with drainage pipes backed with rubble acting as weep holes
Centre: Stone-faced cavity wall with concrete foundation
Right: A brick wall with concrete foundation

1 *Weep holes*
2 *Expansion joint*
3 *Slate or tile coping*
4 *Cavity to prevent moisture staining the stone facing*
5 *Damp-proof course*
6 *Waterproof rendering (bitumen or asphalt) to prevent staining of the brickwork*

Weep holes

All retaining walls outside, particularly those without a damp-proof course, should have weep holes in them to allow surplus water behind the wall to escape. Weep holes should be placed 6 in. above ground level at approximately

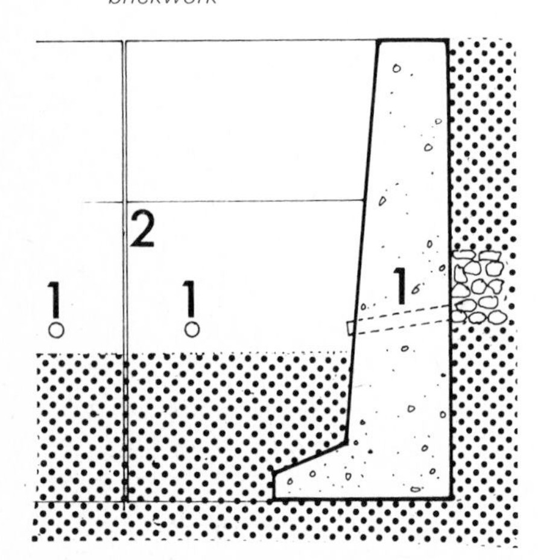

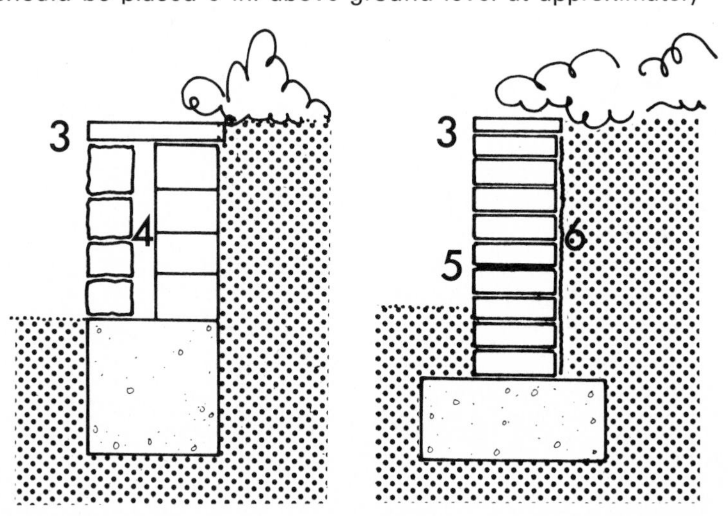

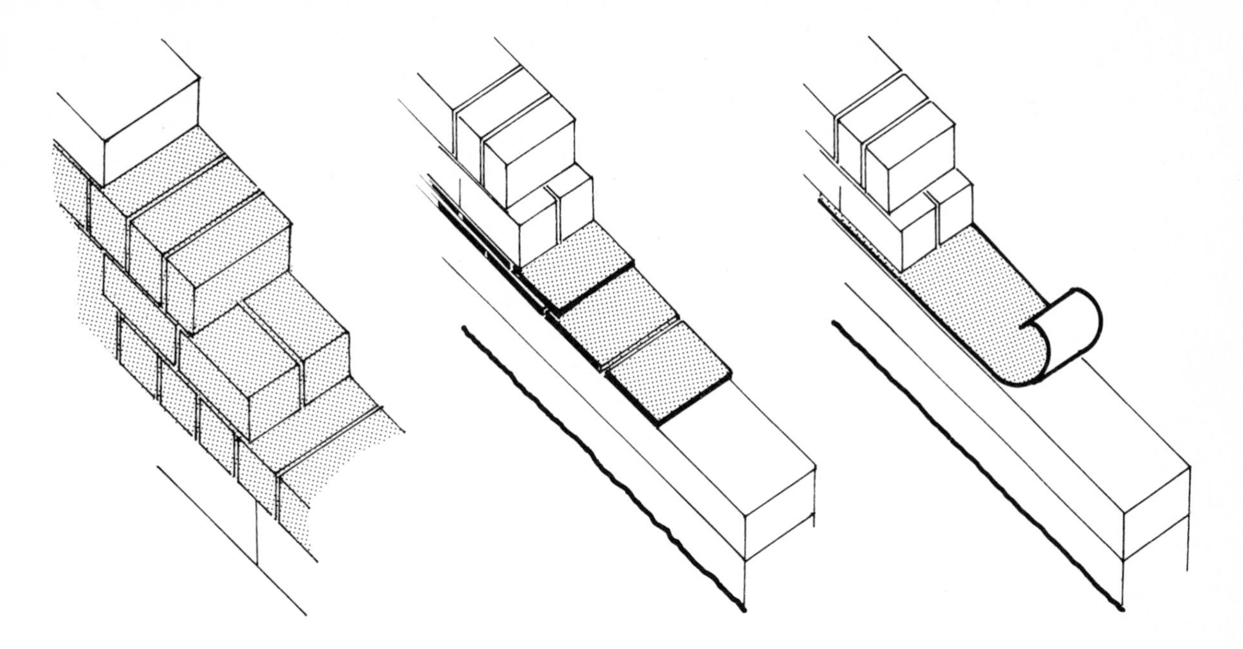

6 ft intervals in the wall run. They are easily constructed by leaving out some of the vertical jointing between the stones or bricks, though where a random material is being used it might be simpler to incorporate the odd earthenware drain-pipe in the structure instead.

129–131 Damp-proof course materials
Left: Three courses of brick
Centre: Two courses of slate laid in breaking joints
Right: Lead or copper strip

Coping

It is easy to destroy the simple line of a good wall by the use of an ill-proportioned coping, so care should be taken in its detail. The ideal coping or capping for a brick wall is the same brick set on edge with or without a tile creasing course. This is the simplest solution, but where a damp-proof course has been included a more weather-proof type of coping might be required – metal, stone, concrete or clayware. Circumstances might arise where the coping needs to fit in with local tradition or with the type used by the architect on the house.

132–134 Bull-nosed brick edgings
Left: External return laid on the flat
Centre: External return laid on edge
Right: Internal return laid on edge

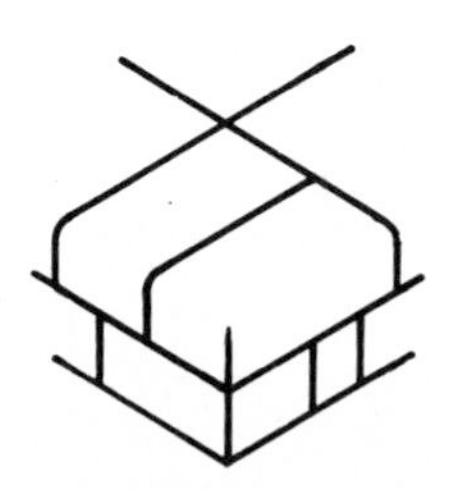

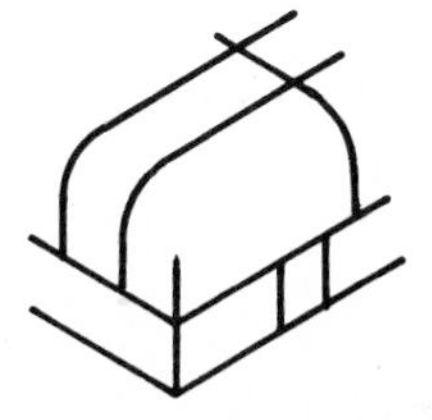

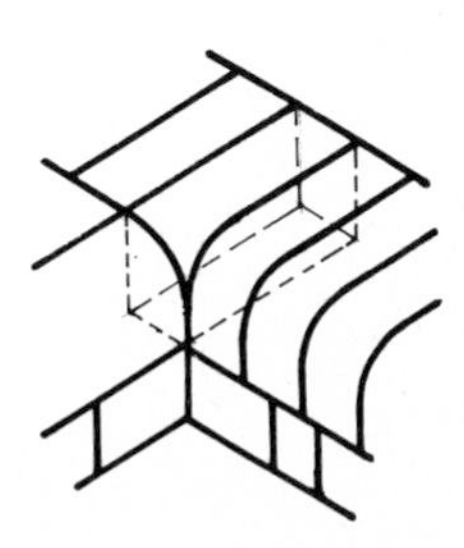

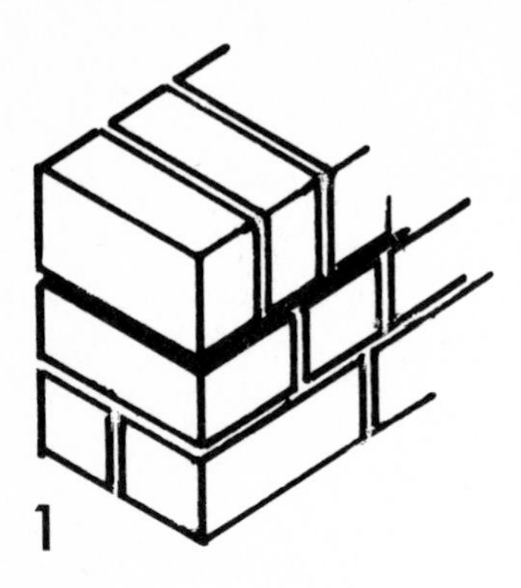

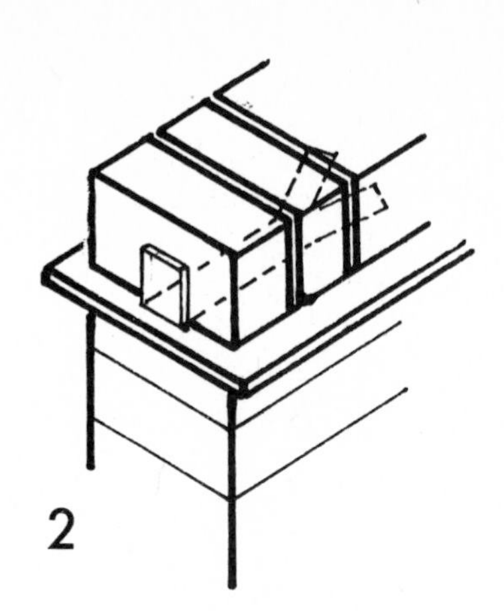

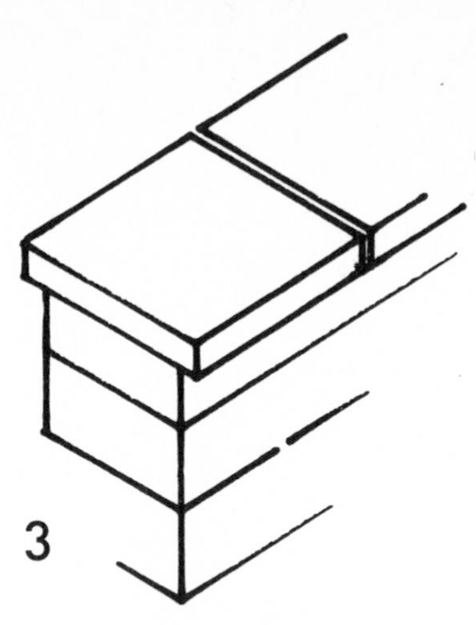

135–146 Wall copings

1 *Bricks set on edge*
2 *Brick with tile creasing course and securing iron*
3 *Paver or tile coping*
4 *Metal (copper or zinc) capping*
5 *Tile or stone with a creasing course of metal strip*
6 *Squared slate*
7 *Ridged slate with throating groove to prevent dripping*
8 *Stone with creasing course and throating*
9 *Weathered stone with a one-way fall*
10 *Curved stone coping*
11 *Precast concrete coping on a brick wall. Water run-off will stain the brickwork*
12 *Granite wall and coping. Granite does not stain or change colour with weathering*

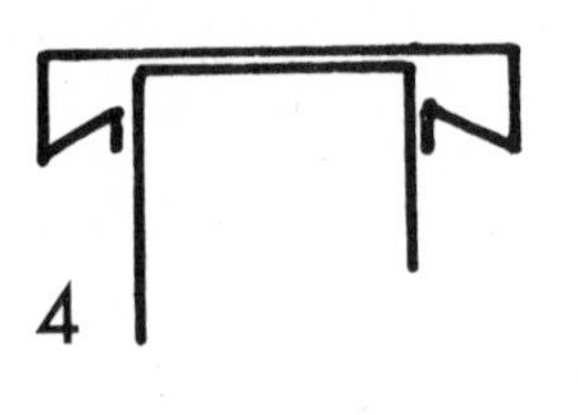

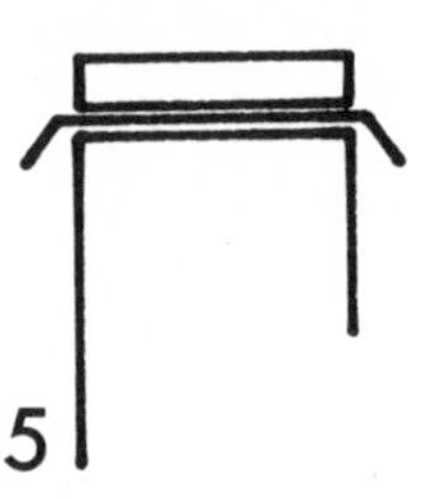

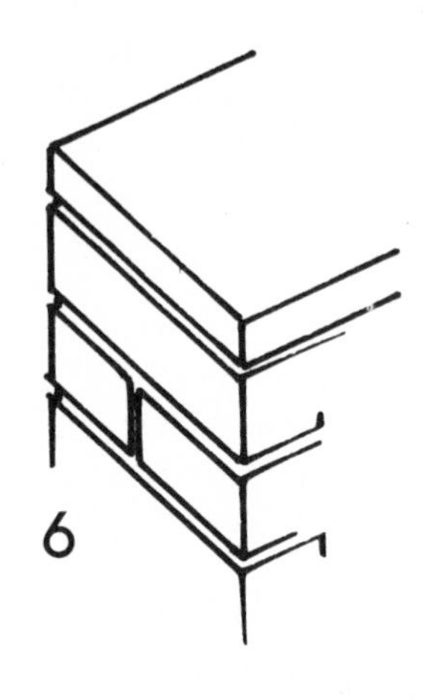

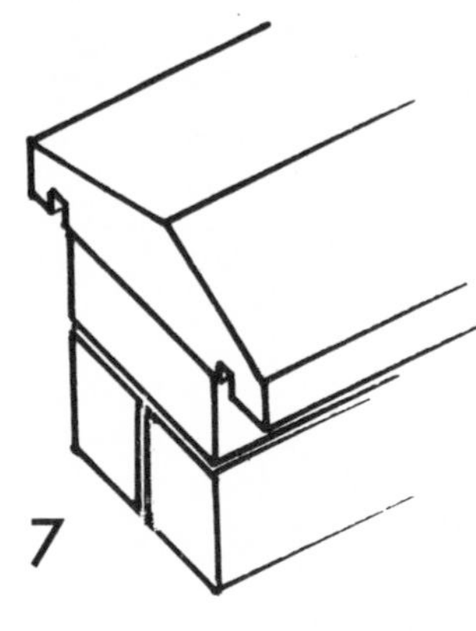

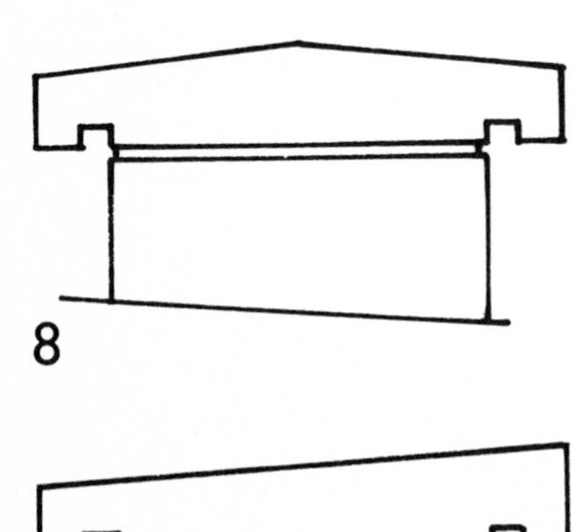

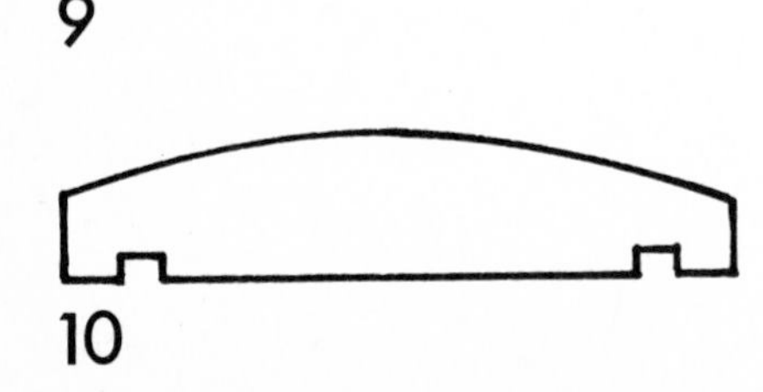

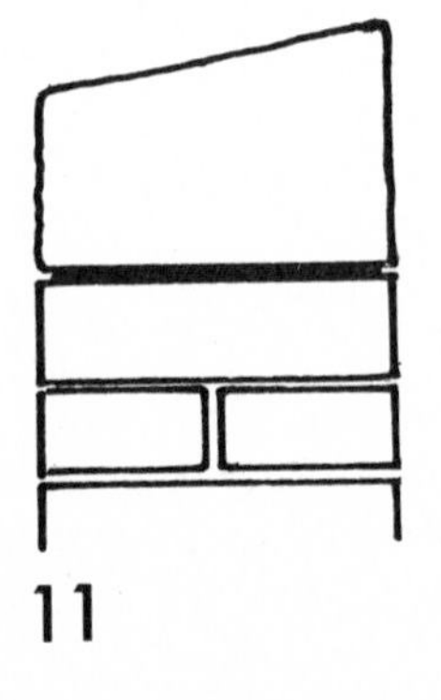

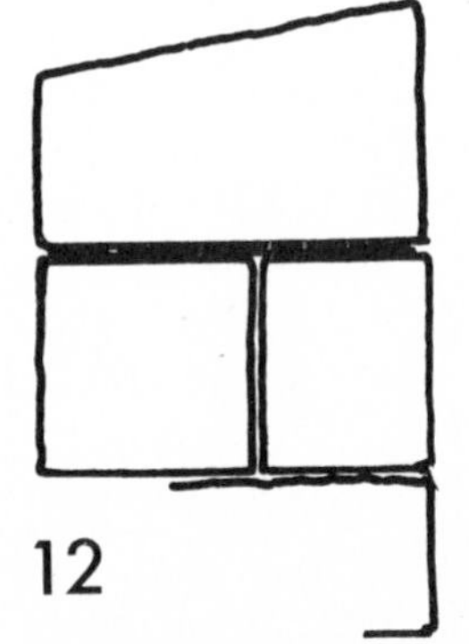

Expansion joints

A free-standing wall is liable to both subsidence and expansion or contraction, due probably to weather and its subsequent effect on the ground if it is poorly drained. Expansion joints should therefore be included in any great length of wall where movement might be expected. A joint should also be made where a wall abuts a structure of the same material – much as it would be desirable, visually, to run the house wall straight on in an unbroken line to form the garden wall, it is probably wiser not to do this in case subsidence should occur.

In order to avoid daylight showing through the expansion joint of a brick wall, thus spoiling a supposedly continuous design, the joint should be made with a staggered break. A gap of ½ in. is enough to allow for settlement and take up expansion if the next break occurs within the recommended distance.

Narrow walls

A one-brick thick wall should not join onto a house as its thinness will be emphasized by the solidity of the building and buttresses will be necessary at 6–8 ft intervals according to the height of the wall. Coping is difficult for such a wall; but probably precast concrete strip would be most suitable or bricks set on end. The curving or serpentine thin wall has greater strength than a straight run, but again the coping presents a problem – though left with no top the wall looks very unfinished and unsatisfactory. In the right position a narrow honeycomb can look attractive in combination with plants, but again buttressing will be necessary, though not at such close intervals, for wind-resistance has been considerably reduced – and so, incidentally, has one's privacy.

Concrete or cinder block wall

If it is the right colour and is suitably capped, a concrete block wall can be appropriate in town and country. The plain block wall is often used inside the garden for partitions but, like the thin brick wall, is too thin for a boundary. The hollow plain blocks, grey cinder blocks, or breeze blocks are very suitable for a solid boundary or screen wall. It should be laid on a concrete foundation and needs no buttressing. This type has an added advantage over a brick wall in that it can be reinforced if necessary with rods running from the foundation up through the hollow blocks and concreted in place, though this strengthening will not normally be necessary for a simple boundary. Capping of these blocks is

147 *A honeycomb brick wall*

difficult and probably precast slab is again the most suitable – if paving slab of the type employed on an adjoining terrace can be used, so much the better.

The colour of these walls and any other concrete structure in the garden needs careful consideration in order to avoid a harsh, tawdry effect which will draw the eye. This question will be referred to later (Chapter 12).

Stone walling

In country districts, where stone is much used locally, the indigenous type of walling cannot be beaten for both visual compatibility with the site and effective screening if this is needed. Types of stone wall vary in different parts of the world and constructional methods should be left to the craftsman erecting it. Broadly, however, the types of stone wall are as follows: regular and irregular coursed rubble, where stones are used like bricks with the occasional one taking up two or three courses, giving a broken effect; square uncoursed rubble which is self-explanatory; or coursed random rubble, where irregular stones are sandwiched between regular layers which give stability. Uncoursed random rubble walls are probably not suitable for the garden as they are built without mortar and are unstable unless they have large keystones (which are not always available) running through the wall at regular intervals. The type of coping for any of these walls should follow the local tradition.

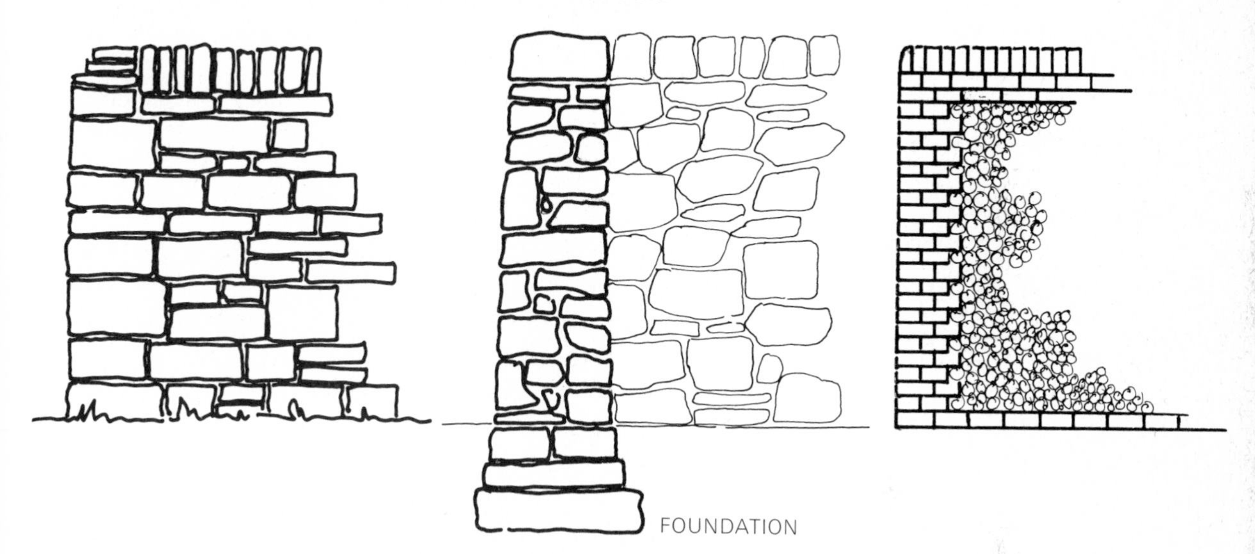

148–150 Fieldstone walls
Left: Coursed random rubble
Centre: Uncoursed random rubble. Note the slight batter
Right: Flint with brick quoins

The unsuitability of this type of walling in an urban setting, or even in the countryside if the stone used is alien, should speak for itself. Sadly it does not always seem to, and local authorities, who should know better, erect walling, round traffic islands, for instance, which is quite out of character with its setting. Do consider, therefore, whether the particular type of walling you saw on holiday and liked so much is suitable to surround your own garden. Use it inside the garden if you must – but not where other people have to look at it.

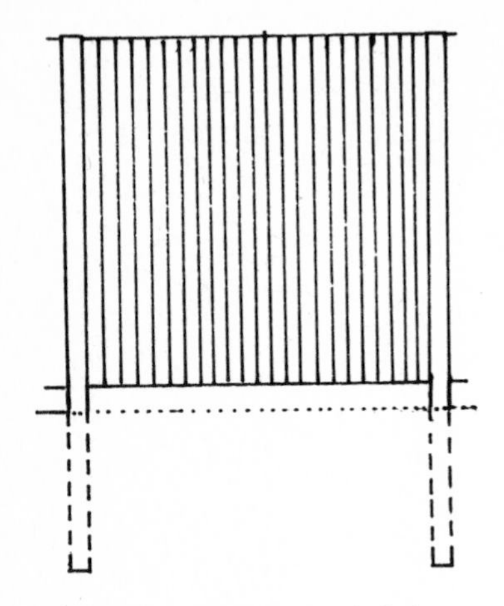

151, 152 Above and below: Vertical and horizontal close board fencing

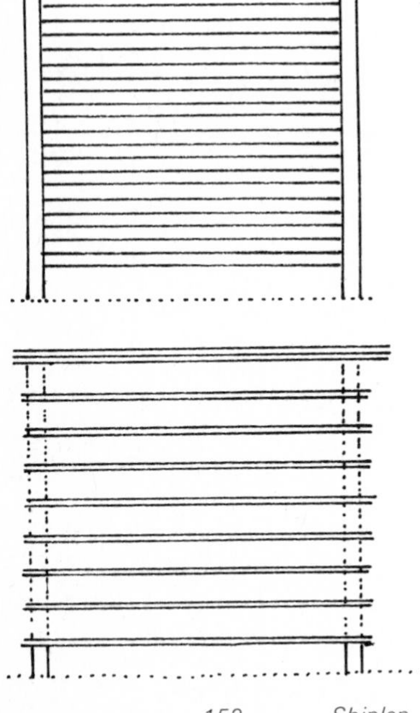

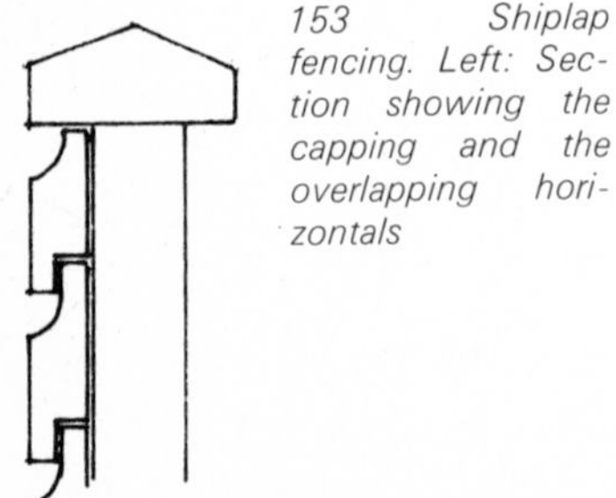

153 Shiplap fencing. Left: Section showing the capping and the overlapping horizontals

BOUNDARY FENCING

Wood fencing, so popular everywhere, is a practical and usually cheaper solution for the demarcation of a boundary. It can be an open fence, such as post and rail fencing, or solid. What timber fencing may lack in longevity or providing privacy is often repaid in appearance. Whether painted or treated with preservative, the more solid timber screens will need a certain amount of maintenance, and access should be left to them for that purpose. The cheaper forms of wattle or split bamboo screening have only a limited life but this could be quite long enough for an evergreen shrub screen to grow up on the inside and render replacement unnecessary.

Remember that plants do not like fresh timber preservative and will die through contact with it. It sometimes takes a year or so before the toxicity of the preservative becomes sufficiently neutralized for climbers to grow on a treated fence.

Woods suitable for fencing include cedar, pine, redwood, Douglas fir and spruce among the conifers, and ash, elm, beech, birch, hornbeam, lime, sycamore and sapwood or oak among the hardwoods.

The types of fencing in different parts of the world and the woods used are as variable as the types of stone and methods of wall construction. It is usually economic, therefore, to use the local style and timber if available. Avoid conscious rusticity at all costs and do not use timber with bark on it. The bark dies, forming a trap for moisture and then decays to provide a retreat for all manner of insects.

Simplicity of detailing and sound construction will produce the most satisfactory results. There are, of course, all sorts of timber fences, but the common types which can be bought by the yard fairly universally are shown here.

Close board fencing

This type provides a solid barrier around a site and is the nearest to a wall one can get in timber. If the solid face of the fence is turned outwards, with the post and rails on the inside, an unclimbable face is presented to the world. It is in fact usually assumed in this country that the structural framework of a fence should be on the owner's side.

Ideally an easily replaceable gravel board should run along the base of the fence – the area most likely to decay. Without this, odd rotting panels in the verticals are difficult to take

out and, when broken at the bottom, provide an entrance for animals.
A capping board like a coping, running along the top of the fence, will help to lengthen its life by preventing the end grain of the verticals being exposed to rain.
The verticals of this type of fence, or any other for that matter, should not protrude beyond the top line of the fence. They should be made, if not of the same timber as the fence, then certainly of timber and not concrete in order to create an unbroken run of fencing rather than a series of separate panels.

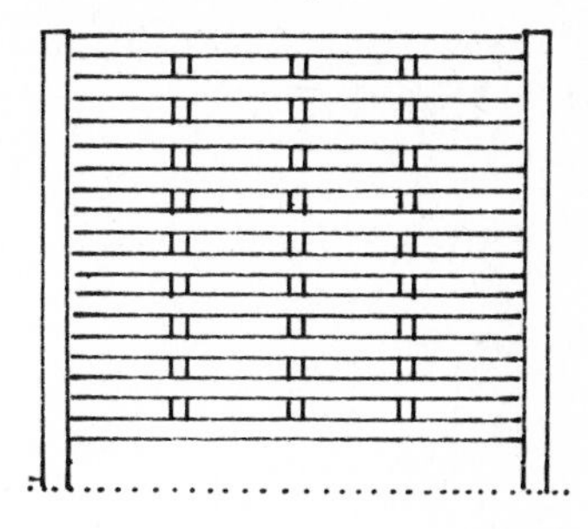

154, 155 Interwoven fencing panels
Above: Interface
Below: Overlap

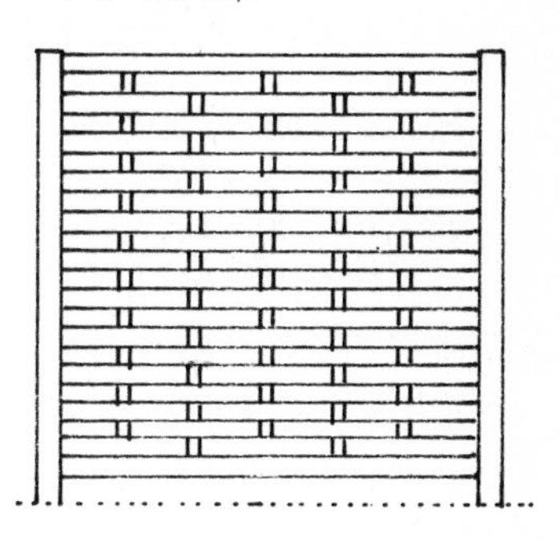

Interwoven fencing

A series of panels is unavoidable, however, if interwoven fencing is used. This type of fence is more suitable for urban use and comes in two types – interface panelling and overlap panelling. The latter is usually more expensive, being the stronger of the two. The life span of the panel type of fence is considerably lengthened when plants are not grown directly upon it but are trained on wires an inch or two away from it. These wires can be fixed to the verticals which support the panels.

Wattle hurdles in hazel

A similar type of fence, more frequently found in England, is the wattle hurdle. This was used originally, and indeed is still used, to enclose flocks of sheep and to provide windbreaks on exposed uplands. The panels come in 6 ft lengths and various heights, and should be supported by stakes driven into the ground. Their length of life is approximately five years.

156 Reed fencing makes an excellent backing for plants and provides good support for climbers

Osier and reed hurdles

Similar hurdles are sometimes made from osier or willow and their weave is much closer than that of hazel hurdles. A finer type still can be made *in situ* of vertically placed reeds held in place by horizontal fence rails. Where reeds are readily available, this is a very cheap method of producing a reasonably solid fence. It will not, however, withstand the attacks of children or dogs.

None of the hurdle fences looks well when used to divide up suburban gardens, since their character is alien to the setting. Woven panels are considerably better for this purpose and probably more durable.

157 Split bamboo makes a good, if short-lived, screen but needs to be supported by chicken wire

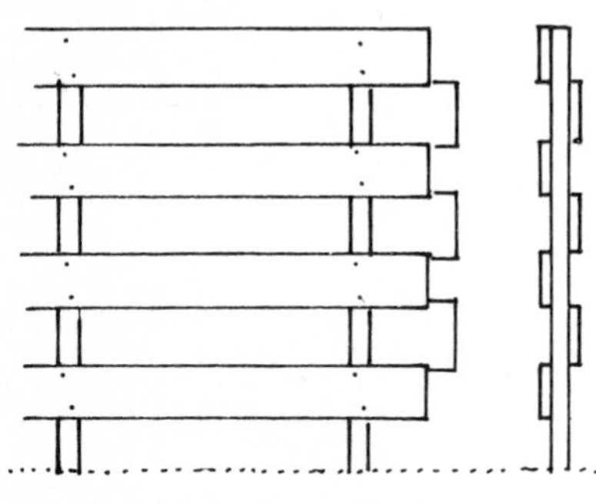

158 Above: Ranch fencing with the rails fixed horizontally on alternate sides of the verticals

159, 160 Below: Split wood or cleft chestnut paling
Left: Strained wire with a strut supporting the corner post
Right: Nailed to horizontal rails

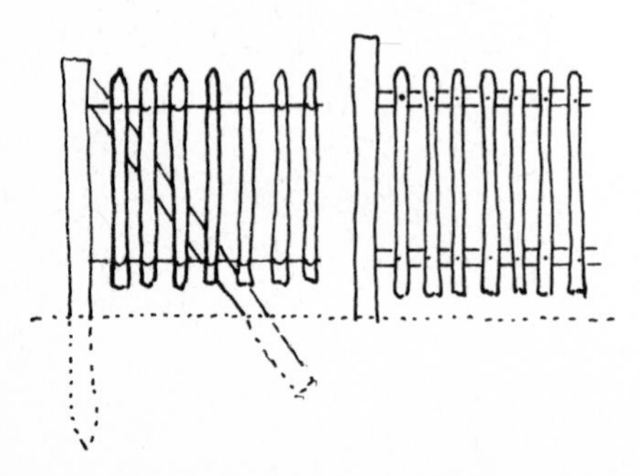

Split bamboo screening

A still cheaper type of fence is the split bamboo which is sometimes used to cover greenhouses or car-parking spaces. This kind of screen comes in rolls of various lengths and gives complete privacy, but it only has a short life span. A rigid supporting skeleton of coarse wire netting is necessary. This is attached to the verticals, and the split bamboo is sewn on to it with wire or tarred string. Being very light, this type of fence can be used as a temporary extension to give added height where necessary. Its use is perhaps limited, however, as the superstructure necessary to support it is unsightly.

Ranch fencing

This type is often used to separate terrace areas in new housing developments. Surrounding a whole garden it can appear somewhat cumbersome, although when properly used it has a clean, trim look about it.

Softwood rails are fixed on alternate sides of their supports either horizontally, when they are attached to the verticals themselves, or vertically, when they are attached to the cross-pieces between the verticals; either way a sort of louvred effect is produced. Being made of softwood, this type of fence needs frequent painting, which can be difficult after a time when plants are growing through the rails. The effect, however, is most attractive.

Chestnut or split cedar fencing

Chestnut or cedar paling can be supported by galvanized wire fixed and strained between timber verticals or by horizontal rail fencing. Both methods produce a very strong and durable fence if properly erected, but give little privacy or shelter. They are, however, 'unclimbable'. The second type is the more robust and stronger looking of the two, but it is accordingly more expensive, though still cheaper than ranch or hurdle fencing. The distances between the pales can vary from practically nothing to about 5 in.

This paling, strung on two or three strands of galvanized wire, can be bought in 50 ft rolls from 2 ft to 6 ft high. To ensure that the paling is taut when erected, stout intermediate straining poles at 6 ft intervals are necessary with struts to give added support at the corners. The pales should be slung a few inches off the ground to prevent them rotting.

161–163 *Palisade or picket fencing*
Right: The low type with rounded or pointed verticals
Below: The tall urban type with a gravel board along the bottom

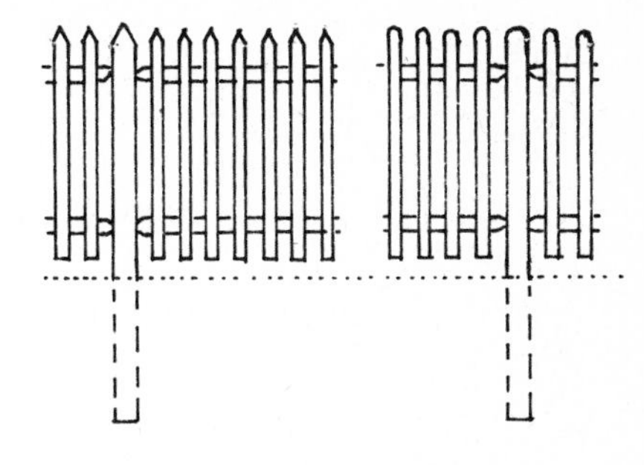

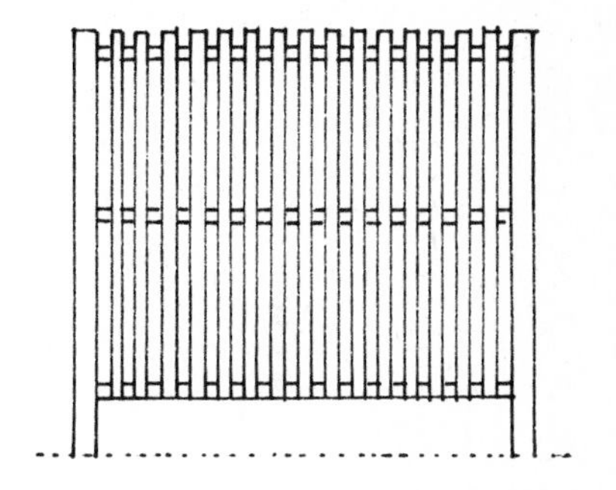

Palisade or picket fencing

This is the type, low and often white painted, usually seen surrounding front gardens. It has a slightly cottagey feel about it but is very attractive when well maintained. The palisade verticals measure approximately $2\frac{1}{2} \times \frac{3}{4}$ in., are spaced about $2\frac{1}{2}$ in. apart and fixed at top and bottom to an arras rail. The top end can be rounded or pointed and the lower should again be a few inches off the ground.
Less often seen is the tall fence, up to 6 ft high, which is perhaps the urban equivalent of the split pale fence. In this case the pickets should be approximately 2×2 in. and have a 2 in. gap between.

Post and rail fencing

Natural split cedar post and rail fencing is particularly popular in America, both as a practical barrier for cattle in ranch lands, and as a simple but most pleasing rustic divider in the country garden. It also has the advantage of being relatively inexpensive. When smooth sawn horizontals are used they can be narrow as shown in the diagram at right, or broad as in the photograph on page 16.
The good post and rail fence, whether treated with preservative or planed and painted, should be mortise-joined at the hardwood verticals. These should be spaced at roughly 9 ft intervals with two smaller prick posts set in between. There should be three horizontals with the lowest one approximately 2 ft 6 in. off the ground.
A cheaper form has only two softwood horizontals nailed to the verticals at closer intervals. Nails should always be galvanized when used outside so as to prevent liquid rust staining the timber.

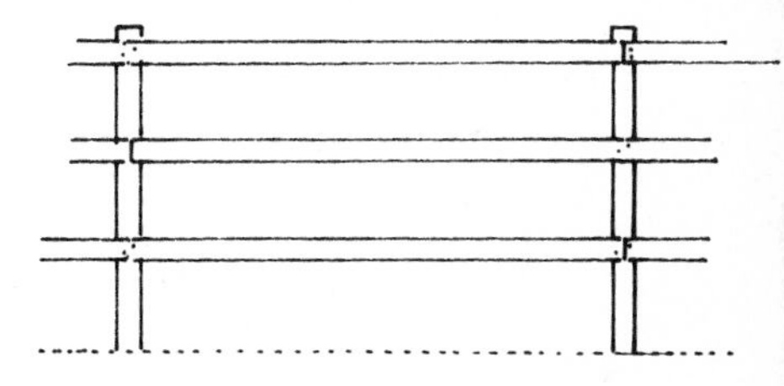

164, 165 *Post and rail fences*
Above: Sawn horizontals
Below: Split horizontals. In background, close split wood paling

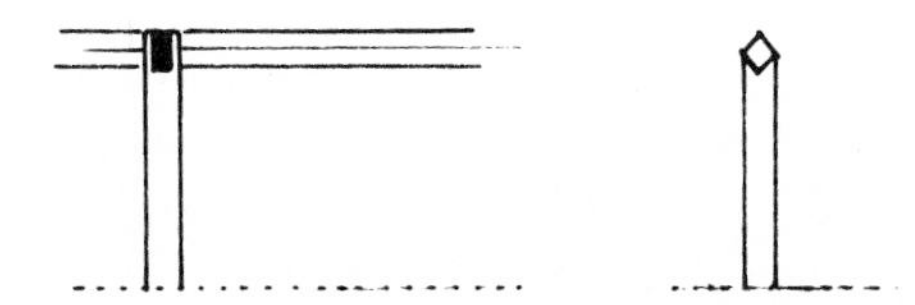

166 *Single rail fence for demarcation purposes*

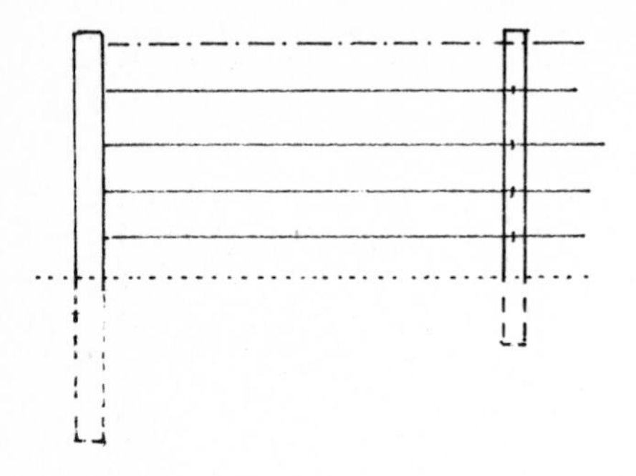

167 *Post and wire fencing*

168, 169 *Metal bar fences*
Below: The rural type with horizontal rails
Bottom: The urban palisade type which provides a very effective physical barrier

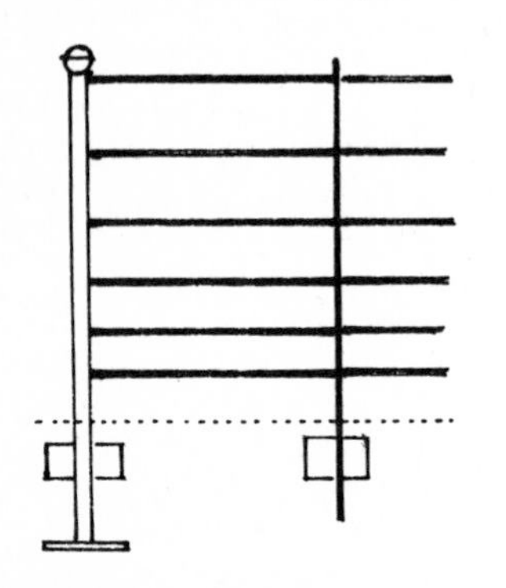

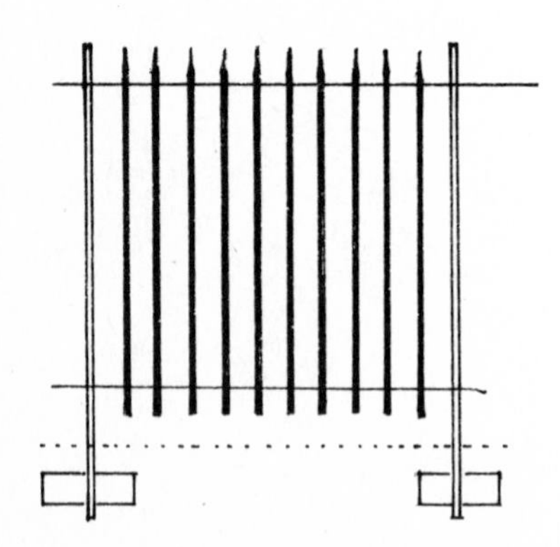

Timber and wire fencing

Fencing made of galvanized wire strained between sawn posts of hardwood is not really at all suitable for the garden. Its use is primarily agricultural, as a cattle fence in some areas, but it could have a domestic use in rural areas if walling is impracticable. It could also be used where a secure boundary is necessary with minimum visual obstruction in order to avoid blocking a view.

The holes for the verticals of any type of timber fence should be made as small as possible, and earth should be packed tightly round the posts when they are in place. If the soil is peaty, sandy or wet, and cannot hold the posts firmly enough to take the strain of the fence and of children or animals pushing against it, the posts should be concreted in. This is done by inserting the post in the hole, half filling it with concrete and then replacing the soil.

In a domestic setting concrete verticals are most unsympathetic with any type of fence, as they have a hard look which does not weather away. There is, however, an economic case for their use where a hedge or evergreen boundary planting will screen them.

Concrete posts are usually used with galvanized wire or chain link stretched between them, but the effect is more in keeping with the prison yard than a domestic garden – developers, please note.

Metal fencing

For domestic use the only other acceptable fencing on the market is the metal-bar type. Its use is either strongly rural or strongly urban.

Continuous metal bar fencing – the sort used in parkland estates – is traditionally of mild steel or wrought iron with round bars running through flat metal vertical standards. Light and thin in appearance, it allows the country feeling to run through it without providing a visual obstruction, yet at the same time it is tough and long-lived and provides a very satisfactory physical enclosure.

In an urban setting, vertical bar railings provide a light-looking structure, which is both strong and unclimbable. The height varies from 4 ft to 7 ft, and the thickness of the vertical bars and the type of capping also differ.

8 HARD SURFACING

With the type of boundary chosen, the next step is to decide on the infilling of the area: the amount of soft surfacing (lawn or ground cover) and hard surfacing, and the proportion of one to the other.
The size and variety of the component elements of a hard surface determine its characteristics. The greater the size and the smaller the variety, the better the wear resistance and the speed at which one can travel over it. The hardest-wearing and hardest-looking surfaces (tarmac and concrete) are for vehicular use, precast concrete slabs are good for fast walking, granite setts are slower and cobbles say, 'Keep off'. The smaller the size of the components and the greater their variety, the more appropriate the surface will be to a garden setting, but the cost, both of materials and of labour to lay them, will also be greater.
Whatever type of surfacing is used, it should, if possible, link up with the materials used either in the house or the boundary. If this is not possible – brick paving for instance is expensive – the linking material can be used as an edging or

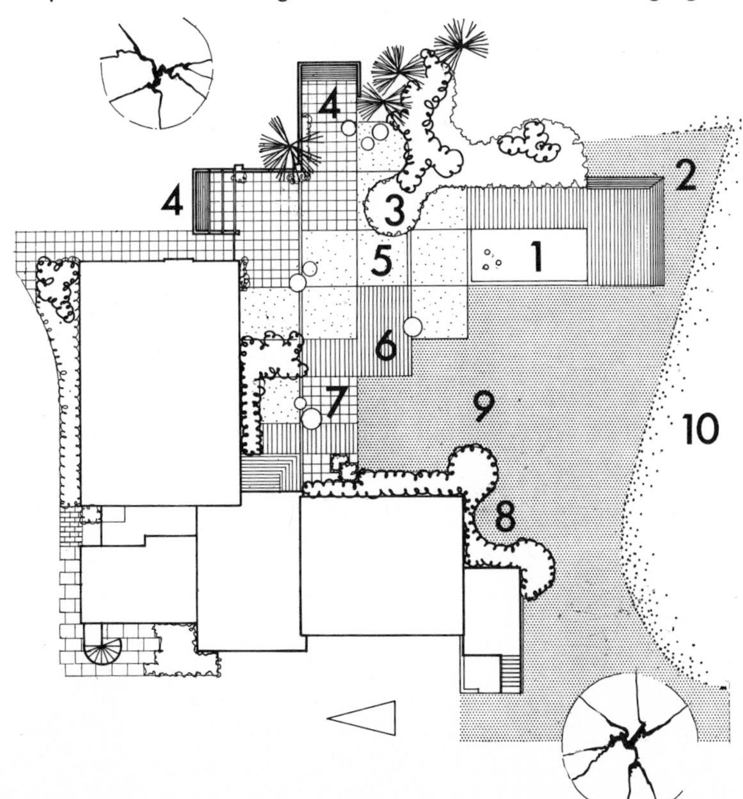

170, 171 Left and above: A terrace for open-air entertaining. The surfacing is a mixture of hard red brick, brushed in situ *concrete and precast concrete slabs*

1 *Pool and fountains*
2 *Timber bench seat*
3 *Bed of heather*
4 *Sitting bays*
5 In situ *concrete*
6 *Brick paving*
7 *Precast concrete slabs*
8 *Mixed planting*
9 *Lawn*
10 *View down hill*

in combination with another surface material. Interesting pavement treatments which illustrate this can be seen in all the new towns and indeed in most new developments.
It is far better, however, to understate surface materials than to overdo them and produce what the architectural magazines would call a 'floorscape'. The over-designed floorscape is as indigestible as the over-patterned carpet, which creates an unsettling effect in a small room and detracts from the furniture standing upon it.
It goes without saying that the hard surfacing you select should substantiate and realize the pattern you have worked out on paper. Where the pattern is a curving one, however, it should be remembered that it is costly to cut paving slabs of any kind to a curve and indeed will probably not be possible if the material is a soft one. Furthermore, the regular line of the paving joints will counteract the sweep of the curve. Concrete and tarmac, however, can run to a curve, provided they are retained by a material which will take the curve, such as metal strip or timber shuttering. The smaller paving elements, setts and bricks, can be laid in a curve as

172, 173 Two stages in the laying of a curved path. The spaces between the precast concrete slabs are filled with small stones

174, 175 Sound terrace flooring is essential on both the public and the private scale
Left: A café with flagstones
Below: A slate and brick terrace

long as consideration is given to the open joints on the outer side of the curve.

Before starting to lay the hard surfacing, peg out the design on site with string and stakes. Mark out the whole area even if you are not laying it all at the first stage, and try to visualize whether the plan works, for it will probably need adjustment at this stage to make it practicable.

The actual area of hard surfacing needed will depend on the

activities for which it is to be used but the function of any paving should be to provide a hard, dry, non-slip surface. A good general principle is to be generous with the areas of hard surfacing, whatever their type or function. To avoid an arid look, the types of surfacing can be varied and areas of planting introduced. The paving should blend into the general layout, and not be an eye-catching excrescence.

Paths should be not less than 3 ft wide to allow easy manœuvring of wheelbarrows, carts or lawn mowers both on the straights and round the corners. Bear in mind that if plants are to be grown on one or both sides of the path they should flop over, and a greater width will be necessary. Where a path runs round the walls of a building, forming a sort of plinth, there seems to be an optimum width proportionate to the height of the structure, and this can be judged only by eye.

For sitting space a minimum width of 6 ft is usually necessary, so that one's feet or the chair legs remain on the paved surface, and there should be room for a table as well. It is essential that the terrace is well laid as nothing is more irritating than a wobbling chair or spilled coffee.

Where children will use the terrace, allow a good radius for tricycle turning, and where paving surrounds a sand-pit, allow plenty of space for overflow.

If the terrace is to function all the year – and it can well do so if adequately sheltered – it must dry as quickly as possible after rain. A crossfall of approximately 1 in. in 6 ft will therefore be necessary to take off surplus rainwater. In the average domestic situation rainwater can simply run off on to the surrounding beds or grass if the dispersal is general, but if the fall is so channelled as to create a current, a gulley will be necessary. This can be a simple metal grating linked to a laid drain, the house rainwater system, or a prepared soakaway (see Chapter 6).

CONCRETE

On a domestic scale concrete, laid *in situ* as a paving material, is not usually satisfactory unless the surface is given some finish, and the whole broken into smaller elements to prevent cracking.

Developers have a habit of leaving a 3 ft wide strip round a new house as their contribution to 'landscape'. It is of course cheap but is usually badly laid on too coarse a foundation and very soon cracks and becomes slippery.

If, however, the concrete area is divided into 8 ft squares – not larger, or reinforcement will be necessary to prevent

cracking – with a brick, granite sett, or hardwood pattern, the scale is reduced and with it the tendency to crack. An infilling to divide the squares is not necessary if the concrete is laid in sections 8 ft square and each is allowed to set before laying the next one.
A coarse gravel aggregate used in the concrete mix and brushed when 'green' will give an attractive broken surface.

LAYING An average mix for domestic garden use, for paths, pools, steps, frames, edging, etc., would be:

1 part cement, 2 parts sand, 3 parts coarse aggregate (all parts by volume).

Cement is the binding element of concrete. It is not a surfacing material on its own.
Avoid using too much water when mixing, as this will weaken the concrete and cause shrinkage when it dries; on the other hand the mix must be workable enough to be put into moulds without developing air bubbles.
In most districts it is possible to obtain ready-mixed concrete from firms specializing in this product. They will usually deliver within a five-mile radius, and the minimum quantity supplied is generally three or four cubic yards. It is, of course, wise to check that they can supply the right mix for the job.
If the aggregate is to be exposed, the surface should be brushed with a soft broom to remove surplus mortar about an hour after the concrete has been laid. When the concrete has hardened sufficiently for the stones of the aggregate not to be dislodged, the surface should be brushed again, this time with a stiff broom, leaving the stones slightly proud of the surface, and finally sprayed with water. Coloured cements, however, should not be sprayed in cold, damp weather, because there is a danger of a white film forming. In general avoid laying concrete in frosty weather, when it will crack as it sets, or in very hot weather, when it will dry out far too quickly unless protected by damp sacking.

176, 177 To expose the aggregate of in situ *concrete, scrub or brush the surface when the mix is partially dry, using plenty of water; repeat at intervals. The result will be a pebbled or marbled effect depending on the type of aggregate used*

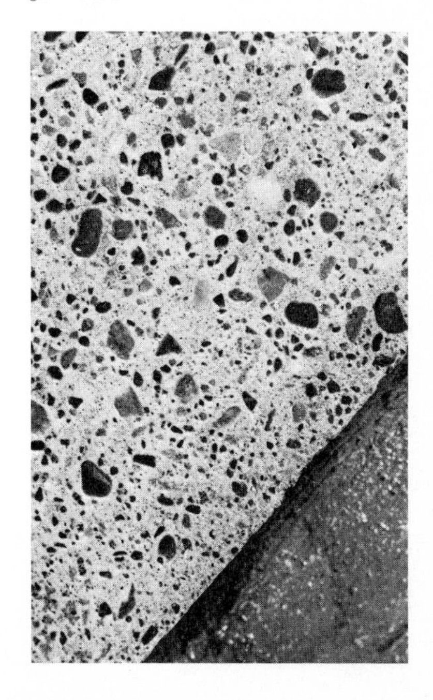

ASPHALT (TARMACADAM)

A bitumen or tarmacadam surface is seldom needed except perhaps in the largest garden as a filler between the concrete or stone slabs of a path (when a cold bituminous emulsion would be used anyway). It can be used for the surface of a drive, but price is usually a prohibiting factor and such a hard and durable surface is seldom necessary for light traffic. Access for oil tankers might call for a better surfacing, although often the length of pipe available overcomes this.

178 A pattern of precast concrete slabs with a tarmacadam infill gives a hard-wearing surface and a contrast of colour and texture

This type of surfacing needs expert laying and base preparation and a contractor should be called in to do the job. Various finishes can be achieved, either smooth or non-slip, through the addition of different surface dressings and chippings.

COLD ASPHALT

This is a mixture of bitumen and crushed rock. It is more likely to be used on a small scale, and can be laid anywhere where there is adequate manœuvring space for a roller to provide the thorough compaction necessary.

	Drives	*Footpaths*
Base	6 in. maximum of hoggin, crushed stone or quarry shale	6 in. maximum of hoggin, crushed stone or quarry shale
Top layer of base	2 in. layer of $1\frac{1}{2}$–2 in. stone consolidated with 6–8 ton roller	$\frac{3}{4}$ in. chippings at 1 ton to 30 sq. yd. Water, consolidate with 10–15 cwt roller

First coat cold bituminous emulsion	$\frac{3}{4}$ gal. per sq. yd $\frac{1}{2}$–$\frac{3}{8}$ in. thick	$\frac{1}{2}$–$\frac{3}{4}$ gal. per sq. yd $\frac{1}{4}$ in. thick
Spread chippings	1 ton to 90 sq. yd	1 ton to 120 sq. yd
	Roll immediately and also next morning. Close drive for a few days	Leave for 2–3 days
Sealing coat of cold bituminous emulsion	$\frac{1}{2}$ gal. per sq. yd	$\frac{1}{3}$ to $\frac{1}{4}$ gal. per sq. yd
Surface chippings, spread immediately and roll	$\frac{3}{8}$–$\frac{1}{4}$ in. thick, 1 ton to 130 sq. yd	$\frac{1}{4}$ in. thick, 1 ton to 150 sq. yd

Cold bituminous emulsion can also be used to bind and seal compacted gravel, but it will not take heavy wear and will no longer be porous.
There are a number of proprietary brands of cold bituminous emulsion on the market and the instructions for each should be followed.

PRECAST SLABS

By far the most commonly used hard garden material is the precast concrete slab which is comparatively cheap and easy to lay and provides a non-slip, dry and durable surface. Be careful to check that the slab you choose will take the necessary weight (e.g., a car) and see that it is well laid.
The sizes generally available are:
$1\frac{1}{2}$ in. thick . . . . . . 1 ft×6 in. or 1 ft×1 ft
2 in. thick . . . . . . 9 in.×9 in. or 9 in.×1 ft 6 in.
1 ft×1 ft 6 in. or 1 ft×2 ft or 1 ft×3 ft
1 ft 6 in.×1 ft 6 in. or 1 ft 6 in.×2 ft or 1 ft 6 in×3 ft
2 ft×2 ft
Not all makes of slab come in all these sizes, however.
The cheapest type is the pale grey slab used for pavements which is available with a smooth finish, a textured surface or a machine-made pattern. The colour is often a little harsh for

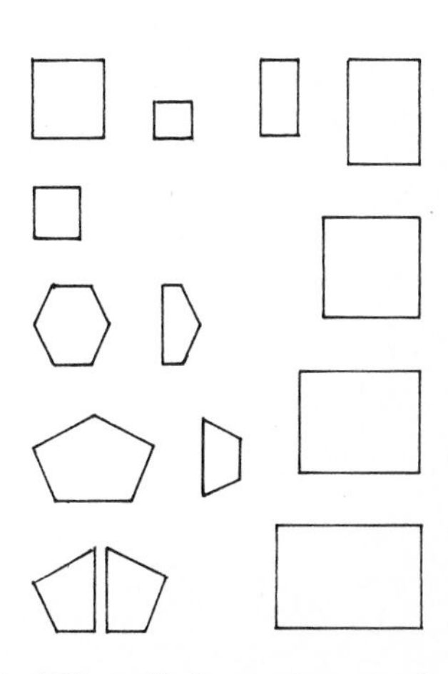

179 Various sizes and shapes of concrete slab

180 *Right: Concrete slabs used in conjunction with loose cobbles*

181–185 *Patterns which can be made with precast concrete slabs*

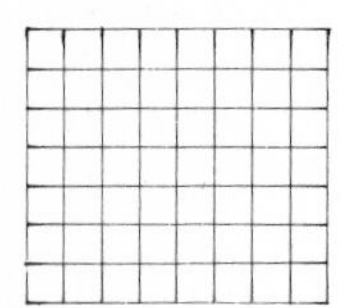

Regular pattern of squares

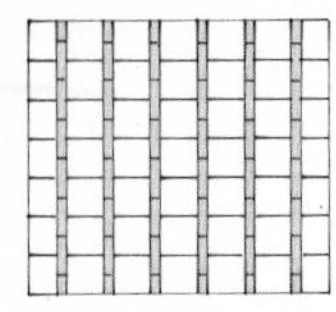

Square slabs separated by bricks or granite setts

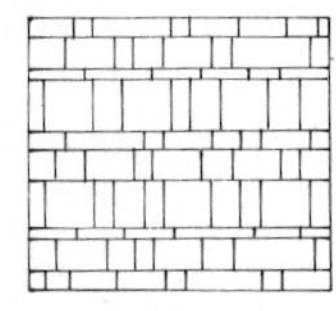

Random pattern using different sized slabs

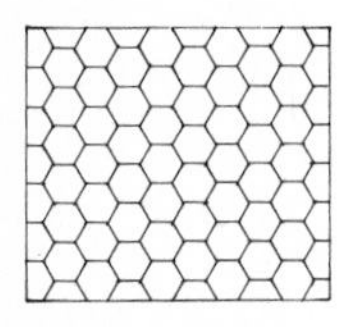

Hexagonal slabs

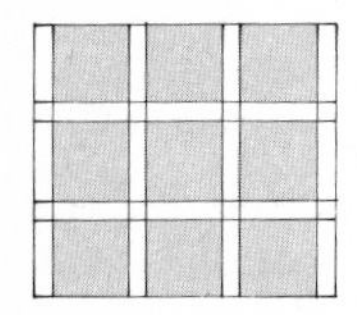

Pattern of square slabs infilled with tarmac

186 *Below: Method of laying a paving slab as a mowing stone. This avoids plants which flop out of their beds being mown with the grass*

a domestic area, although the textured slab is better than the smooth. Other precast slabs are produced in a variety of colours and textures.

As with all else outside, the simpler the solution the better. Many of the proprietary slabs have a colour that is far too garish and demanding for general application and when these are mixed with other colours in a pattern the result is often repellent. When selecting a slab, test its colour when both wet and dry; spit on a small corner and it will be seen how a colour which is comparatively quiet when dry becomes quite loud when wet. A fairly plain dark slab with a slight texture seems to be ideal for a garden in full sunlight, and pale creamy ones will reflect the light and brighten shaded areas.

Slabs can be laid in a variety of patterns by using different sizes. The jointing is important; rubbing back the mortar $\frac{1}{8}$ in. or so between the slabs shows them up to better advantage, but the joint should not be wide enough or deep enough to trap an umbrella stick or stiletto heel.

There are hexagonal, circular and free-shaped slabs on the market as well as the regular squares and oblongs, but to me they look rather too self-conscious and the result is invariably disappointing. Also available are slabs which have a very coarse aggregate in them resembling small cobbles. This is far cheaper than laying cobble stones, but the result is a compromise and looks like bars of nut milk chocolate.

Whatever fancy shape is used the pattern should be finished with half-slabs at the edge to avoid a serrated effect.

LAYING Excavate to a depth and gradient to allow for the hardcore base, sand layer and slab thickness to bring the finished surface layer up to the height you require. Where

the surface will abut a lawn, ensure that it is ½ in. below the grass level for ease of mowing.
Allow for a 3 in. layer of consolidated hardcore, or ash. If using coarse hardcore or rubble as a base, ensure that the final surface is smooth by breaking up the large lumps or covering over with ash.

1 Slabs can now be laid on a 1 in. bed of sand over the base, if there is no danger of the sand washing out and away.
2 A safer and more durable method of laying is to bed the slabs in concrete and joint them with mortar. The actual mix of mortar should be dictated by the type of slab, but in general a 1:5 mix (one part of cement to five of sand) would be suitable.
3 Spot bedding on dots of mortar over a sand base is another method that avoids the undersides of the slabs getting covered with mortar and makes them easier to lift, clean and re-lay.

Generally it is better to allow whoever is laying the slab to do it his way, but discover what this is, and make it clear at the time how much traffic the area will have to take.

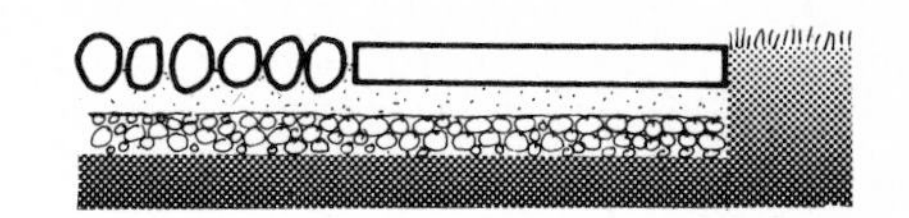

187 Above: A concrete slab laid instead of curbing to retain the grass surrounding a cobbled area

A regular pattern of rectangles

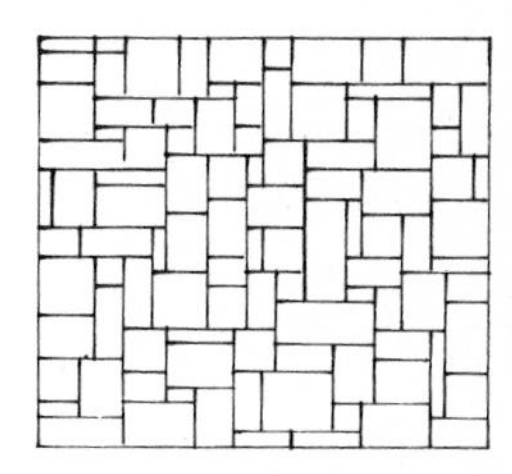

Random pattern

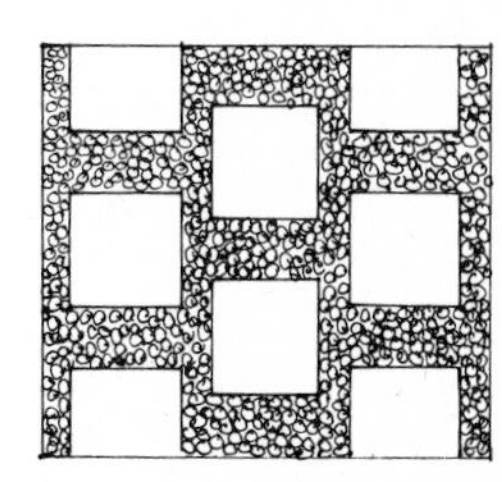

Regularly shaped slabs set in cobble stones

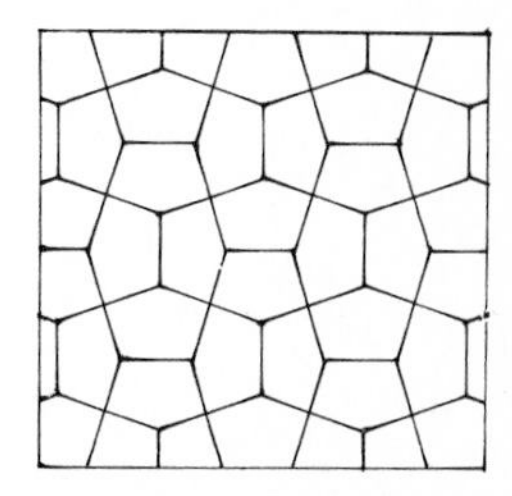

'Pentahex' slabs

188–191 Above: Further patterns which can be made with concrete slabs

192 Left: Circular paving slabs filled in with granite chips

JOINTING

Butt-jointing This is putting the slabs as close together as possible and infilling with mortar – this prevents water percolating through or weeds growing up between them.

Dry mix A clean finish to the slab is achieved by brushing a dry mixture of sand and cement, at the rate of 5:1 (5 sand: 1 cement) between the joints when the slabs are laid. This can be lightly sprayed with water afterwards and allowed to set.

Grouting Where a smooth-surfaced slab is being used a liquid grout can be poured between the joints, but it is essential that any overflow is cleaned off by soaking it up with a coarse aggregate. Grout is a liquid mixture of sand and cement.

Open jointing In the right position it is feasible to leave open joints between the slabs or to brush in sand only. Plants will establish themselves, however, and they can be difficult to eradicate once they have put down taproots. If there are children and pets about, it is not always easy to apply weedkiller safely.

It is difficult to use slabs for a curved edge without having to cut them, and many of the proprietary brands of slab, having a coarse aggregate composition, are difficult to cut cleanly anyway and tend to crack. It is therefore possible to make a path of unsquared slabs laid on a radius with earth or grass coming in between the joints. Grass should be half an inch above the level of the slabs so that it is still quite easy to mow. Such a path, however, should not need to take heavy wear, as the grass or plants will suffer if constantly trodden on and they will provide an obstacle over which the infirm might stumble.

Paving regularly interspersed with plant material is more satisfactory and safer than that dotted with rock plants at random. The latter, like the over-fancy floorscape, attracts the eye down to details when it should be encouraged to look outwards to the remainder of the site. Crazy paving made of broken slabs is unsuitable for the same reason – it is too fussy and is invariably hazardous to negotiate.

STEPPING STONES

Individual slabs can be laid as stepping stones over grass, planted or gravelled areas. Where they are laid in grass there is a tendency, with frequent use, for worn, muddy patches to develop between the slabs which makes this

193 *Sawing a slab to shape*

194 *Circular slab paving with a regular planting pattern superimposed*

195 *Precast concrete discs set in stones*

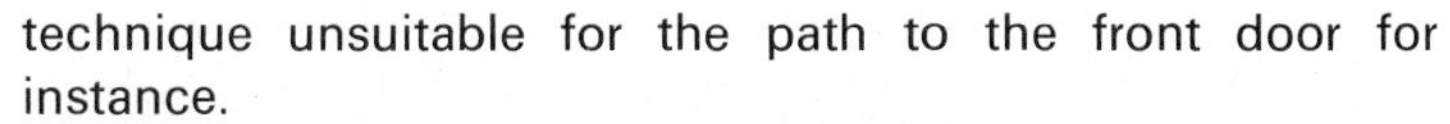

technique unsuitable for the path to the front door for instance.

It is essential that a mower should be able to run between and over the edges of the slabs without blunting its blades.

The spacing of the slabs also depends on their size, and usually 2 ft slabs with a 6 in. gap between will cater for the average length of stride. With stepping stones, as with steps, the user should not be conscious of having to regulate his stride.

LAYING Cut and lift a turf the size of the slab. Excavate down to the subsoil. If this is deeper than the 5 in. or so necessary for the slab and base, allow for 3 in. consolidated rubble. On this lay 3 in. concrete (1:2:4 mix) and then the slab, ensuring that its surface is just below the level of the grass.

STONE PAVING

Flagstone and slate for paving come in both square and rectangular shapes and are laid in a similar manner to precast concrete slabs. New stone paving is apt to be of a regular thickness, but old stones or slate are not, and the foundation levels should be altered accordingly. Where large heavy slabs are being laid a mortar bed is often unnecessary.

There can be no doubt that the look of stone paving cannot be surpassed in a rural or old urban setting. If second-hand stone is being used, the surface is often not smooth, but this is more than outweighed by its mellow character. Old stone paving is becoming more and more difficult to obtain, but one can be lucky when local authorities take up an old pavement to replace it with concrete slabs.

196 A pattern of old stone slabs laid in gravel (Ian Mylles)

LAYING There is an art in laying stone paving over a large area: this is to put them down in areas round a key stone. On a smaller area stones should be laid with as little cutting as possible and with courses not running into each other. The random appearance of the stone is emphasized if the edge of the paving is not formalized but allowed to run at random into an adjoining bed. It is important when laying stone to ensure that the joints are always rubbed back a little so that one sees each piece of stone and the whole pattern clearly.

197 Stone slabs laid without jointing

198 A brick path creates a strong directional line in a garden by A. du Gard Pasley

199–203 Brick paving patterns

Stretcher bond

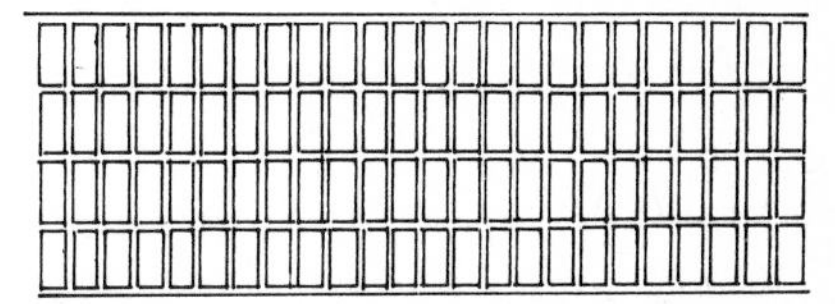

Soldier courses

Herringbone

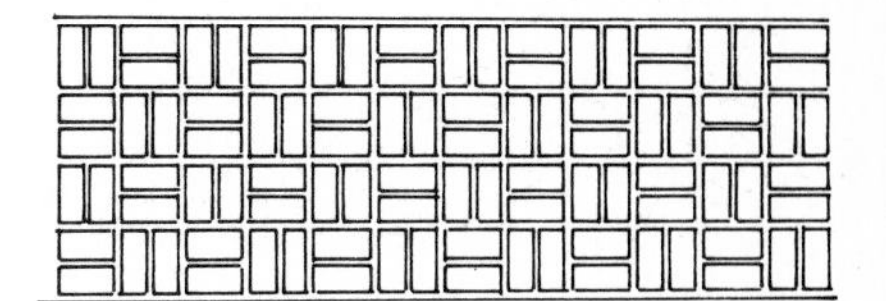

Basket weave

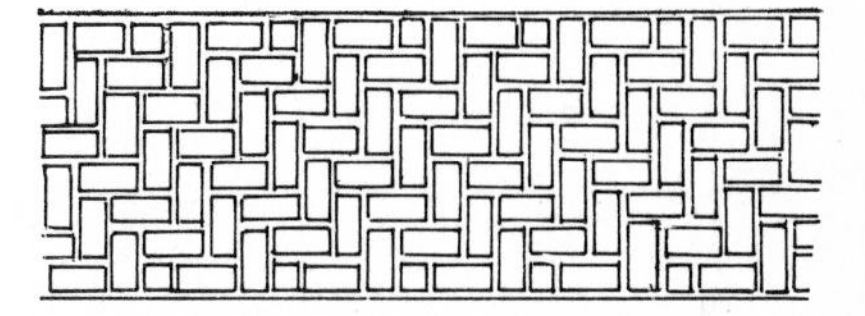

Herringbone pattern set at right angles

BRICK PAVING

Brick paving, unfortunately, is expensive since not only is the material costly, but also the labour of laying it. Even if one buys second-hand bricks one has to pay for the labour of cleaning the mortar off them. Nevertheless, there is often no substitute for the sharp outline, the colour and the patterns one can make with bricks. The brighter-coloured engineering brick usually needs careful positioning as, like coloured slabs, it can be too harsh and unsympathetic; but in general brick is ideal for use in combination with any other hard flooring material. It can be used to change the scale and, if only a little is used, can bring some of the feeling of an adjacent brick structure down into the second dimension.

The small size of bricks allows for gradual changes of level in a paved area, as on a slope, and on an inclined surface one can even lay the bricks slightly tilted so that one edge forms a foothold (when laid this way, they are said to be

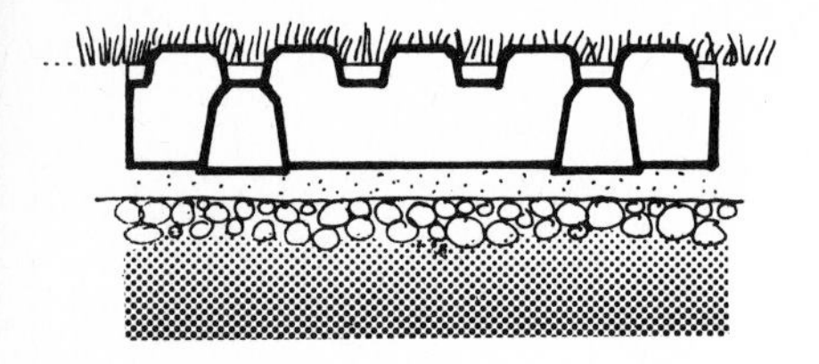

204–206 Mono slabs: grass or plants can grow through the holes in the slabs. These are useful when access for wheeled vehicles is occasionally needed over a planted area and they are also ideal for rough drives, play areas or for retaining rough banks

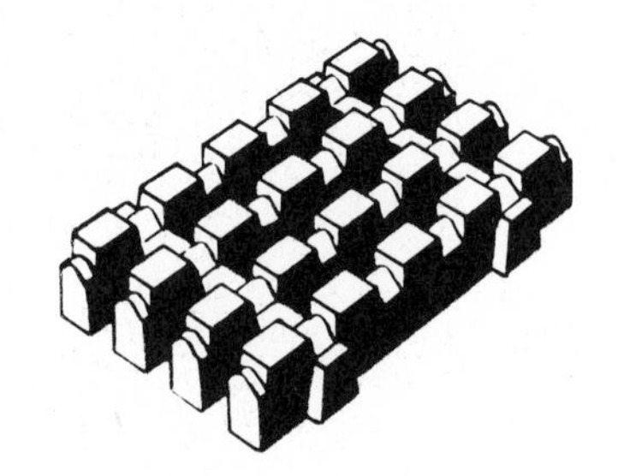

207, 208 Concrete firepath pots, often used as an alternative to mono slabs where fire-engine access is needed over a grassed public area

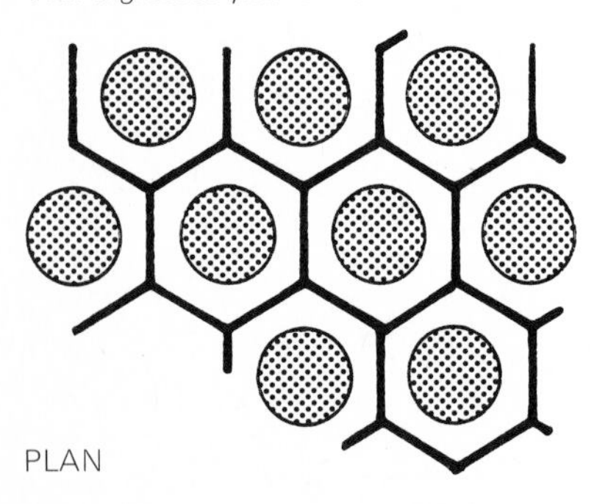

'haunched up'). Bricks are also useful for making curving paths without creating the large V-shaped joints which occur when other larger-sized materials are used.

Bricks used for paving, unlike those in a wall, will be damp most of the time and it is therefore important to select a type which can withstand damp and frost. Always check with a builders' supplier whether the particular brick is suitable. If you want to use the same brick for paving that you have used in a wall but find it is too soft, the choice is so wide that you will probably find another, harder, brick of similar colour which will do the job. A well-fired brick is generally suitable for garden work, so long as it will not have to take vehicular traffic. Over-fired bricks can be cheaper and when used *en masse* will give a brindled effect which is not unattractive.

Bricks can be hand-made, pressed or wirecut. Some types have a hollow area called a frog on the broad side which prohibits the use of this face for paving.

Wirecut bricks have no frog but are not suitable for outside use with the laminated side uppermost, as water tends to settle in the laminations of the clay and crack it. Pressed bricks generally have frogs on two sides and will therefore have to be laid on edge, which means that more are necessary. Where a hand-made brick with a frog on only one side is being used, or a pressed brick with no frogs, the brick can be laid flat.

Choice of brick

Bricks are available everywhere, but colours and sizes can

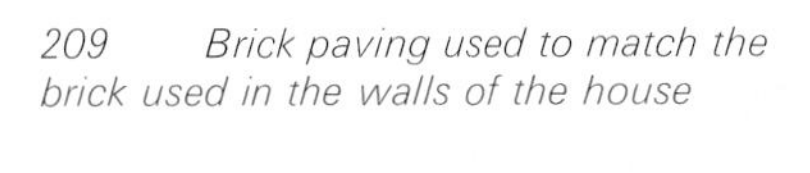

209 Brick paving used to match the brick used in the walls of the house

210 Brick basket weave pattern in a city garden

vary. It should also be noted that some bricks are harder than others and some have smooth and some more textured surfaces. Smooth brick can become slippery, so the textured type is probably safer for most paving surfaces. The best advice is to check your needs with your supplier. Old mellowed bricks, naturally, are more attractive for the garden if you can get them. When used for walling, the hard colour of new bricks can be softened with whitewash if this fits the colour scheme of the environment.

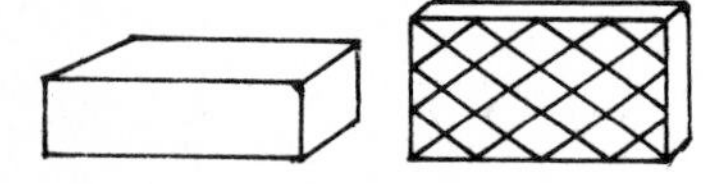

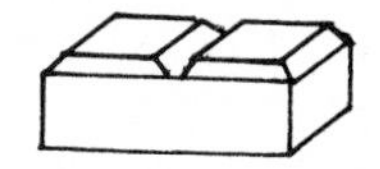

211–213 Types of stable paver
Top: Plain and diamond patterned
Bottom: Panelled (available with two, four, six or eight panels per brick)

Stable paver

Paver brick, also known as stable brick, can be plain, diamond-textured, or panelled so that when laid it looks like chocolate bars. It is always thinner than normal house or engineering brick and can be laid only one way up.

Brick pattern

One of the features of brick paving is the variety of ways in which it can be laid and bonded. The direction of the coursing can be used to emphasize the lines of a garden plan – to give the illusion of width if running from side to side across the viewer, or of depth if running away from him. If a squared pattern is used, it can stabilize an otherwise fluid layout.

214–216 Laying a brick path. The bricks are laid on edge in a 2 in. dry bed of sand and cement; more of the same mixture is brushed into the joints and then sprayed

LAYING After excavation to the required depth, lay a 3 in. foundation, as with concrete slabs, and set the bricks in a bed of mortar (1:4 mix). Joints can be run with grout and rubbed back when nearly set, or coloured jointing can be used as required. The bricks should be left clean after laying.

Granite setts (Belgian block)

Granite setts are roughly the same shape as bricks (although they come in different sizes) and should not be confused with cobbles, which are rounded and egg-shaped.

Large areas of setts – as in old European streets, confusingly called cobbled – are seldom laid now since they do not make the easiest surface to walk on. They also have a cold, grey, hard feel about them which is not very sympathetic for small-scale garden work.

They are, however, valuable in small areas for breaking up another large mass of paving, or they can be used to make a linear pattern which is then infilled with another material. They are quite often used as curbstones for a tarmacadam road or drive, and can be useful to delineate car-parking areas or, when laid in a raised strip across a drive, to jolt oncoming cars and make the drivers aware that they are approaching something requiring extra vigilance. Used in a car-parking bay or up the centre of a drive constructed in another material, their small-scale, irregular pattern can conceal patches of dripping oil. Like bricks, setts can be laid at an angle, or haunched up, to provide a foothold on a slope.

In Europe small granite setts are used quite frequently in a fan pattern on roads and walkways. When laid in this way a reasonable width is necessary to allow the viewer to recognize the recurring pattern.

217 Granite setts used on a gravelled drive to surround a specimen tree

218 Setts haunched up

Setts can sometimes be obtained secondhand during local renewal but, having originally been laid in a roadway, they are likely to be coated with bitumen. Sizes vary from the 4 in. cube up to 12×5×6 in., the ideal size for curbing. New setts, such as those made in Portugal, are not in standard sizes.

LAYING Excavate as before to allow for a 3 in. consolidated base. Lay setts on a 1 in. bed of sand in a breaking bond and ram well. Fill or 'rack' the sett joints with chippings before running with grout.

Cobble stones

Cobbles are rounded, waterworn egg-shaped stones, and, where available, come in sizes from 1 in. up to about 1 ft in diameter. Only in very few cases would one consider cobbles as a paving treatment since it is most difficult to walk over, particularly for those wearing high-heeled shoes. Cobbles are readily available in Europe, and can also be obtained in America at a considerably higher cost, from pits where sand and stone is being quarried.

Cobbles are also useful for infilling awkward corners round an area which has been laid with a larger element that cannot be cut to shape. Do not use them, however, to infill random gaps in areas of paving which have not been laid properly, as they then become as much of a hazard as the hummock of a plant.

219 A cobble infill between concrete slabs provides a contrast in textures

220 Cobbles used outside a garage to conceal the oil drip from standing cars

LAYING Cobbles can be laid close together set on end in a dry bed of concrete or mortar, over a prepared and consolidated foundation, and then watered in with a spray after laying. This way the stones are kept clean, which is important, since nothing is more indicative of sloppy workmanship than mortar adhering to cobbles and paving.

An alternative method of laying is to prepare the consolidated base, and lay a 2 in. bed of concrete (1 : 2 : 4 mix) over a 2 in. bed of sand on the base, pressing the cobbles in by hand, close together, so that they all protrude equally.

It is essential when laying cobbles to see that they are packed close together and that as little as possible of the mortar or grout holding them is visible – odd stones should not float about in a sea of concrete. If a surface is required which is not so discouraging to walk on, the smallest cobbles or pebbles can be used in a concrete mix as aggregate and brushed when dry.

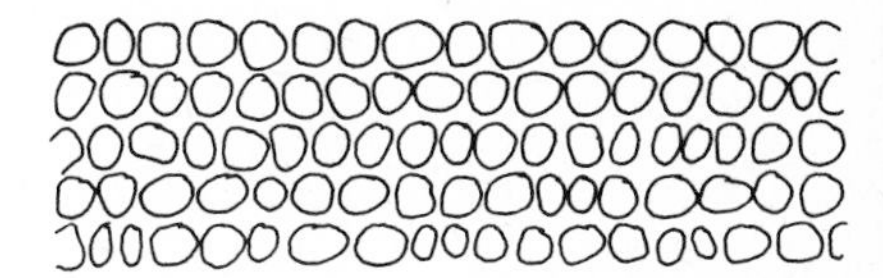

Coursed

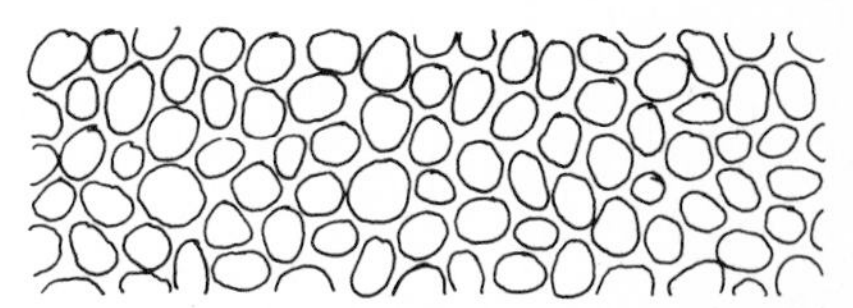

Random

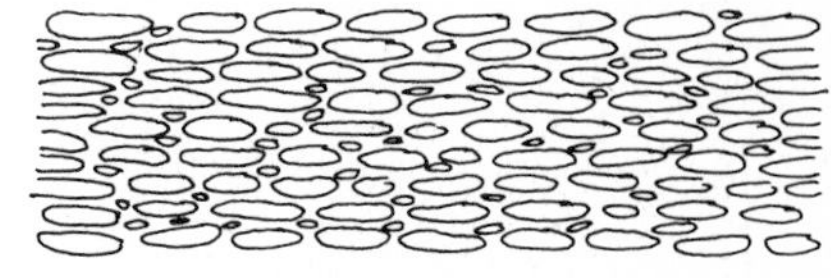

Flat cobbles laid parallel

221–223 Cobble patterns

224 Below: Cobbles in section showing the bed of concrete and the layer of hardcore

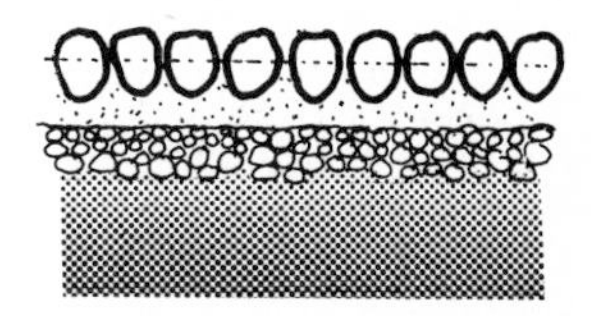

225 Left: A pattern made with flat cobbles laid parallel

226 Loose cobbles with strongly shaped plants growing through them

227 Tiles and concrete slabs of the same colour used to link inside and outside with as little visual interruption as possible

PAVING FOR INSIDE AND OUTSIDE USE

Some paving materials are appropriate for indoor flooring as well. These can be used to link inside and outside – particularly where only a glass door or wall separates the two, or where a sunroom or conservatory joins them – and to integrate the house with its outside room: the garden.

Tiles can produce this effect, and they are ideal for small town terraces, balconies and roof suntraps. They are, however, expensive to lay and, sadly, only some of the varieties on the market are frost-proof. They should be laid according to the manufacturer's instructions.

Slate also can be used in this way, being durable and easy to clean, although its cost can be prohibitive for those not living

in an area where it is quarried. Sealed stone, brick or concrete slab are other alternatives.
All these materials were previously considered cold underfoot, but underfloor central heating opens up the possibility of their use on a much wider scale.

GRAVEL

There are positions and situations in the ground pattern of a layout where a broad sweep is needed, but paving treatments would be too hard and grass either out of character or impossible to grow. In such cases loose gravel can be used.
The grass lawn is most successful in regions where the climate is not too hot or dry. In many regions, gravel or brick dust has been used instead for both formal and informal situations where it would not be subjected to excessive wear.
Gravel has a trim, easily maintained neatness that is difficult to surpass and avoids both the bareness of paving and the limited resistance to wear of grass. It can be laid cheaply and in bold sweeps difficult to achieve with a hard paving line. These advantages far outweigh the great disadvantage that it is difficult to walk on when newly laid or wet: with rolling and use it soon packs down.

228 A terrace paved with slate

229 Gravel edged with brick provides an undemanding contrast to a perennial border (Design by A. du Gard Pasley)

230 White gravel chippings used to brighten a city garden

How sensible if half the pocket-handkerchief lawns one sees, riddled with wormcasts and spotted with rose beds, were laid with gravel. Shrubs, herbaceous plants and bulbs can grow in it (although the last will usually not flourish in their second year after planting) and annuals or biennials like evening primrose will seed in it. It comes in various shapes, colours and sizes, blending with whatever one grows beside it, and is altogether more desirable than tradition leads us to suppose.

Types of gravel

It is obviously cheaper if one uses the local type. Washed pea gravel, in various shades of gold and brown and in various gauges, comes from gravel-pits and river beds.
There is on the market a white gravel chipping, not marble but an industrial extract, which provides a superb flooring material in a dark situation, bringing light down into the area. It can, however, be dazzling in bright sunlight.

LAYING It is essential to lay gravel well with a fall of 1 in 30, otherwise areas of moisture form and the gravel will sink into them giving an uneven surface.
For garden use excavate for and lay a 3 in. consolidated hardcore base. Lay two separate layers of gravel each rolled to 2 in. thickness. The hardcore can be omitted at intervals where planting is to grow through the gravel.

To lay a drive-way subject to considerably heavier wear:
1 Prepare a thicker consolidated hardcore base, 6 to 8 in. deep, unless the subsoil is particularly strong.
2 Spread gravel, passed through a 2 in. screen, to a rolled depth of 2 in.
3 Spread fine gravel with a hoggin binding medium (clay and brick dust) to a rolled depth of 1 in.
4 Finish with a layer of $\frac{3}{4}$ in. gauge fine gravel raked to a thickness of approximately 1 in.

HOGGIN

An alternative surfacing to gravel, though not a practical one, is hoggin. Hoggin is a mixture of brick dust and clay which, when dry and laid over a consolidated hardcore base, provides a fairly cheap semi-hard material – used sometimes for tennis courts.
The reason why it is not used more generally on the domestic scale is that when wet the material can stick to people's shoes leaving behind a broken surface which needs further treatment.

231 Brick paving on a California patio

CURBS

Curbing is necessary only to prevent soil from overflowing on to a hard surfaced area, or to contain tarmacadam, concrete, stones or gravel. It is not necessary to have a curb surrounding a paved area, since the edge of the paving itself provides the retainer. This seems obvious until one sees the unnecessary expense to which local authorities and private individuals have gone in laying a curb where none is needed.

Often where a curb is necessary an element of the surfacing, such as brick or setts, can be used without importing another material which would spoil the simplicity of the original scheme. The harshness of a new precast curb can ruin the subtlety of a softer material beside it.

Granite sett curb

On a domestic or small scale the granite curb is seldom necessary except perhaps to edge a driveway. Where a retainer of this strength is necessary, the largest granite sett is admirable. It should be laid in a concrete foundation.

Concrete curb

Concrete curbs are probably the cheapest. Since they are manufactured in various sizes, radii, colours, shapes and finishes, a suitable type can be found for almost any situation where a fairly heavy-duty edging is needed. They should be set in 4–6 in. concrete if they are to take heavy wear, with the concrete haunched up at the back.

Concrete edging

Concrete curbing should not be confused with concrete edging which, if it were less harsh in colour, would be admirable for the average domestic situation. Concrete edging is finished with a rounded, bull-nosed edge on one side, but this can be sunk into the ground if the flatter profile is required. Always set in concrete and haunch up at the rear of the edging.

Brick curbing

Bricks or blocks with a bull-nose or rounded edge are best for use in curbs. The square-edged variety is liable to be broken with constant buffeting, and can be too sharp and possibly dangerous. Lay in concrete. Building brick and setts can also be used, laid lengthwise, for a narrow curb.

MIXING MATERIALS

A layout combining any of the foregoing paving or surfacing materials can be very satisfactory with different materials serving different uses. This type of treatment is seen in new town centres, where sitting, playing, walking, and possibly even dancing are all catered for within a restricted area.

232 Sawn logs used as a flooring medium in a garden by Ursula Seleger Hansen

233 Left: A mixture of traditional paving materials and (above) a more modern approach

Ample planting is needed, however, to soften large areas of hard surfacing and to form a green connecting link between them. Well-grouped clusters of pots and the occasional bench seat will humanize and furnish the area as well.

There are other forms of surfacing which are not widely available, and it is up to the individual to use them if they are obtainable and economic to lay in his particular area.

In regions where it is plentiful, wood is frequently used as a paving medium. It is very attractive and, in a reasonably dry climate, it is quite practical.

Wood can be laid as duckboarding, for example – narrow slatted boards with a hardwood frame for decking – or in heavier pieces, more widely spaced for an attractive random roadway with grass coming up between the joints. Log cross-sections of varying sizes can also be used to make a circular pattern.

Pottery filling tiles from old kilns make an attractive path material, and even roofing tiles or slates can be used if taking no weight.

If you are moving to a new neighbourhood, it is always a good idea to see how others have solved their paving problems, presumably with available local materials that are characteristic and therefore suitable.

MANHOLE COVERS

The occurrence of manhole covers in a garden area is a problem for some, one or more, may be sited at the wrong angle in an area which is to be paved or turfed. Sometimes the direction of the drain leaves no alternative, but too often it is the result of lack of thought. So if you are building or carrying out extensive alterations, check this problem with your builder, and try and get him to site the manholes where they will not interfere with the garden layout.

There are various ways of dealing with the problem of misplaced manholes. It is a very easy operation to alter the level of a manhole cover by simply adding or subtracting courses in the brickwork under the cover itself; and it is sometimes possible to alter the orientation of the cover slightly, but the structure must remain sound, and access should not be impeded.

The usual flat metal manhole cover can be replaced with one in the form of a tray which will take a paving slab, cut to size, or bricks or cobbles. It is too shallow, however, to take turf, except in the most exceptional circumstances where

adequate maintenance and watering of the turf can be ensured.
Where the manhole cover cannot be worked into the paving, an irregular pattern can be created round it and infilled with gravel – covering the manhole too if need be – or an easily removable pot or tub can be placed on top. Where the manhole is a small distance from a paved area, and it is not feasible to plant out the cover, lead the paving to it, and make a feature of it as on right.
Manhole covers and septic tanks in the more open parts of the garden can be screened with planting, and this is one of the features which should be considered in the general shaping of the ground plan.
It should always be borne in mind that access is occasionally necessary to these services, and anything used to cover them should be light and easily removable. Trailing plants over a manhole might do a good job until access is needed, when they will have to be lifted.

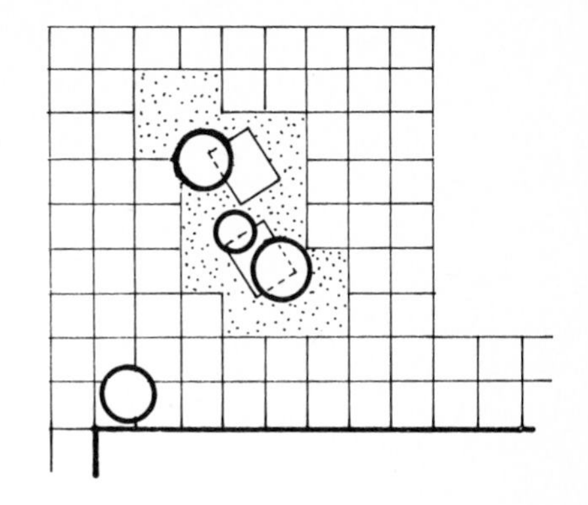

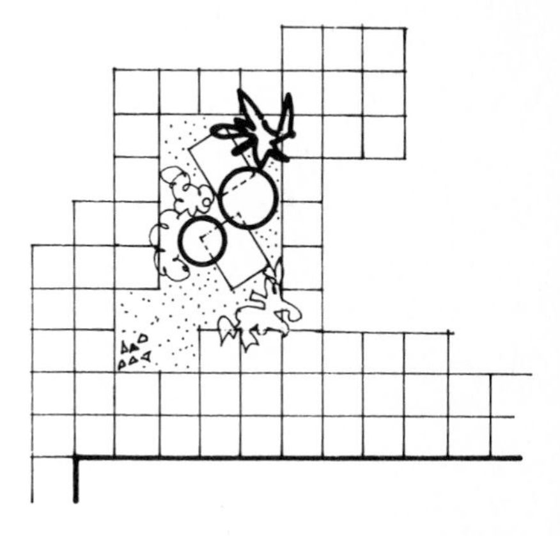

234, 235 Two methods of disguising manhole covers
Top: Enclosing them in a gravelled area which is then planted and framed by paving of irregular outline
Above: Surrounding the gravelled area with formal paving and standing pots of bulbs and annuals on it

CHANGES OF LEVEL IN THE HARD GROUND PATTERN

I tried to show in Chapter 3 that any change of level in a garden area is a feature to be preserved, and later developed. Ground shaping and working with contours to produce a roll in the ground is one way of doing this, but obviously a change of level in the hard ground pattern must be effected by means of a retaining wall, steps, a ramp or a combination of all three.

Steps

It is unnecessary to deal with the theatricality of long flights of steps in this context. When one thinks of famous steps, they invariably belong to or are adjacent to a building. They are architecture and the architectural rule-of-thumb methods for designing steps are nonsense when applied outside.
Broadly speaking, progress up and down steps outside should be slow. Shallow treads and steep risers make for speed, and this is not wanted in a place for relaxation. (The tread is the flat part of the step; the riser the vertical between the treads.)
Invariably the dimensions of steps have to be dictated by the angle of the slope unless one is prepared to alter a whole bank. In general, however, the depth of tread should not be less than 12 in., the ideal being perhaps 18 in. Riser heights should be between 4 in. and 6 in. Steps outside, if they are

236–241 *Step details*

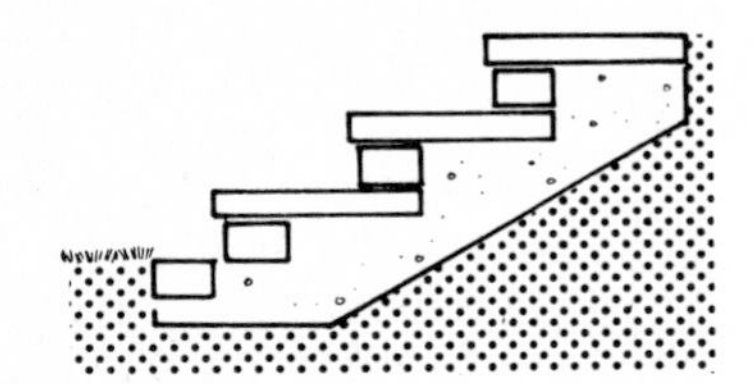

Brick risers with precast concrete slab treads overhanging by 1 in.

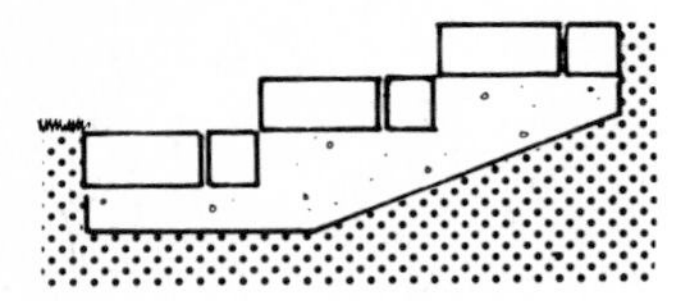

Brick steps, using bricks set on edge to increase the length of the tread

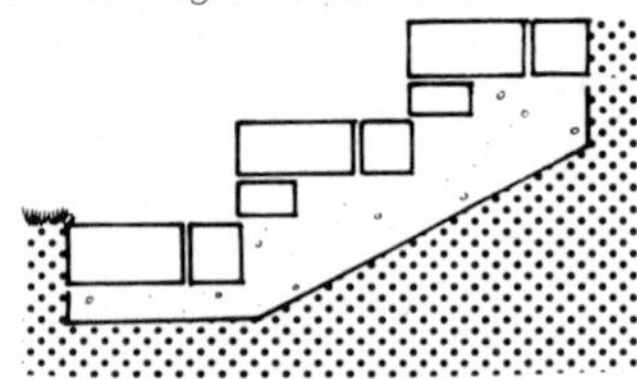

Steeper brick steps with a slip course of bricks or tiles to make up the riser height to 6 in.

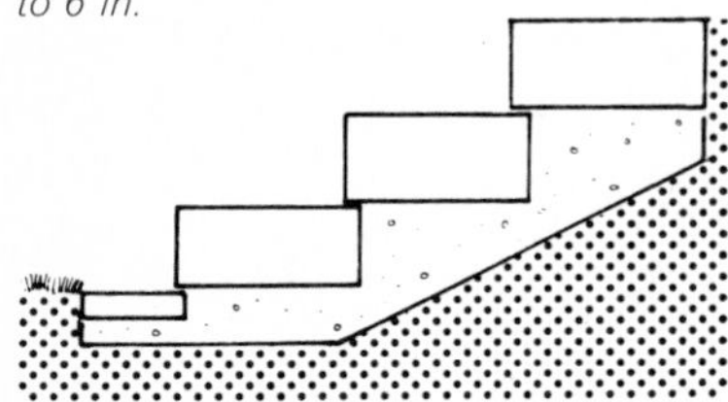

Solid stone blocks

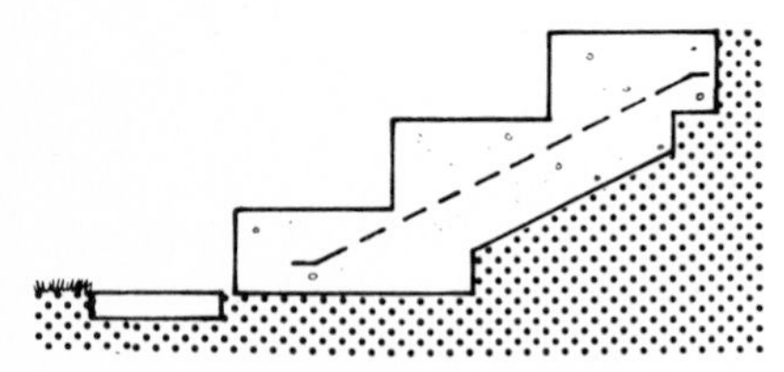

In situ *concrete. This will need reinforcement*

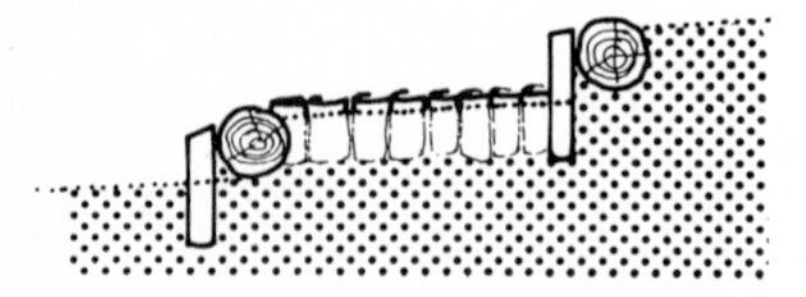

Log steps. Lengths of paling at the sides of the steps hold the risers in place

in the sun, often double up as occasional sitting places, so the deeper the tread the better.

Where a long flight is contemplated it should be broken up every ten to fourteen steps with a landing. Aesthetically the landing looks well if it is square – the flight width squared, in fact.

Steps need not always be considered as narrow flights, breaking through an adjoining retaining wall; for comparatively little extra money, the flight can run along the length of the retaining wall. Where steps lead down into a confined terrace or basement area, far more light will penetrate that area if the steps run down the retaining wall and tubs or pots are stood about on them as a decorative feature.

Steps can be faced with most of the materials used for paving and, when used to join two paved areas, should generally be made of the same material. Methods of construction vary from steps cut into parent rock, cantilevered steps, or normal cut-and-fill steps, to flights made of wood or metal built over the fall of the ground. All are valid in the right situation.

Stepped ramp

Where a long shallow slope is involved, the stepped ramp is ideal as it gives a more easily managed gradient between each step. It is commonplace in Mediterranean hill towns, where an ascent by mule or donkey used to be necessary. A minimum distance of three paces should be allowed between each riser.

Ramp

In new town developments and at entrances to pedestrian underpasses both ramps and steps are usually provided. The ramp is an ideal solution in a garden where there are prams or invalid carriages or children with tricycles, but they are dangerous if too steep and, unless laid with care, can become slippery. An angle of 1:10 is usually the maximum gradient for prams and tricycles, although this is rather steep for a laden wheelbarrow.

CONSTRUCTION Steps should always be constructed in a non-slip material and if this is the same as that on the adjoining path or terrace so much the better. The faster steps drain, the quicker they will become dry, so that construction with the correct fall to each side is essential.

242, 243 Above left: Concrete treads with brick risers
Above right: Stone treads and brick risers (J. St Bodfan Gruffydd)

244 *Stone treads cut to a curve*

245 *Concrete treads and risers*

246 *Above: Concrete steps, precast as a complete unit, make an interesting pattern at Halun Siedlung*

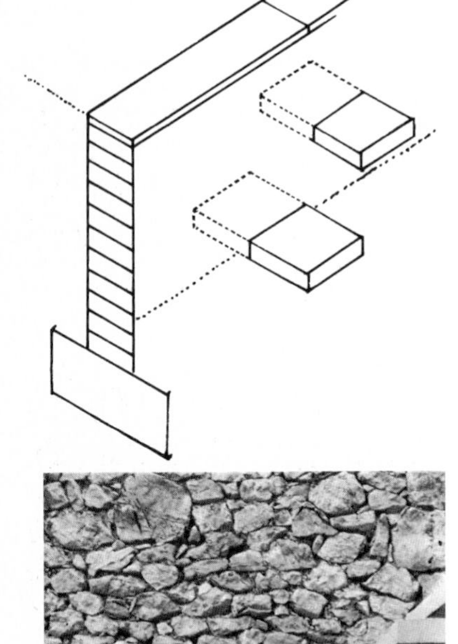

247–249 *Top: Diagram showing method of building cantilevered steps into the structure of the wall*
Above: Concrete beams cantilevered from a random rubble wall
Right: Stone steps cantilevered from a wall of blocks

The majority of steps that one is likely to construct on the domestic scale will be in concrete slab, stone, brick or wood, depending on the situation. Stone and brick have either an urban or a rural association, while *in situ* concrete or concrete flags are best in a suburban setting. Wood is solely rural and is used only for risers – the infill of packed earth forming the treads. (Such steps can, of course, only stand light wear when wet.) The permutations of different varieties of these materials are numerous.

The actual profile of the step can be very crisp, with no overlap of the tread over the riser, or there can be an overlap of several inches which casts a shadow over the riser and gives a more gentle effect. If treads are cantilevered from an adjoining wall there is no riser at all.

The ramp and stepped ramp can be constructed in the same materials as steps, with the obvious addition of gravel, tarmac, *in situ* concrete or bricks haunched up to give a better foothold. Whatever the surfacing for a ramp, it looks better to have a continuous gradient which does not alter throughout its length.

WALLS INSIDE THE GARDEN

The fewer retaining walls there are in a garden the better, since they tend to break up and punctuate the general flow; for the same reason the simpler their construction the better. A retaining wall should do only what its name suggests, and this only where a smooth gradient is impossible.

The methods of constructing a retaining wall are similar to those listed in the previous chapters dealing with boundary walling. Precautions should be taken, however, to prevent moisture penetrating the structure by inserting a vertical damp-proof course between the wall and the earth it retains, building a cavity wall, or waterproofing the rear of the wall with a bitumen preparation. Weep holes should be made in the lower brick courses to facilitate drainage if no damp-proof course is included in the construction.

There seems to be an increasing tendency to construct mean and purposeless dwarf walls all over the garden, but where a division is really necessary the pierced screen wall could be considered.

Pierced screen walling

This is a development which originated in the hotter climates, where some seclusion is necessary but a through draught essential.

In a temperate climate the application of such walling is limited but, where it is used with discretion and in association with good planting, the effect can be most attractive. It should be supported at each end by brick buttresses, and only short lengths of the screening should be used since the pattern is so strong that over-use can ruin its effect.

The great advantage of this type of screen, when used internally, is that it allows one garden space to flow into another through the wall, with only a slight visual check. This same advantage will, however, make it unsuitable for use as a boundary wall, where privacy or solid shelter is needed.

The geometric shape of the panels makes a good contrast to bold foliage planting and also provides a useful support for climbers which can weave their way in and out of the wall, softening the often hard outlines.

This type of walling is quite easy to erect and reinforcement is not usually necessary. Blocks are available in several standard designs, but in general they are approximately 12 in. square, and 4 in. thick. Colour and finish vary according to the manufacturer. Plinth, pilaster and coping units are

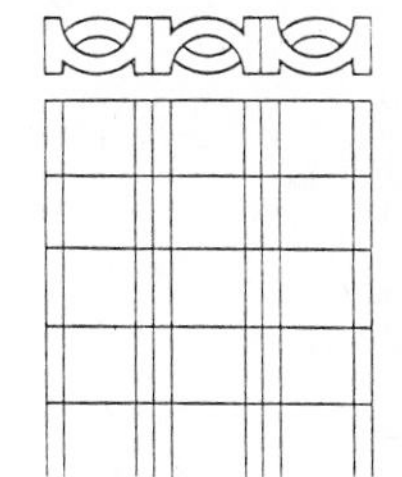

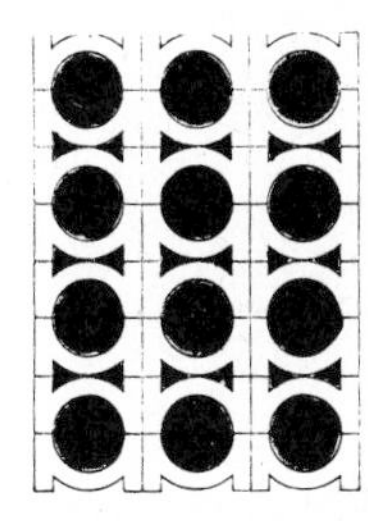

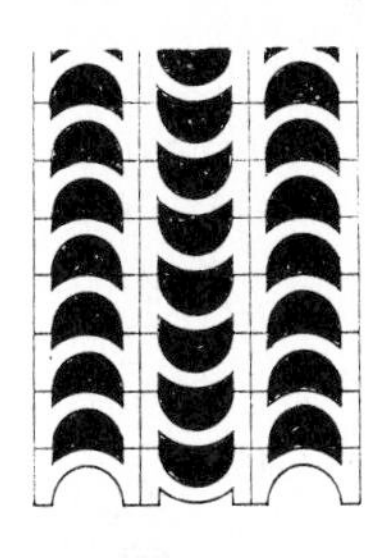

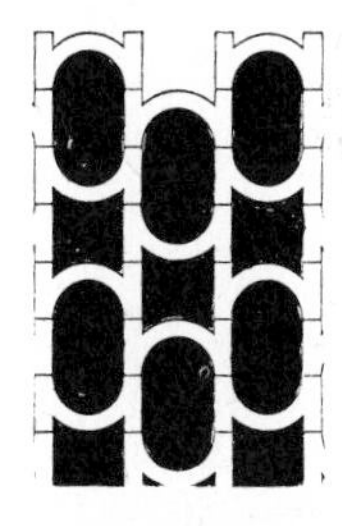

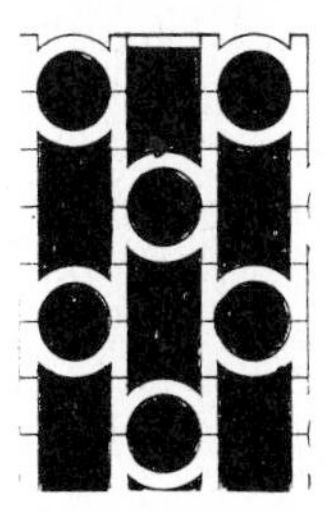

250–259 Some of the patterned blocks available for pierced screen walling

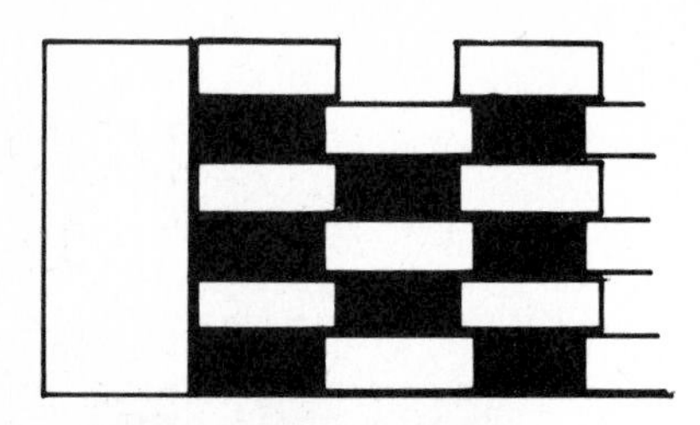

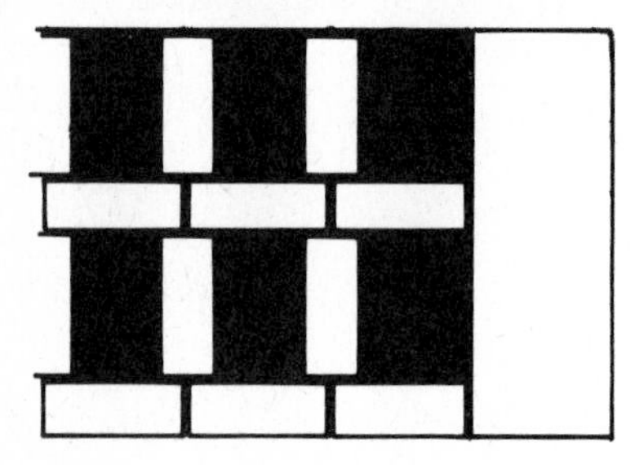

260, 261 Above: Honeycomb brick patterns for pierced screen walling

available which give greater stability and neatness of appearance.

Similar units and blocks are available in asbestos. These are of course far thinner and would be ideal for use where lightness in weight is an essential requirement – in roof gardens for instance.

One or two sculptors have experimented with this type of panel, as the permutations and variations possible are enormous.

262 Right: An interesting timber screen by Victor Pasmore

263 A concrete wall panel by Paul Mount

264 Another concrete wall unit of modern design

265–267 *Above left and right: Patterned concrete wall-cladding panels*
Below left: An iron screen

Timber screens can be used to divide up areas in the garden, either supported on posts or as vertical, louvred infill panels between brick piers.

There are a number of suitable materials which can be used decoratively when supported between piers, including corrugated or patterned vinyl sheeting (of various colours), tiles of various patterns, plastic-coated wire mesh and even, occasionally, mirrors. Walls can be rendered and painted either all in one bright colour, or in patterns. We tend to be very hidebound and unoriginal in garden thinking and it is on the structure of internal walls that the imagination can be let loose. The result does not need to be garish, however, and should marry with neighbouring planting.

268, 269 Below: Logs of different heights used to make an interesting screen
Bottom: Sawn logs used as a retaining wall. Garden by Ernst Baumann

9 SOFT GROUND SURFACING

Not all the garden will be hard surfaced, if a back-yard feeling is to be avoided.

After areas for planting have been designated, there will still be the remainder. Too often this is just put down to lawn when, with a little imagination, either the grass could be treated in a different way or areas of ground cover could be planted instead – or a combination of both. Too small an area of grass is seldom worth while either visually or practically, being difficult to negotiate for maintenance.

The beauty of a lawn is that it provides a unifying base medium. The simpler the shape, therefore, and the less the expanse is broken up with island beds, the better it will do its job. Isolated strips of mown grass taking considerable wear should be avoided, as they are likely to become muddy in wet climates and too dry in others. Likewise a serpentine edge to a lawn is difficult to maintain.

When planning your lawn, consider its shape in terms of the machine you will use to cut it: the cable run for an electric machine, or the turning circle of a motor one. A grassed bank should obviously be on a gradient negotiable for a mower (approximately 30°) and small irregularities should be avoided, as large mowers will 'leap' them. The type of grass cutter which floats on a pocket of air is ideal for an irregular bank.

The fine sward of grass in a mature garden is superb, but it would be foolish to suppose that it is achieved with little attention. There are, however, various schools of thought on the standard of the sward which needs to be achieved, though all insist that drainage should be good.

For the family lawn which will have to take heavy wear in summer, a very fine lawn is not necessary. The odd weed is not a horticultural calamity – indeed, it is probably appreciated by young children who love making daisy chains – and a mixed lawn of this sort can take quite heavy treatment without being harmed. If moss is growing in it, however, this will easily be kicked up by children, leaving a nasty hole, so the cause of moss growth should be ascertained and remedial treatment given. Just killing the moss is not enough, as it will soon reappear.

A finer lawn and a level surface is necessary if croquet or similar games will be played on it.
Above all, the gardener should be the master of his lawn, and not its slave, since setting oneself too high a standard of turf culture can result in the expenditure of a lot of time and money on maintenance later on.
When contemplating a new lawn one should consider the relative merits and demerits of turfing and seeding.

Turfing

Laying turf is the more expensive operation initially. Against this, less initial preparation of the area is needed and considerably less aftercare over the comparatively short period until the lawn is usable. It is important to ensure that the turf being laid is of the standard you wish to achieve. Always ask about the source of turf if the work is being completed by contract, and see a sample, or better still the actual field from which it will be cut as, after clearing your site of pernicious weed before turfing, you do not wish to reintroduce it with the sods themselves.
Another advantage of turf is that provided there is a water supply accessible one can lay turf at almost any time of the year when the weather is open.

270 Daisies are in no sense a disaster in a lawn intended to take wear – as long as paving slabs are laid just below the level of the grass the mower will run straight over them without damaging the blades

271 *A broad sweep of lawn in a garden by Roland Weber*

Seeding

Seeding, on the other hand, should generally be done in early autumn, or in spring when the worst frosts have passed. Initial preparation of the ground should involve not only levelling, cultivating and fertilizing, but removing small stones as well. The type of seed selected for the lawn will depend on the quality of the grass you wish to achieve. The finer the grass the more expensive it will be. On the other hand, it will need less mowing in the end.

Coarser grasses will take heavier wear, and there are various mixtures of seed on the market suitable for different situations, from the family lawn to the football field.

The better seed mixtures will not include rye grass. This grows in tufts if left undisturbed, not knitting together laterally, and its flower heads are particularly difficult to cut as the mower simply flattens them, and they spring up again after it has passed.

There are some seed mixtures on the market which are suitable for grass growing in shade. When using one of these in conjunction with another mixture for a lighter part of the garden, however, check with your seedman that both will produce a similar green colour.

There are now bird repellents on the market which can be mixed and sown with the seed to prevent it being eaten before rooting.
After seeding, a lawn should not be subjected to heavy wear for its first season, and considerable maintenance will be necessary during that time: weeding, rolling and watering.

Rough grass

Much mowing can be saved by allowing areas of grass to become rough, though this solution is more satisfactory in a large garden than a small one.
Rough grass needs only rough cutting two or three times a year with a scythe, rough-cut mower, or an ordinary mower with the blades set high, and spring and autumn bulbs can grow in it with a crop of wild flowers between. The time of cutting, however, is crucial. The first cut comes as the spring bulbs die down, the second during August after the field daisies, for instance, have flowered, and the third some time in September before autumn crocus and colchicum leaves come up. One should only attempt to cultivate wild flowers which can compete with rough grass, and which one sees growing naturally.

272, 273 Flowers growing informally in rough grass
Below: Spring (tulips)
Opposite: Summer
These pictures and No. 274 are of a garden by Taylor and Green

274 *Mowing stones alongside the lawn prevent the need for edging*

The edge of rough grass, where it borders the smooth lawn area, can be one of the basic lines in the design of your garden. Furthermore, it can be changed as desired each year simply by mowing, provided naturalized bulbs are not in the way. This is one of the lines in a garden that can be made to swoop and curve in a way which is very difficult to achieve with hard surfacing.
When trying to establish a rough grass area within a newly seeded lawn, the whole area should be established as a lawn sward, before allowing some of the grass to get longer. This way one will get a close-grown and dense rough-grass area.

Camomile lawn
In areas where camomile grows, this can solve the mowing problem. Camomile is very fragrant to walk on and blooms from mid-summer until the first frosts, producing daisy-shaped white and yellow flowers. The leaves are light green and feather-shaped. It should get plenty of sun, although it seems to do quite well in not too heavy shade. Once established, a camomile lawn is self-seeding and needs no mowing, but on the other hand, it will take very little wear. Ground cover planting, which is considerably more attractive, seems, therefore, a better solution.

Ground cover planting in the open
Sometimes a level area of infilling is needed in the garden pattern which is too small for a lawn. If it will not be used regularly and the trouble of maintenance is not wanted, open ground cover planting should be considered. The initial plant cost of such a solution is compensated by the subsequent lack of maintenance and it is an ideal treatment for small front gardens or small urban public areas.
The use of ground cover planted under shrubs as a means of cutting down on bed management, is dealt with in a later chapter, and many of the same species will grow in the open.
For areas of low planting basically a crawling evergreen plant is needed which will cover a large area. This makes economic sense and is practical as well, since too long a period of maintenance before plants knit together is not wanted. Check garden catalogues and your local nursery for suggestions.
Generally the larger the stretch of a single plant the more arresting its appearance, but care has to be taken to select a type of ground cover which is not too rampant

*275, 276 Areas of ground cover (*Festuca *and* Polygonum*) in the garden of architect P. Beyersdorf*

for the area it will cover. The occasional specimen can grow through the ground cover provided it can hold its own, and bulbs also can be planted and will force their way through.

It is almost more essential than when preparing ground for a lawn to clear the site of weeds with running roots, since they are almost impossible to extract once the ground cover is established.

Carpet bedding, of which the Victorians were so fond, is in fact ground cover planting to a prescribed and figurative pattern. There is no reason why this type of planting cannot be incorporated in a more up-to-date and imaginative design, where the site can take it. In so doing, however, the character of the plant is being subordinated to the pattern of the whole, avoiding the horticulturalist's approach to gardening. Such a pattern can also combine interplanting with paving – to make, in its simplest form, a chequer-board for instance. The South American garden designer, Burle Marx, uses his plants on these lines in some layouts, producing broad sensuous sweeps of colour and texture.

Where the pattern becomes too intricate, some provision has to be made to prevent the different varieties of plant from growing into each other and becoming inextricably entangled.

277 A swirling pattern of ground cover planting in a South American zoo garden by Roberto Burle Marx

10 BASIC PLANTING

CULTIVATION

Initial cultivation of the areas to be planted is vitally important and should be considered before we turn to the selection of the plants themselves. It cannot be overemphasized that time and money spent on turning over the ground properly and feeding it with manures and fertilizers is never wasted. The aim is to provide a suitable medium, in its best physical condition and improved by the incorporation of manure and fertilizers, so that the young plants are better able to take root and subsequently develop to full maturity. Enough water should be retained for the plants' well-being, but it should nevertheless drain away freely.

The type of topsoil with which you start on a site (see Chapter 3) dictates the cultivation and treatment necessary to achieve the most manageable and productive growing medium. For those with no topsoil left after the ravages of the developer or builder, it will be necessary to import some, after first eradicating any pernicious weeds still struggling for survival. Care should be taken when importing topsoil both to break up any compaction of the soil on to which the new material is being laid and to avoid over-compacting the imported soil during the spreading operation.

Ideally, the greater the depth of topsoil the better, and the process of cultivation is intended to increase this. But when importing soil, because of its price the purchaser will want to know what is the minimum amount with which he can make do.

For a lawn, at least 2 in. of topsoil is needed, and drainage beneath, and the more rampant ground covers will survive with this depth of soil as well. Some of the surface-rooting herbaceous plants can survive in 6 in. of topsoil, and many shrubs in 9 in. Trees, of course, need a greater depth, but individual planting positions can be made for them using more topsoil. On the other hand, there are dozens of situations in which shrubs seem to survive in the cracks of walls and among ruins on a fractional amount of soil; the secret must be that, although they have very little soil, their roots are able to penetrate into the soft brick or rubble and gain a foothold where there is adequate moisture and yet excellent drainage.

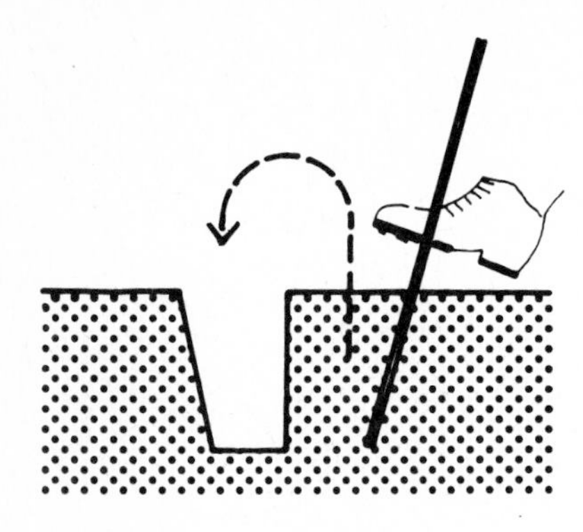

278 Digging one spade length deep

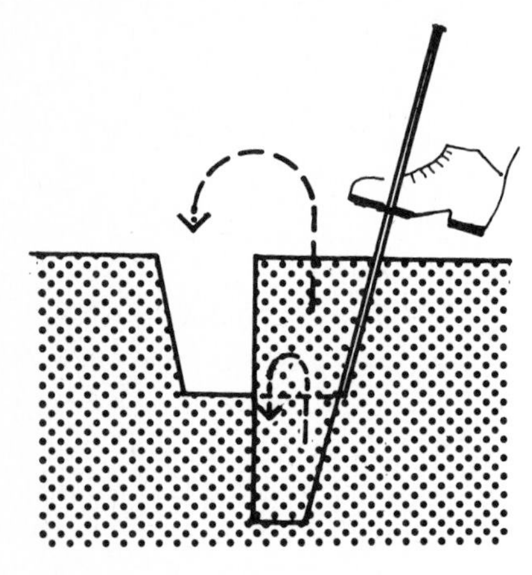

279 Double digging. The earth at the lower level is turned over (but not brought to the surface) and organic manure is incorporated at both levels

Cultivation of any sort of soil should involve digging to a depth of one or two spits below the surface in order to break up the top layer of the subsoil. This will increase the root penetration of the plants and will also assist the organic changes involved in the evolution of subsoil into topsoil. Care should be taken, however, to see that no subsoil comes to the surface in the process.

Cultivation by hand

On the domestic scale hand-cultivation still cannot be beaten, for by this method the gardener can ensure equal soil penetration and spread of manure, and the removal of stones, weeds and builders' rubble. It is a slow, back-breaking process, but gives a good foundation on which to build.

There are two methods of digging: double digging which goes two spade lengths deep, and single-spit digging. Forking and raking also come under the heading of hand-cultivation.

By machine

Mechanical cultivation may include ploughing, disking to break up the earth, and harrowing. Light mechanical cultivators with a rotary blade action do the whole operation in one. Generally, however, these cannot penetrate to a sufficient depth to break up the soil in a new garden to a manageable tilth, and only succeed in chopping up invasive weed roots, which grow again twice as quickly. This type of pernicious weed root can, however, be killed by repeating the rotary treatment two or three times at intervals of a fortnight or three weeks.

MANURES AND FERTILIZERS

A plant is a living organism, and it reacts to conditions around it in the same way as any other living thing. It also needs food. A fertilizer provides this, but organic manure provides this and a soil conditioner as well.

Plants can require up to sixteen chemical elements for their food, and most of these have to come from the soil. Nitrogen (N), phosphorus (P) (as phosphates) and potash (K) are the ones needed in the largest quantities, and it is these we supply in organic manures or inorganic fertilizers.

Organic manures

These have a fairly low and unbalanced food content, but have a great beneficial effect on soil structure, aeration and water-holding capacity, and they also promote microbial activity (see Chapter 3). Concentrated forms of organic manure release their nutrients over a far longer period.

Inorganic fertilizers

These are useful for application to a soil where the organic or humus content is already high, as they supply only plant foods but in concentrated form. It is essential to apply them according to the instructions on the container.

LIME

In the past, when its function was not fully understood, lime was often applied too liberally to the soil. Lime is not a plant food; to a certain extent it is useful as a conditioner for clay soil, but by far its most important use is for improving the pH value of an acid soil. It should be used, however, with extreme caution, as excessive application will make the soil too alkaline and it will be a long and painstaking job to restore the balance.

PEAT

Unlike other organic substances, peat contains few, if any, nutrients and is used only as a conditioner, either to improve the texture of a heavy soil or to retain moisture in a light one.

FACTORS INFLUENCING PLANT SELECTION

I have tried to approach each aspect of garden layout as one would approach the making of a new outside room. The selection of plants comes only after all the other basic work is completed and is the carrot which dangles in front of the new gardener to spur him through the initial hard work. But even at this stage the plants selected will form only the skeleton for, with first-stage planting, the voids and the masses are built up, areas of shelter, privacy and shade are created and views blocked or directed – the original conception is carried through into the third, vertical, dimension.

The plants selected at this stage have a practical purpose, and their decorative qualities are secondary. They act as a background in front of which the remainder of the planting is grouped.

Certain factors outside the site will affect the basic planting in it:

Wind

One of the major hazards of the new garden is wind, particularly in a newly developed area where natural vegetation has been removed, and the only protection round the garden is a chain-link fence. It is being realized more and more how wind passages can be created, particularly among large blocks of buildings, which are quite different from prevailing winds.

The answer to this problem is to plant a dense windbreak of trees or shrubs to shelter the garden and those who use it. As a rough guide, shelter planting can be assumed to give protection at ground level over a downwind distance of five to ten times its own height. When used on a large scale, however – round an orchard for instance – the planting should rise gradually from the upwind side to its maximum height. This will avoid the turbulence and downdraughts on the lee side which the sudden checking of the wind by a sheer face can create.

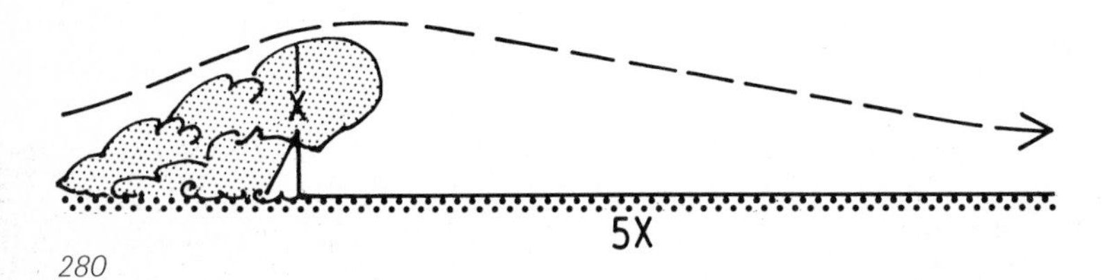

280

Evergreen shrubs provide excellent shelter, though there is a great antipathy to them, probably because the extent of their variety is not appreciated. The old urban park, the rectory drive and cat-infested town garden are associated with *Aucuba*, privet and grime-covered *Fatsia* leaves. But the camellia, the rhododendron and many of the cotoneasters are evergreen, while some of the laurels and privets are most handsome when used in another context.

Coastal winds present another problem, as they are salt-laden. However, there are several shrubs which can survive in these conditions and are admirable for providing shelter.

When planting fast-growing shrubs, it is as well to realize that they won't necessarily stop when the required height is reached (so do not select a variety which is too vigorous), and that, although the recommended planting distances seem far too far apart when putting in the miserable twigs the nursery delivers, shrubs grow sideways as fast as they grow upwards. It is, however, an easy matter to thin out original plantings if you put too many in for a start.

Frost

Plants seem to be very variable in their resistance to frost, some varieties thriving for a considerable number of winters only to die suddenly and leave a hole in a rapidly developing group. It is helpful, when selecting reliable plant material, to choose from the varieties which are known to grow well locally and are therefore hardy. It is better to plant a hardy shrub than a sad thing which has to be covered with a plastic bag all winter!

Shade

Shade may be caused by neighbouring trees or buildings. The amount of sunlight excluded from the garden will vary not only according to the size of the neighbour, but also, less obviously, according to the time of the year, for the high summer sun will often shine over the top of an obstacle while the low winter sun will not. Plants that will grow, therefore, will depend on other factors besides their ability to withstand shade. Lack of water will often affect them, and loss of nutriment taken by the shade-inducing neighbour.
Nevertheless, there is a surprising amount that will grow in quite dense shade – think of woodlands!

281 Living in a temperate climate, we tend to forget that there are places where shade is needed and plants that give protection from the sun are welcomed. Lattice screens and eucalyptus foliage in an Australian courtyard house (Design by Andrew Young)

Conifers generally will not grow in shade. Plants with silver variegations do better than those with gold, which often revert to green, and bright colour is difficult to achieve, since the majority of flowers need sunlight.

Atmosphere

In some urban areas smoke pollution or the heavy chemical content of the atmosphere are injurious to many plants. Generally evergreens and conifers suffer most under these conditions since the atmospheric deposits prevent them breathing through their leaves. Deciduous plants which lose their leaves regularly are therefore more reliable in such cases.

Noise

This is a fairly new hazard of modern living, which one needs increasingly to hold at bay. A thick planting of evergreen shrubs and trees combined with ground shaping provides an excellent baffle and cuts down noise considerably.

While planting can be used to block an unsightly view it can equally well bring a good view into the garden, or disguise a physical boundary by linking the planting inside the site with that outside. If garden planting is to be linked with natural planting the shrubs selected will have to be ecologically correct, becoming gradually more 'domesticated' as they approach the viewpoint.

PLANT SELECTION AND NUMBERS

The types of shrubs and trees selected will vary according to soil, situation, aspect, site characteristics, etc., but the manner in which they are sited will be the same, since at this stage, they are serving the practical purpose of building up a preconceived pattern and should not detract from it. The occasional large tree of a particular shape or variegated shrub group, as a point of emphasis, if part of the conceived pattern, will be part of this skeleton planting but the majority of it may be fairly mundane, acting as a backing to more colourful and interesting planting in front. To that end one should not plant one of this and one of that, giving a restless, spotty effect, but should plant in bold groups of three or four in the small garden and perhaps twenty or thirty in the largest. The overall shape of each group should be similar to that of the individual shrubs, and a good proportion of them should be evergreen, so that the planting can be effective the whole year round.

It might be necessary, if rapid results are required, to interplant the basic screening material with faster-growing specimens. These will have a comparatively short life, after which they can be removed to allow the more slowly maturing varieties to come through. Forsythia and buddleias are good examples of shrubs which give very quick results, but buddleias have a fairly limited life span. Laurustinus (*Viburnum tinus*), on the other hand, is an ideal evergreen, growing up to ten or twelve feet high, but taking time to do it.

Conifers, when used in the skeleton planting, are too often placed in positions quite unsuitable for them. The vast majority are specimen trees with a strong vertical emphasis which is strengthened by their intense green, or blue. Both qualities are fine if properly used but when they are mixed at random with deciduous specimens or more rounded shrubs the effect is most unsettling. The conifers used in rural gardens are, moreover, generally alien varieties and make an unsettling punctuation mark in the landscape. The indigenous conifers – pine, larch, yew or juniper – while still being visually strong, fit in far better. One has to admit, however, that in maturity conifers do provide an admirable, if a singularly dark and dreary, screen.

282, 283 Two stages in the laying out of the skeleton planting
Left: Skeleton planting of trees, evergreens and large deciduous shrubs
Right: Subsequent planting of smaller deciduous shrubs and perennials

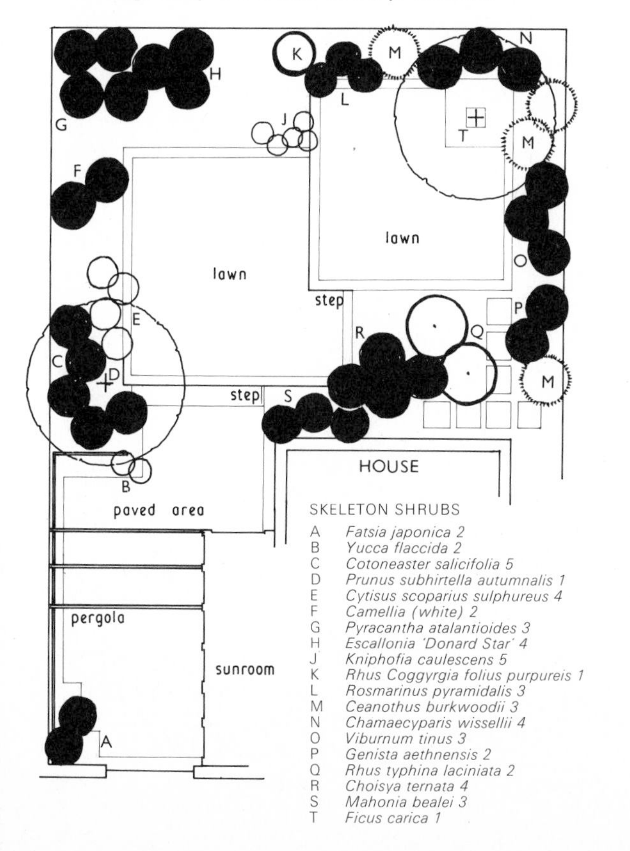

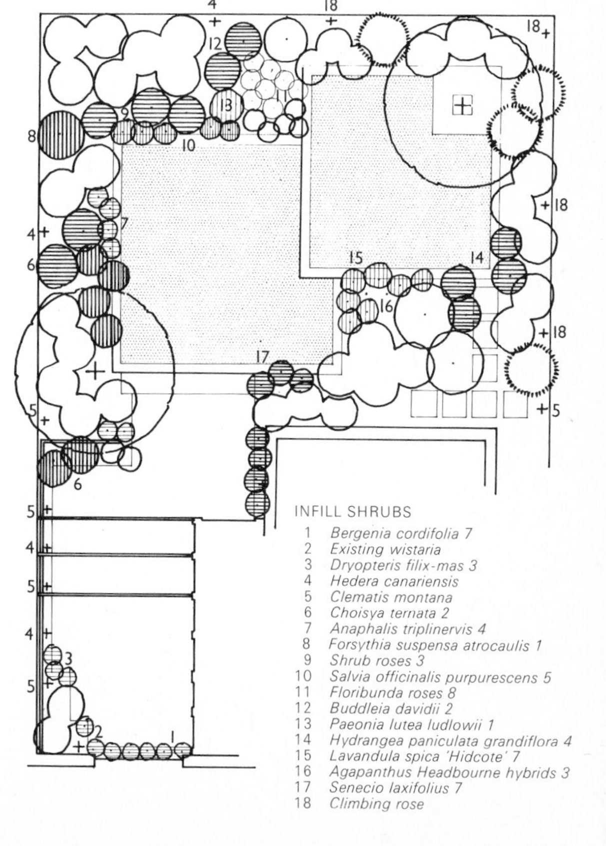

PLANTING AND THE ESTABLISHMENT OF PLANTS

Type of plant	Main planting season in temperate climates
Deciduous trees and shrubs; roses	End of October – end of March to middle of April
Evergreen shrubs and conifers	End of September – early May
Herbaceous perennials	September – end of April
Alpines and rock plants	End of August – end of October or March – April
Pot-grown plants and plants in containers	Throughout the year, preferably September – early May
Water lilies and marginal aquatics	March or April – early June
Bulbs	Early September – October

Plant		Distance apart (inches)	Number of plants per sq. yd
Shrubs –	dwarf and slow-growing	18–24	2–4
	medium	36–48	1
	vigorous	60–72	2–3
Bush roses		18–24	3–4
Herbaceous perennials –			
	vigorous	24–48	1–3
	average	12–18	4–9
Small herbaceous and ground cover		8–12	9–25
Bulbs –	large, e.g. narcissus	8–12	9–25
	small, e.g. crocus	6–8	25–36
Hedging –			
	privet, quickthorn	9–18	—
	beech, hornbeam	12–24	—
	yew, holly	18–30	—

TREES

Trees are planted at this stage to reinforce the shrubs and give a greater height to the skeleton planting of the garden area. The types of tree used for the purpose will, in the main, be smaller-growing and faster-maturing than the free-standing specimens planted singly or in groups.

The scope for planting forest trees in a domestic setting is sadly limited. Nothing is finer and more lasting than a good specimen tree, but nothing more depressing than a mutilated one which has been tailored down to fit a small space.

Careful consideration should, therefore, be given to the siting of any tree, its eventual height, girth and root run being taken into account and the sort of shade it will give. Its winter form should be thought of as well, for there are few large evergreen trees, and none which grow at a fast enough rate for home planting. There are occasions when, if access is available, the importation of a fully or partly-grown specimen tree might be considered at this stage. The cost and likely result of the process should be set against that of planting healthy young tree stocks which will not have to suffer any root check through being moved, and will grow away quickly without much maintenance.

Trees can be roughly divided into three groups in this context:

Large forest trees

In this group are the largest trees and the slowest to mature. They are the superb specimens that are characteristic of the northern countryside and parkland. Many have taken two or three hundred years to mature and it is a sad reflection on modern society and its demand for a quick return on expenditure that they are not being replaced in the same numbers as in former years.

Because of their size and scale such trees are invaluable in the overall development of any area, but their planting *en masse* is probably more appropriate to public parks than to any but the largest private grounds.

Individual trees, however, can be planted as specimen trees and would come into the next category.

Specimen trees and shrubs

Specimen trees are those planted as a focal point, or to serve a particular purpose, and many of the more exotic varieties come into this category. They should be allowed to develop unhindered and unrivalled by surrounding trees as the point of a specimen is lost if a number of different trees

284, 285 Above: A specimen oak which acts as the focal point of a whole road
Right: In this garden by A. du Gard Pasley a copper beach was retained to provide a point of interest. Note the transition from sunlight, through the shade under the tree, to sunlight again in the field beyond

are planted too close together, each vying with the others to catch the eye.

A specimen tree should be chosen so that its eventual size will be in keeping with the scale of the surrounding layout. All too often one sees a weeping willow planted in a position not only out of character with the tree itself, but completely out of scale with it as well. A willow is not a tree for the centre of the front garden!

A specimen tree group of one variety should have the same shape on maturity as an individual tree of the group, only on a larger scale.

Small and flowering trees

These are the trees which achieve maturity in a comparatively short time. They can be used with shrubs as screening, or to direct the eye; they can be used as individual specimens, or they can be used in a group, whether of uniform or mixed varieties.

Because of their adaptability, these are the trees most often misplanted. If they are to be grouped with shrubs, they should extend the characteristics of the group, and their shape, foliage or flower colour should match or contrast suitably. If used as specimens, whether individually or in groups, they should be sited as explained above.

HEDGES

As a visual screen, noise baffle, security precaution, and shelter-provider, a good hedge can hardly be bettered. It need not be used only to define the garden boundary but can be employed in the internal composition of the layout and can carry the structural lines of the house out into the garden in the same way as a wall. Structurally a hedge can break up an area like an internal wall, not necessarily into complete garden rooms – the area has to be pretty large for this – but partially, so that the remainder of the garden flows round it (see page 29). It can screen a junk area, washing-line run or vegetable plot, or it can also be used like the wings of a stage, curving round and varying in height.

The type chosen must depend on the ultimate height needed and on what will grow best in the selected position. A hedge can be either loose or clipped. If one plants any group of shrubs in a line, the ensuing mass becomes a loose hedge. In the context of skeleton planting, however, the hedge will generally be more formal.

The value of a good hedge is often overlooked in the desire to avoid upkeep, but this in itself depends on the type of hedging planted. Privet, for instance, is planted far too often; not only does it grow too quickly, needing endless clipping and clearing (although there is a growth stopper on the market) but it is a gross feeder, taking nutriment from quite a large area of adjoining ground. Privet also tends to be an urban plant, as it can endure considerable atmospheric pollution.

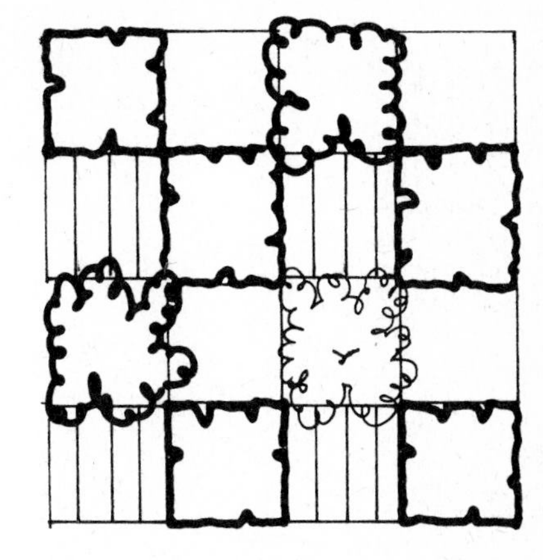

286 Above: Clumps of contrasting evergreens used to form an abstract pattern

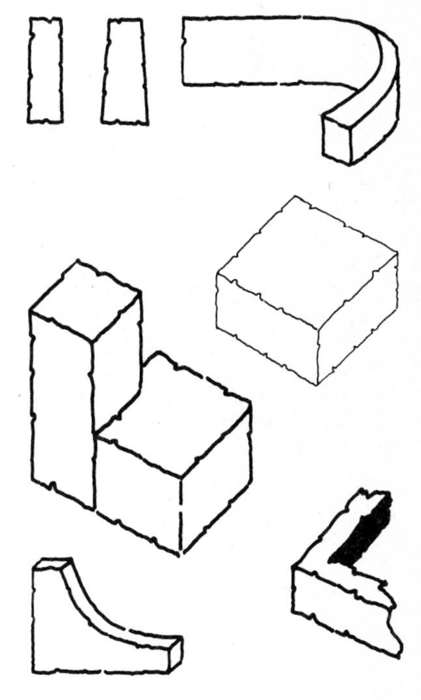

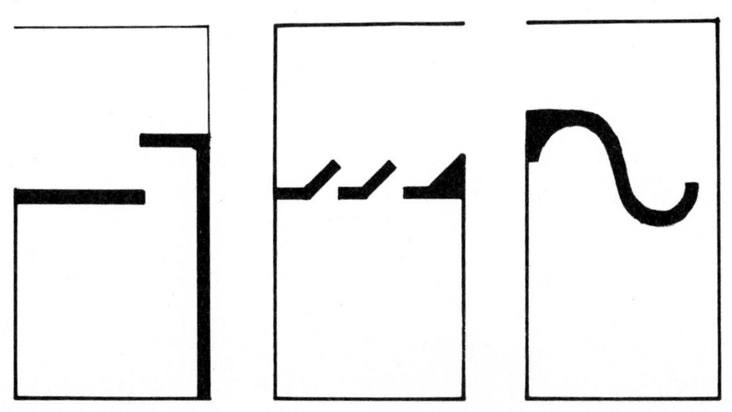

287–290 Above: The height of a hedge need not always be uniform, but can be varied to provide added visual interest. The type of plant used should, however, be one which is amenable to this treatment

Left: Hedges do not have to be used as boundaries. They can be part of the sweep of the internal design and can serve to direct the eye or form a partial block like the wings of a stage

291, 292 *Above and below: Hedges used as walls to divide up an area into 'rooms'*

Beech and hornbeam, on the other hand, provide a reasonably quick-growing hedge, needing much less clipping than privet and, although deciduous, they retain many of their brown leaves throughout the winter if planted in a not too exposed position. Both have a satisfying toughness about their growth and are excellent for chalk or any well-drained soil.

Thorn hedging has the feeling of the countryside about it. It is best utilized as the outer defences of a large rural garden, as its thorns make it difficult to penetrate and it grows well down to the ground. When it grows too high or too thickly, the hedge can be laid to rejuvenate it, although this is an expert's job.

Nothing beats the dignity of a yew hedge, which provides an ideal foil for other plants in front of it. Contrary to popular opinion, I have always found that yew grows reasonably quickly when well looked after, putting on 6 to 9 in. per year. If large specimens are bought, 4 or 5 ft high, it is essential to ensure that growth is reasonably full right down to the ground.

Box hedging makes a dense barrier for an urban garden, as will some berberis, cotoneaster and laurel. *Lonicera nitida*

293 *Right: Topiary in an English cottage garden*

294 Topiary on a grander scale at Levens Hall, Westmorland, England

(same family as honeysuckle though quite, quite different) will do the same, although when mature it tends to flop in a high wind or under any weight of snow.

Where an informal hedge is needed yew, hornbeam, forsythia or mountain laurel can be used in various combinations.

Like all other plants in a garden, hedges need maintenance: watering when young, and feeding at regular intervals as they mature. If this is overlooked, growth will be slowed down.

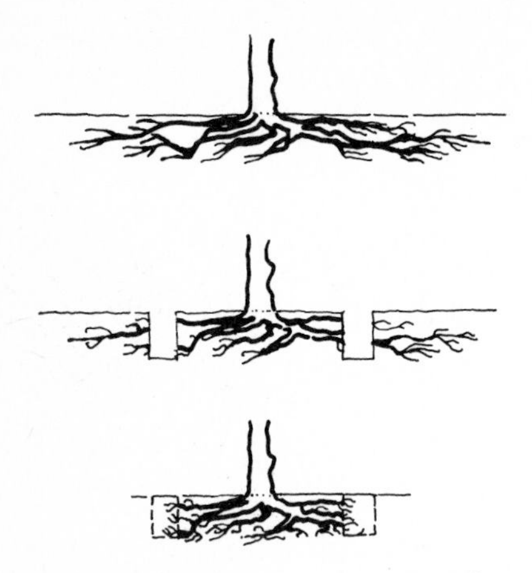

295–297 Preparing the roots prior to transplanting a tree. Ideally this process should start two years before the tree is moved
Top: Normal root spread
Centre: The original roots should be severed by a channel surrounding the trunk. This is then filled with a mixture of loam, peat and sand in order to encourage a system of fine fibrous roots to develop
Above: When the fine roots are established, the tree can be lifted

TRANSPLANTING SEMI-MATURE TREES

There is a tendency nowadays to expect immediate results from whatever is being undertaken, and the garden is no exception. The desire for semi-mature trees seems to be growing and it will be at the skeleton planting stage that large trees are brought in. The process of transplanting large trees – that is, those over about 20 ft in height and over 4 in. in stem diameter, is comparatively new, and long-term results cannot yet be assessed. Short-term results would seem to be good, however, *provided the correct preparation is carried out before lifting the tree and provided it is properly maintained for approximately three years after planting.*

The moving of large trees has been carried out for many years on private estates, with infinite trouble and at great cost, but we are concerned with the commercial process. Not all firms will give a guarantee of survival of the tree which they have moved, and if they do the price will rise accordingly.

The size of tree which can be used for a particular position depends not only on its availability but also on the access to the site. A large tree is pretty heavy and machine access is therefore necessary to the position in which it is to be planted. The tree itself should be young and vigorous and, where possible, it is a good idea to see the tree *in situ* before commissioning anyone to move it.

Getting the type of tree you want may be a problem as there is a general shortage of prepared stock. Prices will also vary and the cost of machinery and of cartage over a long distance can come to more than the cost of the tree itself.

Preparation

It is advantageous if the tree root is prepared or pruned as much as two years before its removal, so that small fibrous or feeding roots are encouraged to grow within the area of soil that will be lifted with the tree. If the root has not been prepared and these are severed, the tree will obviously suffer a serious check.

The more soil and the bigger the root ball that can come with the tree, the less likely it will be to suffer a check. Trees growing in a heavy soil are more likely to lift cleanly, leaving the fine roots intact, than those growing in a light soil, which falls away and leaves everything exposed. When trees are being removed out of season, and in leaf, the tree head should be sprayed with an anti-transpirant so that moisture will be retained in the leaves.

Methods

There are currently three methods of moving large trees, each involving different machinery:

CRANE This is the oldest method of lifting. After digging, the root ball is securely wrapped and the tree lifted by its stem and put on a truck. The process is reversed for planting.

NEWMAN TRAILER A simple method but one which has the disadvantage of being suitable only for trees with a stem diameter that will fit the securing clamp – approximately 12 in. – and not weighing more than four tons.

POWER TRANSPLANTER A hydraulically operated trowel-shaped blade mounted on the front of a high-powered four-wheel drive tractor, scoops out tree and root in one process, after initially cutting round the tree root. The tree travels on the blade and is finally deposited into its prepared hole. This is a simple method of lifting, and usually enjoys a high degree of success, because of the amount of root that can be taken. Its disadvantage is the limited distance over which the machine can carry the tree. It is ideal, however, for short runs.

Replanting

The hole for the new tree should be 2 to 3 ft wider than the root ball itself. The depth should allow for drainage, according to the soil type, and approximately 6 in. of vegetable topsoil should be laid in it before placing the tree.
Backfill round the root with good topsoil, leaving no air pockets – fertilizer can be included either at this stage or as a top dressing – and *water very well* both during and after planting.
Secure guying is necessary, either with stakes or sunken 'dead-men', and the tree stem should be protected from the chafing of its guy-fixing by cradling the guy in rubber where it meets the stem. Some provision should also be made for tightening the guy.
Trees can also be guyed underground during the planting process so that no wires are visible. Guying is essential so that the tree head remains stable while young fibrous roots grow away.

Maintenance

After planting, adequate watering is essential until the tree has established itself. During the summer months, April to September, an average of forty gallons per tree at three to

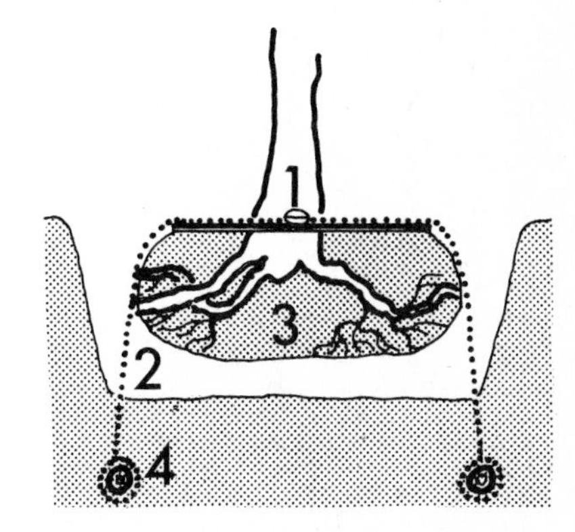

298, 299 Guying a transplanted tree with buried 'dead-men' logs so that the support does not show. Oak, chestnut or larch logs, 6 ft long, should be sunk about 1 ft below the bottom of the hole. A strong wooden frame should be laid on the surface round the tree and galvanized wire laid over it and attached to the anchor logs. This can then be tightened with turnbuckles

1 *turnbuckles*
2 *galvanized wire*
3 *root ball*
4 *anchor logs*
5 *wooden frame*

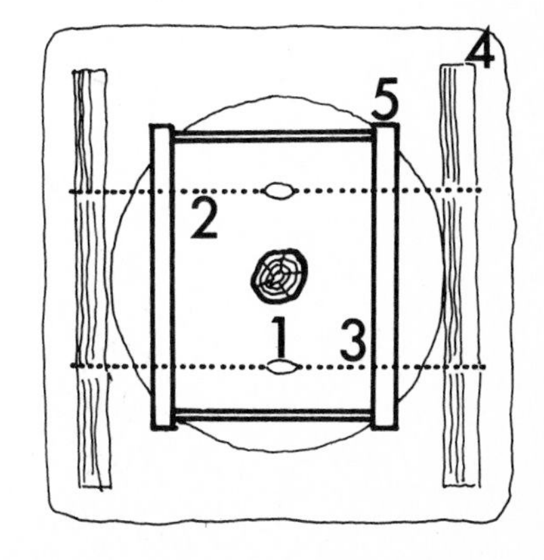

four weekly intervals will be necessary. A 3 in. deep mulch over the roots will help to avoid water evaporating from the soil. This can be well-rotted farmyard manure, compost, damp leaf mould, peat or grass cuttings.
Constant checking of the guys is essential.

CONTAINER-GROWN PLANTS AND PLANTING OUT OF SEASON

Following from the need for mature trees is that for planting the whole year round, which is a good way of creating a quick screen. Nurseries and garden centres are catering for this by growing plants in large containers. These are plunged into the ground, the container gradually rots after contact with moisture in the ground and the plant roots expand outwards. This is of course not possible with plants sold in plastic containers or old tin cans, unless the sides of the container are cut. Root growth will, however, be severely limited and possibly damaged during the cutting process.
As with large trees, *subsequent maintenance and watering is essential* when planting out of season.
When large plants have not been grown in containers and they are to be moved, it is wise to select those with a close-knit fibrous root system and not a straggling one. Top spraying of shrubs to avoid transpiration is desirable before they are lifted – this should be done in dull weather – after thoroughly watering the ground round them beforehand, and the plants should finally be watered into their new positions to settle the soil around the roots. Shrubs which have been moved should be watered well in dry periods, at approximately weekly intervals. A mulch spread on top of the soil will help to conserve moisture. Top spraying the foliage with a fine spray is advisable during weather when the sun is not shining; bear in mind that wind is as drying as sun, and shelter from both would be an advantage.

11 PLANTING DESIGN

If the garden is being used as an outside room, the planting in it should not only provide enclosure and shelter, or frame a view; it should give pleasure as well. Trees, shrubs and flowers should be planted to create a definite composition and their individual characteristics considered to that end. That a plant has the most wonderful flowers for three days in June is not enough – it must work for its keep the other 362 days of the year as well.
What the characteristics of plants are, how they are used by nature and what the gardener can learn from this is worth considering.

300 The fastigiate lombardy poplar is too often used as a screen. In fact it draws rather than deflects the eye

Shape

First, the shape of a plant. Trees with a strong characteristic shape have been considered and given key positions in the skeleton planting of the garden. The weeping form is well known, but there are other forms which trees take in maturity: the umbrella shape, for example, or flat top, and, contrasted with these, the fastigiate (or upright) forms, ranging from the narrow column to the pyramid. Such extreme shapes are only for occasional use as a special point of emphasis, but the contrast of one with the other – a willow and a poplar, for instance, is pure natural sculpture.
The more extreme the climate, the more bizarre and the more diverse the plants which grow in it, since lack of water, great humidity, or strong sun all lead the plant to adapt its shape and leaf to its particular situation.

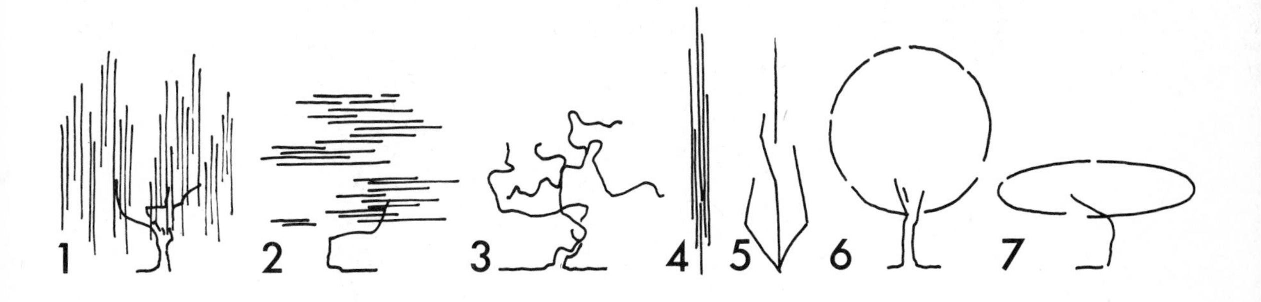

301–307 Tree shapes

1 *weeping*
2 *horizontal*
3 *twisted*
4 *fastigiate*
5 *pyramidal*
6 *round-topped*
7 *flat-topped*

308, 309 Natural sculpture
Above: The contrast of the huge leaves of Gunnera manicata *and the delicacy of a weeping willow*
Right: The spikes of the red hot poker pick up the columnar outline of conifers behind

Lower down the scale, the number of shrubs and herbaceous plants with outstanding form is limited. The sumach (*Rhus*), the yucca, the iris, and the giant cowparsnip (*Heracleum*) spring immediately to mind. These plants are often known as architects' plants, as their strong shape provides a good contrast with that of a building.

Pattern

Akin to the overall form of a plant is its leaf form or pattern. Quite a range of subjects from trees to herbaceous material, while not having a particularly interesting general shape, have leaves, seed heads, twigs or bark which are their main feature: for instance *Aralia*, *Prunus serrula* with its peeling red bark, artichoke, *Acanthus*, and also *Hosta*. These are the plants which can be grouped to give strength and variation to a composition which might otherwise rely too heavily on colour.

310–312 Above left: Iris and Hosta *leaves*
Above right: Yucca filamentosa
Left: Acanthus mollis. *Its leaf was used as the motif of the capitals of corinthian pillars*

313 The grey, furry leaves of Verbascum bombyciferum

Texture

The texture of the leaf of a plant is not only a tactile quality but also a visual one, which can add to the textural quality of the whole garden. Compare the glossy leaves of the laurel with the matt density of yew, the glistening green plates of *Magnolia grandiflora* and the dreary green of the rhododendron. Nearly all the grey-leaved shrubs have a felted, hairy leaf, which makes them a wonderful foil to flower colour and therefore much beloved by flower arrangers.

Colour

The best and most important factor with which one works in building up a satisfactory plant arrangement is colour – flower colour. It is colour that people crave through the dull cold days of winter in temperate climates – much of the craving, one suspects, results from the need for warmth, holidays, sunny climates and bright flowers. When spring comes again and nurserymen's catalogues arrive through the mail, those not living in semi-tropical climates try to create the brightness of such gardens.

Too often the landscape designer is accused of being against colour in the garden. This is far from the case. What he advocates is the *use* of colour together with all the other qualities of a plant – its shape, form and leaf texture – to complete the roundness of his scheme.

There is a vogue at present for white flowers with grey foliage. Certainly none of the marketable washing powders can come up to the pristine whiteness of nature, but it is to be hoped that controlled colour will slowly creep back into fashionable gardens to produce viable planting compositions of the extraordinary beauty and balance achieved by the flower arrangers.

Most northern climates allow for the growth of a greater range of plants and a much greater variety of colour than is possible in semi-tropical climates but the intensity of colours is less – for two reasons. First, people tend to use too wide a variety of colours, which are then scattered about so that the effect is much too spotty, and secondly, the humidity of some atmospheres produces a haze which tones down colours outside. In rainy climates bright colour, when attained, has to be used properly, however, if it is not to burn a hole in the overall picture which one is trying to achieve.

It is worth seeing how colour is organized in nature. Very seldom does one see a bold mixture of indigenous colour; the brilliant patchwork display of an uncut hayfield is only visible at close quarters, and even then is diffused throughout the grass. The boldest splashes are either of one or two contrasting colours – or else a variety of shades of one or two seasonal colours – autumnal gold, bronze and russet, for example, or the many and often very beautiful browns and reds of winter.

There is a definite natural colour cycle throughout the year. It starts in spring with white snowdrops, against winter brown; later this shades into yellow-green (*Narcissus bulbocodium*, primrose). Colours intensify in early summer with pink and pale blue (violets, bluebells), getting stronger towards autumn after a gap in high summer. Early autumn yellows and golds turn to russet and red, and then to the brown and grey of winter.

Plant hybridization and imports have disturbed this natural cycle, but it can act as a good basic guide to the colour

314 A beautifully graded and contrasted mixed border by Christopher Lloyd

selection of garden plants. Another method of restricting one's natural impulse to pick one of this and one of that from a catalogue regardless of its colour, is to decide on a garden of, say, three basic flower colours – yellow, white and red, perhaps – using different foliage colours to supplement this. Pink, blue and white, with grey and purple foliage, would be another combination.

Probably only in the largest garden can one select and use the colour of plants as one would use oils in a painting. Gertrude Jekyll, who was influenced by the French Impressionists, used this technique in the design of her herbaceous borders at the turn of the century. To avoid strong colour 'boring a hole in her scheme' she generally sited the golds and scarlets in the foreground and faded the colours through blues to pinks and whites in the distance. This technique tends to give greater depth to the area, whereas a splodge of scarlet at the furthest corner of a garden will rivet the eye to that spot, and appear to shorten the area.

The rules for plant selection work in the same way for any type of vegetation in any climate. In a hot climate colour can be used to cool: brilliant splashes in full sunshine, pale colours in shadow. Cacti in a desert garden should, however, be grouped according to their shape; one variety contrasting with another, with occasional points of interest counterbalanced and steadied down with a less spectacular group.

Because of climatic conditions or maintenance time, it is often impossible or undesirable to have a garden area with flowering plants throughout. All that can be managed may be groups of pots on a paved area, backed by less spectacular but equally rewarding shrubs. The grouping of colour and selection of plants in this case will work in the same way as normal plantings – usually one colour, or shape, per pot. Using different heights and sizes of pot, it is possible to build up an arrangement which can easily be adjusted at will, or as the various varieties go out of flower (see Chapter 14).

Shade

There are many, including the elderly, who cannot sit in full sun, and welcome shade. It is not always an adverse characteristic in a garden and should be considered with planting design. In a temperate climate shade is needed more often than is realized, for the sun does not have to be shining for the glare from white paving or new concrete walls to be uncomfortable. This can be relieved by planting.

315, 316 *Areas of shadow break up regular outlines and add interest to a garden by Gordon Patterson. The tree in the picture above is* Catalpa bignonioides

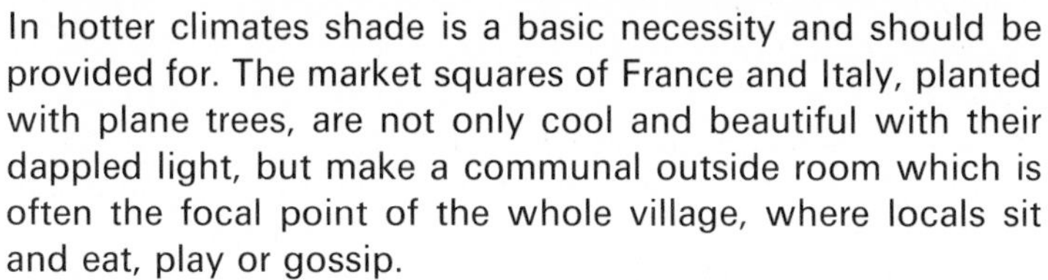

In hotter climates shade is a basic necessity and should be provided for. The market squares of France and Italy, planted with plane trees, are not only cool and beautiful with their dappled light, but make a communal outside room which is often the focal point of the whole village, where locals sit and eat, play or gossip.

In the Renaissance gardens of Italy shade was often used to frame a sunlit view beyond, and in England the eighteenth-century gardeners used the shadow of trees to mask the boundary of a site.

Before cutting down a fine specimen tree, or before planting a new one, consider what effect its shadow will have, and how it could be turned to advantage.

317 *Below: For maximum safety a tree should be planted at a distance from the house equivalent to its ultimate height*

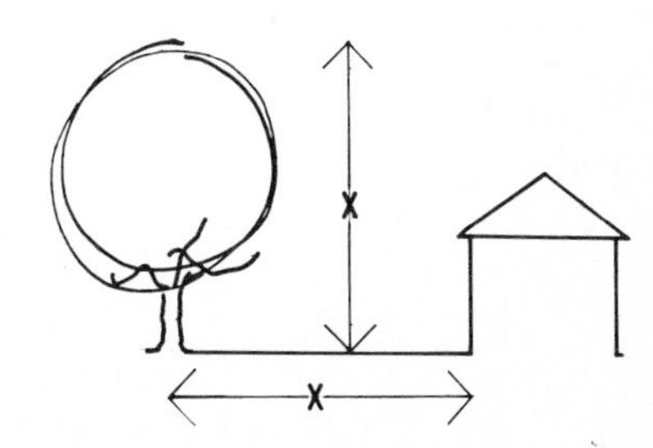

PLANTING TREES

Forest trees and specimen trees are either so big, or hold such a key position in maturity, that their positioning in the garden should be considered in the initial stages of skeleton planting.

The more decorative of the small trees, the flowering ones, should be considered at this stage for use as infillers, either with our indigenous small trees, or in conjunction with shrubs. In either case the way they grow naturally should be copied as far as possible.

Silver birches, when growing in the wild, rise out of ferns and low ground cover. They grow with other small trees and are seldom seen in conjunction with shrubs – the mixed rhododendron or laurel and silver birch planting is not always an indigenous grouping, although it is on its way to becoming one wherever this material will grow well. Maples and, in some regions, dogwood, occur naturally in groups making brilliant autumnal splashes of fruit and leaf. The flowering trees which grow wild in temperate climates are usually white or pink, like the crab-apple, the thorn, or the wild cherry, and this should be borne in mind when trying to link domestic planting with wild, or when including flowering trees in skeleton shrub planting.

When grouping trees, use only two or three species and weave and interplant them as naturally as possible in the plan. Refrain at all costs from planting one of this and one of that to no conceived plan, if an unrestful look is to be avoided, and, when small trees are being contrasted with large ones, drift them in groups at the edge of the planting, the way wild cherry trees cling to the edge of a beech wood.

The more exotic and bizarre the colour of the tree, the nearer it should be to the beholder, or it will dominate the whole area. The classic example is the sugar pink of some of the Japanese cherry varieties, which does not marry well with the vivid fresh green of spring. This is far too often set against the orange and yellow stripes of the Kaiser Kroon tulip, and perhaps the yellow of a laburnum as well: one would not consider such colour clashes in one's home or on one's person, and they should not be inflicted on nature.

Standard

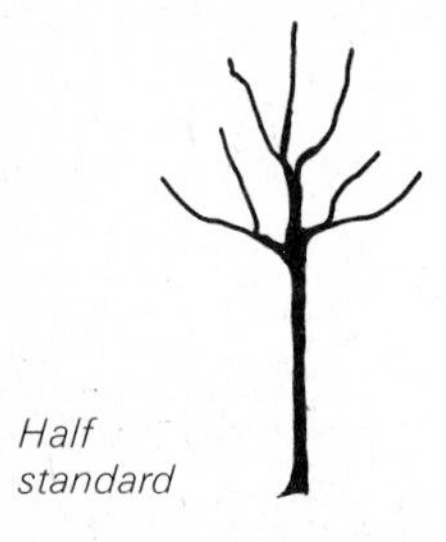

Half standard

Bush

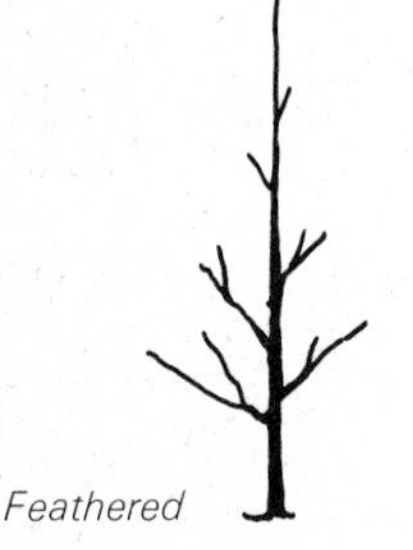

Feathered

318–321 The usual tree types. Note the straight central leader in the standard (top)

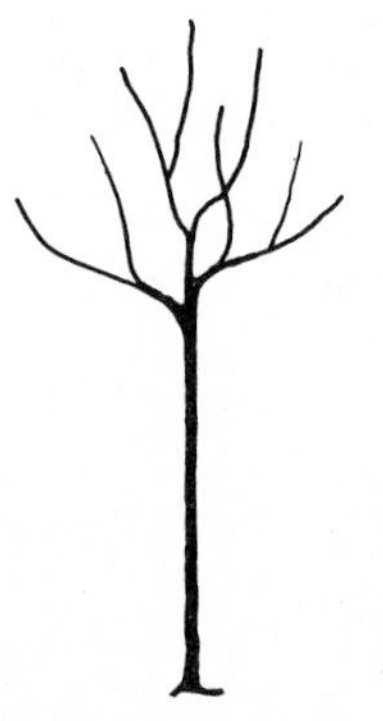

Standard

Cordon

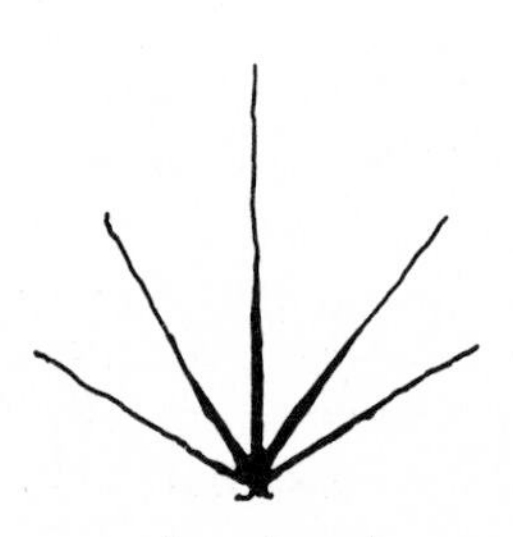

Fan-shaped

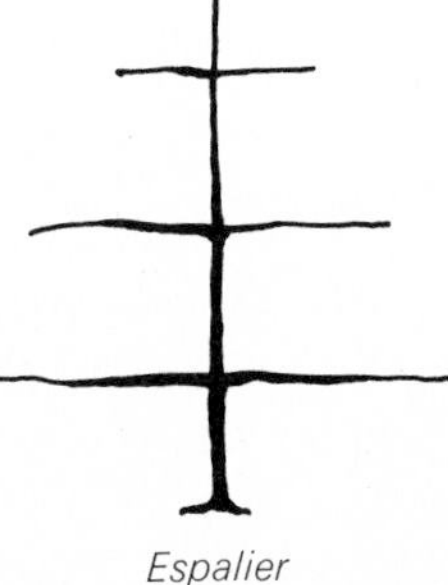

Espalier

322–325 Methods of training trees. Note that in this example the standard does not have a straight leader

326 A natural grouping of silver birches

Used well, however, set against dark green shrubs with a touch of grey, white tulips and blue forget-me-nots, a pink cherry would look superb, as would a laburnum sited against a group of dark yews.

Think carefully before mixing your tree colours, and blend them with the remainder of your planting. Trees with variegated foliage and yellow or purple leaves need most careful siting. The rich, purple spring foliage of a *Prunus* can become overpoweringly dull by late summer if the colour has not been blended in a special group.

COMPARATIVE GROWTH OF TREES

	Expected height in 20 years		Expected height in 50 years
LESS THAN 20 FEET	Almond	LESS THAN 40 FEET	Almond
	Arbutus		Arbutus
	Catalpa		
	Cedar		
	Crab-apple		Crab-apple
	Dogwood		
			Eucalyptus
	Gleditsia		Gleditsia
	Hawthorn		Hawthorn
			Holly
	Hornbeam		
	Japanese cherry		Japanese cherry
	Laburnum		Laburnum
	Magnolia (various kinds)		Magnolia (various kinds)
	Maple (various kinds)		Maple (various kinds)
	Oak		
	Plane		
	Rowan (Mountain ash)		Rowan (Mountain ash)
	Whitebeam		Whitebeam
	White birch		
	Yew		Yew
20 TO 40 FEET	Ailanthus	40 TO 60 FEET	
	Alder		Alder
	Ash		Ash
	Beech		Beech
	Birch		
			Catalpa
			Cedar
	Horse-chestnut		Horse-chestnut
	Swamp cypress		Swamp cypress
	Elm		Elm
	Eucalyptus		
	Gean		
	Gingko		
	Holly		

	(in 20 years)		(in 50 years)
			Hornbeam
	Larch		
	Lime (Linden)		Lime
	Maple (various kinds)		Silver maple
	Oak (various kinds)		Oak (various kinds)
	Corsican pine		
	Scots pine		Scots pine
			Plane (Sycamore)
	Spruce		
	Sycamore		
	Walnut		Walnut
	Willow		Willow
OVER 40 FEET		OVER 60 FEET	Ailanthus
			Birch
			Wych elm
	Fir		Fir
	Giant arbor vitae		Giant arbor vitae
			Gingko
			Larch
			Black oak
			White pine
	Grey poplar		
			Spruce
			Sycamore
	Tsuga (Hemlock)		
	Tulip tree		Tulip tree
	Willow		Willow
OVER 60 FEET	Douglas fir	OVER 80 FEET	Douglas fir
	Giant fir		Giant fir
			Giant sequoia
	Black poplar		Black poplar
			Grey poplar
	Lombardy poplar		Lombardy poplar
	Sitka spruce		Sitka spruce
			Tsuga (Hemlock)
			Tulip tree
			White willow

327–329 *Planting in interlocking groups for maximum effect of colour, height and texture*
Below: Ideal for public areas; planting in masses is easier but lacks subtlety

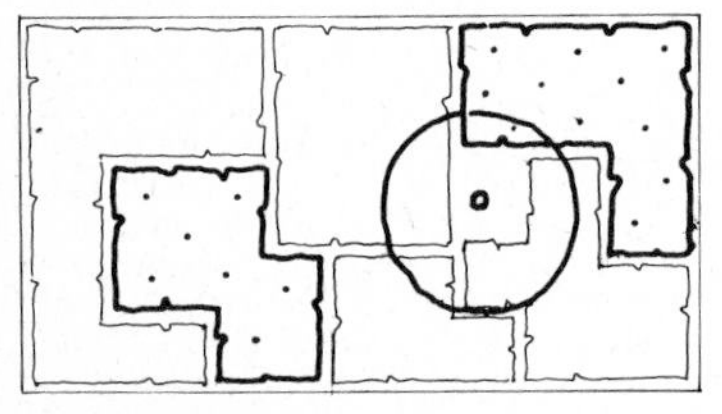

330 *A mixed border which appears to burst out of its bed*

MIXED SHRUB PLANTING

The technique of background planting should also extend to the more decorative foreground shrubs. The number of varieties involved might be less, but they should still be planted in groups of one variety rather than as single specimens.

The effect to aim at when planning a plant group is one of fullness, with shrubs almost bursting out of their containing beds: ideally one should see no bed at all. In addition to its aesthetic appeal, this arrangement has the more practical advantage of helping to keep down weeds.

As with trees, shrub groups will interweave with one another, contrasting in overall shape, leaf texture and flower colour to produce a considered scheme providing interest throughout the year.

To achieve this it is necessary to put in some hours looking at mature shrubs in parks and in other people's gardens, preferably with a plant catalogue in your hand so that you know what the plant will do at other times of the year. The need for this background work seems to surprise many people, although just as much exploratory work goes into selecting a new car or stove, and mastering the correct

331 *A border almost entirely composed of different coloured foliages, such as the one below, provides interest throughout the season. This one includes the grey of* Hippophaë rhamnoides, Sambucus nigra aurea *(gold),* Cornus alba sibirica variegata *(silver variegated),* Salvia purpurascens *and* Ajuga reptans *(purple), with low, grey* Phlomis fruticosa *and* Stachys lanata

332 *A white cherry in spring, with very pale pink tree heath in the foreground*

name, variety and size before ordering it. The vagueness on plant nomenclature of many people who in all other respects consider themselves good gardeners is amazing.

Nomenclature

A plant name works as follows – taking the Japanese maple as an example:

Acer is the generic name; *palmatum* the species.

Subsequent names denote different varieties or the cultivar of the species.

If any of these is missed out when ordering, or if only its English name is given, one cannot blame the nurseryman for giving you the least distinguished form of maple, or even a Norway maple, which is a forest tree. When ordering a plant be quite definite what you want – give all its names – and do not take a suggested substitute until you have looked it

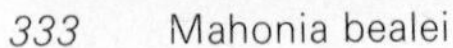

333 Mahonia bealei

334 *Fig* – Ficus carica

335 *Spurge* – Euphorbia wulfenii

336 Viburnum davidii

337 Yucca flaccida

333–337 Some strongly-shaped plants

up. There are three common species of *Buddleia*, for example: *davidii*, *globosa* and *alternifolia*, and all are quite different. Alternative roses are often suggested; the colour of the variety proposed might be what you wanted, but how about its height, scent, foliage, or resistance to mildew?

When collecting new shrubs avoid at all costs accepting cuttings from friends, who may be giving you something that they would otherwise have thrown out. Refuse it unless you particularly want it for your plant composition – or accept if it is easier, but pass it on at the earliest possible opportunity. It is all too easy to amass a collection of friends' 'throw-outs'.

The mixed border, that is, a combination of herbaceous plants and shrubs, is nowadays a more practical proposition than keeping the two separate. Few people have enough time for the maintenance and work involved in keeping a solely herbaceous border in trim – endless tying, dividing, staking and cutting down – and it will provide little winter interest for your pains. By mixing herbaceous plants with shrubs, some of the tying and staking work is eliminated, as the shrubs themselves will support their weaker neighbours and give shelter from the wind. When the individual blooms are over, immediate attention is not so necessary, as the flower heads blend into surrounding greenery, and eventually die down.

A mixed border would also include, for example, lilies, spring bulbs, and the occasional spot filled with annuals. Some of the most suitable shrubs are: tree peonies, lavender, rosemary and *Santolina* – all invaluable for foliage as well as flower.

Positioning should still be organized on the same lines, with similar-coloured plants clustered in groups.
When trying to work out a mixed border on a plan, it is not a bad idea to discipline yourself, when you think you have finished, by taking out nearly half of what you had put in. This way you will probably avoid the pepper and salt effect which ruins this type of border. The effect should look very simple when established and provide interest throughout the year – strong plant forms, splashes of colour blending with the foliage and specimens on the edge of the border flopping out on to the surrounding surfacing.
The plants should not be graded in rows of increasing height to form a bank, but should vary in size as much as in colour and texture. Large background shrubs should occasionally come to the fore to break up the run of the border and create definite areas.

338 A good combination of mixed planting by A. du Gard Pasley

NORMAL HEIGHTS OF TREES AND SHRUBS

FORM	*HEIGHT FROM GROUND LEVEL TO LOWEST BRANCH*
Bush	1 ft 0 in.–2 ft 6 in.
Half standard	3 ft 6 in.–4 ft 6 in.
Three-quarter standard	4 ft 9 in.–5 ft 3 in.
Standard	5 ft 6 in.–6 ft 0 in.
Tall standard	6 ft 3 in.–7 ft 0 in.
Weeping standard	minimum 5 ft 6 in.

HERBACEOUS (PERENNIAL) BORDERS

Where the herbaceous border is planted only with biennials or perennials, it should, if possible, be sited so that it is not dominant in the overall plan, or is at least partially screened, since it will contain little of interest through the winter months, and can provide no form of enclosure as the shrubs in a mixed border can do.

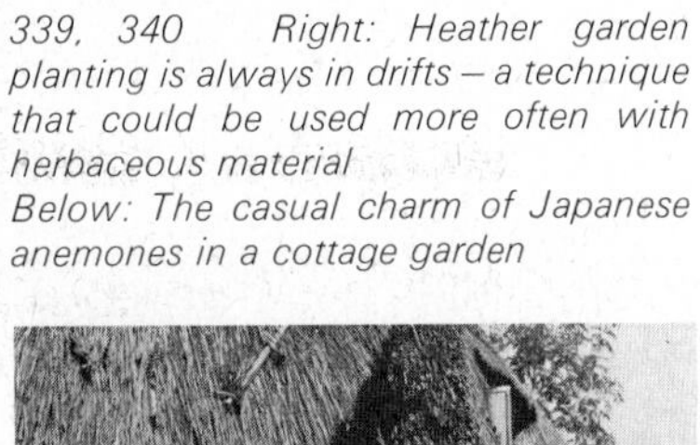

339, 340 Right: Heather garden planting is always in drifts – a technique that could be used more often with herbaceous material
Below: The casual charm of Japanese anemones in a cottage garden

341 Contrasting herbaceous forms

When planning, use plants again in groups, with an eye to flower form, contrasting the spires of hollyhock and *Bocconia* (plume poppy) with low-growing clumps. Control of the colour according to some preconceived design is even more important in a herbaceous border than in a shrubbery or mixed border.

Interplant where possible in the border so that the space is utilized to the full; planting crown imperials through paeonies, for instance – both hate being moved, and one is over before the other shows much life.

342

BULBS

The comparative cheapness and availability of bulbs (tubers, rhizomes, corms, etc.), coupled with their early spring flowering, has led to much misuse in their breeding, hybridization and planting. Anyone who has seen narcissi growing wild, tulips on the hillsides of Turkey, and lilies discreetly crouching in long grass cannot but have been impressed by their simple charm, and noticed how far removed they are from many of our top-heavy, crudely coloured cultivated daffodils and our gross double tulips. This is not to say that many of the cultivated varieties are not admirable for cutting, but for garden cultivation – where the essence of spring is lightness – they are out of place. I have restricted myself more or less to spring bulbs, but it is possible to get a rotation throughout the year of many other less common bulb types.

Bulbs can be used either naturally or formally and the shape of the plant should dictate its position: snowdrops, spring and autumn crocus, fritillary, bluebells and lilies are to my mind essentially informal, and should be grown in drifts in grass, where they can die down naturally; informal groups and not circles round tree stumps. Daffodils or narcissi, because of their informal flopping growth, do not look right in a formal bed and should be planted in grass as well. Lilies can grow through shrubs in a mixed border, but *Galtonia* (summer hyacinth), crown imperial, grape hyacinth and *Allium* are formal in shape and should be planted in beds or tubs. One does see tulips of the lily-flowered type growing in rough grass in continental parks, where they look superb, but these have much more delicate flowers and tend to get smaller (and better) as they get older.

Many of the bulbs we plant are native to the mountainsides of the eastern Mediterranean, and it is their sudden flowering with the first sun after winter snow, before they are burnt up by the subsequent heat, that the Persians wrote about so much. Their brilliant colours when growing naturally are diffused among the fresh grass to produce the effect of a multi-coloured carpet. When such a scene is re-created in a less sunny climate the result can also be breathtaking.

Bulb colours should, however, be carefully chosen, for, when used in an open position as they are in the average garden, mixed bulb groups can often be too loud and demanding at this early time of the year. Many of the blues of crocus and hyacinth are too electric – although when the early ones are consciously used against the brown stems of winter trees they look very fine. The deep yolk-yellow of some daffodils is too strong with fresh grass, whereas the lemon colour of wild narcissi is not. The more bizarre shapes and exotic forms of tulips need careful placing, although as the season creeps on stronger colours are more acceptable.

At the other end of the year, the pale colours of autumn crocus and colchicum always seem insipid against the dying fiery colours of autumn – used on their own, however, or near asters they can look splendid.

GROUND COVER UNDER SHRUBS

Areas of ground cover plants as a lawn substitute have already been considered. There is, however, much to be said for planting ground cover under shrubs in mixed borders. This is a way of keeping down weeds, eliminating digging and providing a permanent mulch to keep moisture in the ground. Furthermore, since ground cover has to be evergreen to be wholly successful, winter interest is added to deciduous shrubs.

343 Mixed ground cover planting in a shady situation – including Lamium maculatum variegatum, Viburnum davidii *and* Megasea (Bergenia)

There are a few shrubs which will provide their own ground cover, having wide branches which are low-growing and sweep the ground. *Viburnum tomentosum* with its varieties *Lanarth*, and the horizontal one *mariesii*, are ideal for this. Hydrangeas are good, although deciduous, while *Juniperus pfitzeriana* and the horizontal yew, *Taxus baccata dovastoni*, are fine if slow-growing evergreens which sweep to the ground. Many rhododendrons, when young, can provide their own ground cover, and two rampant roses, *Rosa paulii* and 'Max Graf', also do so, but their flower is insignificant.
Lower down the scale there are many smaller shrubs which provide good ground cover in different ways. Their forms of growth separate into:

1 Shrubs which make dense small bushes which will link together in time.
2 Those with runners which root into the ground as they spread.
3 Those which spread by means of underground roots.
4 Those which are prostrate growing.

Those with underground roots and runners, however, can be vigorous and invasive.

It is often supposed that only woody specimens are suitable for ground cover, but many perennials both tall and small are equally suitable. Like the shrubs these can also be divided into groups:

1 Those that are clump forming.
2 Those which root into the ground as they spread above it.
3 Those which spread underground.

When selecting suitable varieties for a given position it is essential to choose a plant that will not outgrow its position and swamp its neighbours. Where different groups are being used, clumps of buffer plants should divide up the more invasive varieties: the smaller shrubs and *Bergenia* are ideal for this.

TYPES OF GROUND COVER PLANTS

Rampant
Ajuga reptans
Convallaria majalis (Lily of the valley)
Cornus canadensis (Bunchberry)
Gunnera manicata, 6 ft high
Hedera helix hibernica (Ivy)

Hypericum calycinum (St John's wort)
Luzula maxima, Grass-like
Pachysandra terminalis
Vinca major (Periwinkle)

More sober
Alchemilla mollis (Lady's mantle)
Anaphalis triplinervis, grey leaves
Anchusa myosotidiflora
Anemone hupehensis
Artemisia abrotanum (Southernwood)
Artemisia canescens, grey
Artemisia pontica, grey
Aruncus silvester, Spirea-like
Asperula odorata (Woodruff)
Astilbe
Bergenia (Elephant's ear)
Calluna (Bell heather)
Campanula latiloba
Centaurea dealbata
Cyclamen neapolitanum
Daboecia (Tree heath)
Dianthus Highland Hybrids
Dicentra formosa
Epimedium
Erica (Ling heather)
Eryngium bromelifolium (Thistle family)
Euphorbia robbiae, green flowers
Ferns
Geranium, most herbaceous types
Helleborus, many varieties including the Christmas rose
Hemerocallis (Day lily)
Hosta (Funkia)
Iris, several varieties
Lamium maculatum variegatum (Variegated dead nettle)
Monarda (Bergamot)
Nepeta mussinii (Catmint)
Origanum (Marjoram)
Paeonia
Polygonatum (Solomon's seal)
Polygonum
Pulmonaria
Rodgersia
Ruta graveolens (Rue)
Salvia officinalis (Sage)
Saxifraga geum

Saxifraga umbrosa (London pride)
Stachys lanata (Lamb's ears)
Tiarella cordifolia
Vinca minor and varieties
Viola (violet)

It is also possible to use as ground cover climbing plants, which, instead of going up, are allowed to go along the ground. The number that will do this, however, is limited.
The climbing hydrangea (*Hydrangea petiolaris*), liking shade and a northerly aspect, makes an ideal ground cover. It has a green-cream flower, but is not evergreen. In more open positions on a good soil, *Vitis coignetiae* – a rampant vine with huge leaves which turn scarlet in autumn – will be suitable, and this might be interwoven with a *Clematis montana*.
Ferns also like shade and cool moist places, and make an ideal ground cover plant under shrubs; they are not used enough in the many situations where other plants refuse to grow.

12 MAINTENANCE AND IMPROVEMENT

Maintaining a garden, and ensuring it grows as you had envisaged it, is more of a job than is generally realized. Not only has the pottering to be done, weeding, hoeing, watering and light forking over – much of which can be avoided anyway by mulching and correct planting – but mowing is necessary all through the summer, and in winter the more specialized jobs of thinning, pruning and cutting back have to be done and, ideally, digging or other cultivation of open ground as well.

The design of one's garden should therefore depend to some extent on the amount of time available for these jobs.

Even for those who can afford them, gardeners are few and far between. It is possible to get some help with manual labour – at a price – but many calling themselves gardeners have no conception of pruning or thinning and know little of plants, belonging perhaps to the 'alyssum and lobelia' school.

Firms that specialize in garden maintenance are prepared to do straightforward mowing, edging and sweeping, but treat the whole job as a tactical operation to be done in the shortest possible time. It is too much to expect them to know the whims of individual plants – or to bother with the whims of individual customers either.

The brunt of the specialized maintenance, therefore, invariably falls on the owner of the garden.

If surfacing is well laid initially, if boundaries are constructed of substantial materials, planted areas properly thought out, and grass edging eliminated, maintenance can be cut down considerably, though a good deal will still remain.

Pruning

So much gruesome detail is published about pruning down to specific buds on specific spurs that many people are terrified of planting anything at all but, unless one is concentrating on growing show specimens, the amount of pruning necessary is marginal. All it involves is trimming to produce a nicely shaped head on a tree, or a good bushy plant which is not top-heavy or spindly in growth.

The time to prune depends on the growth. For instance, shrubs which flower on the current year's wood in the late summer will be pruned hard back in the spring (*Buddleia*), while spring-flowering species will need less drastic pruning

when flowering has finished. If a forsythia is cut hard back in spring all its flowers will be lost, or if a *Buddleia* is lightly pruned, it grows up and up, getting more and more top-heavy and putting out no growth at the bottom.
Shrubs that are grown specifically for the stem colouring on the young wood need cutting back (or stooling) in spring, so that by the following winter there are plenty of shoots.

Plant	Method of pruning	Season for pruning
Evergreens including conifers	Shape to natural form	April and throughout summer
Leggy and overgrown evergreens, e.g. yew, holly, box, etc.	Cut hard back into old wood	End of February or early March
Deciduous flowering shrubs, e.g. *Philadelphus, Syringa, Rosa, Weigela*	Thin every three years by cutting back old and weak shoots to base	Dormant season or after flowering
Ground cover, e.g. *Vinca, Hedera, Calluna, Erica, Hypericum calycinum*	Clip over to encourage bushy growth	April
Shrubs grown for foliage effect, e.g. *Ailanthus, Sambucus, Rhus typhina*	Cut hard back to within a bud or two of old wood	March
Shrubs for winter effect of coloured bark, e.g. *Cornus, Salix*	Cut hard back to within a bud or two of old wood	Late March, early April

Dividing herbaceous plants

Herbaceous plants need cutting down during the winter months and dividing every two or three years. The growth of herbaceous plants is outwards and, if it is allowed to go on unchecked the plant develops in a ring with a hole in the middle. The clump is therefore divided every so often to prevent this.
Once the simple mechanics of how a plant grows are understood (and they are so much easier than the mechanics of a household gadget or a car) it all becomes very simple.

The lawn

The same sort of theory applies to lawn maintenance. Where there are bare patches in the grass, either the wrong seed was selected, or the site was not correctly prepared, or the ground is too wet. The presence of moss indicates some basic physiological problem and the site needs closer inspection before giving an application of top dressing or feed, the same way as a child's illness needs diagnosing and curing before a tonic is given. A tonic given to the sick child will not cure it, and a feed alone will not rectify a sick lawn.

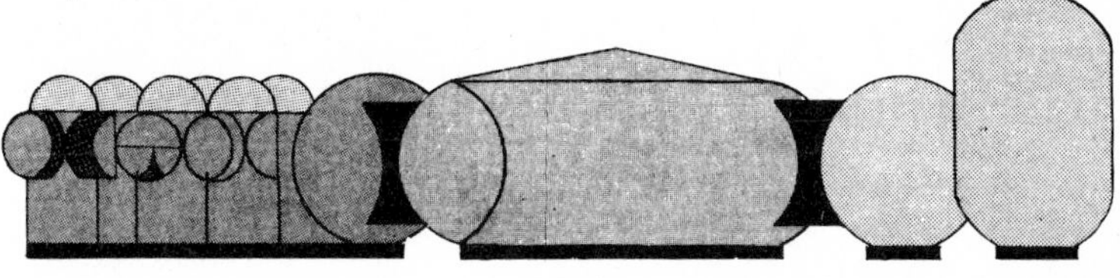

344 *The uses of fibreglass for all manner of structures are still being explored. Keith Albarn has experimented and produced a series of structures which can be used individually or fitted together. With their bright and permanent colours, these would make excellent play houses or shelters*

Structures

There is often great reluctance at the outset to spend money on structural features in a garden. The assorted medley of do-it-yourself huts and greenhouses which one sees in back yards bear witness to this. The maintenance such structures demand is generally considerable, and each remedial effort makes the original look more makeshift than ever.

The architect is at last becoming aware of the fact that a household needs an outside storage place and that, if it is left to his customer, the choice of hut will in all probability do no justice to the lines of his house! The range of outside structures on the market increases annually, so that, by hunting around, it is now possible to find the type of structure needed for a particular position, with windows and doors in the right places. There is, however, a need for a modular system of outside structures to be evolved – not unlike storage units inside – which could be added to at will while still maintaining a unified overall effect.

Greenhouse design seems less adventurous. The pitched-roof type is always difficult to site in the garden and the lean-to type needs a strong wall to support it. There is, however, a circular greenhouse on the market; it is small but would make an attractive feature for house plants or ferns if correctly sited.

345 *Circular greenhouse*

346 *Left: Storage cupboards in a garden by Ursula Seleger Hansen. The floor has been sunk to give them greater height inside and the top is used for growing herbs in pots*

347, 348 Above: Tough lattice-work made of 1 in. square battens
Right: Lattice-work used to make a feature of an old doorway in the garden of Derek Hill

Fencing

Cheap fences need high maintenance – wattle hurdles, for instance, rot quickly, five years being an average lifetime. They still need strong vertical support at regular intervals and, for a little more money initially, a stouter infill makes good sense.

Bought lattice-work usually has a short life span because the individual laths are so thin. During replacement, the inevitable damage to shrubs and climbers which have become entwined with the fence makes the operation a nightmare, and the same objection applies also to trellis-work on walls. There are on the market panels of plastic-coated wire mesh, which are a better solution in some situations.

Support for climbers

Subsequent maintenance can be reduced by providing good support for a climbing plant from the outset, rather than making annual additions as the plant grows. First of all, however, make sure you know what type of support the plant wants. The word 'climber' covers a number of different types of plants which attach themselves to, or grow up, vertical surfaces in different ways. Their method of holding themselves up and their orientation is, of course, the key to getting the right support to do the job.

Some climbers attach themselves by suckers or climbing roots and need a solid face; common ivy is a good example. Others, such as honeysuckle, twist themselves through whatever obstacle they wish to surmount, and others again have grasping tendrils which support the plant – like vines or peas.

Some plants, particularly the more decorative types of ivy, take some time to produce the stems with suckers which attach it to a wall, and the plant initially appears to push itself up the wall.

The true rambler rose has none of these attributes. It is very strong growing and its long whippy branches flop about and will support it on neighbouring shrubs, though when trained up a wall it will need support.

The climbing rose also has no method of attachment. Its wood is harder than that of the rambler and it will support itself for the first year or so, but when a vigorous specimen reaches 20 ft high, it becomes top-heavy and support will obviously be necessary. *Cotoneaster horizontalis*, for instance, like the climbing rose, has no attachment system, and the strength of its own main stem supports it against a wall although, since its form of growth happens to be flat or fan-shaped, it appears to climb.

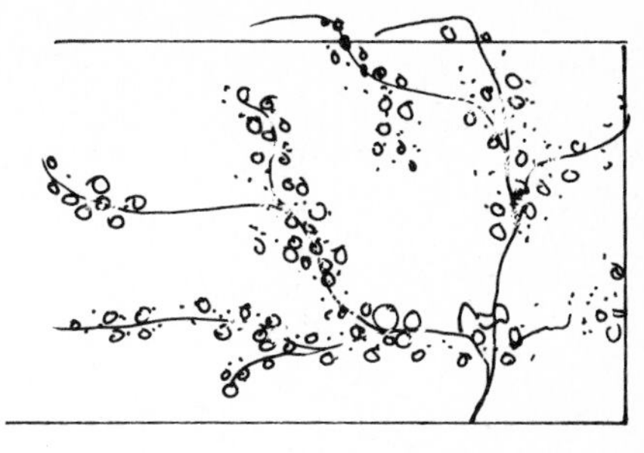

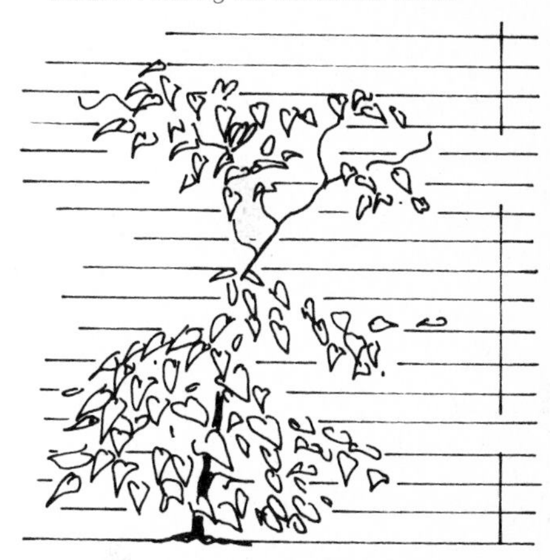

349, 350 Wall supports for climbers
Above: The plant is supported with random vine eyes
Below: Training on horizontal wires

351 Below: Polygonum Aubertie (baldschuanicum), *the silver lace vine, growing on a town house. While not evergreen it is one of the most rampant climbers*

Twisting plants (using their stems for climbing)	Twining plants (with tendrils)	Plants with suckers or climbing roots	Wall species
Honeysuckle	Clematis Vine	Ivy *Hydrangea petiolaris*	Ramblers *Pyracantha*
Morning glory French bean Wistaria Jasmine	Passion flower Pea family		*Ceanothus* Winter jasmine

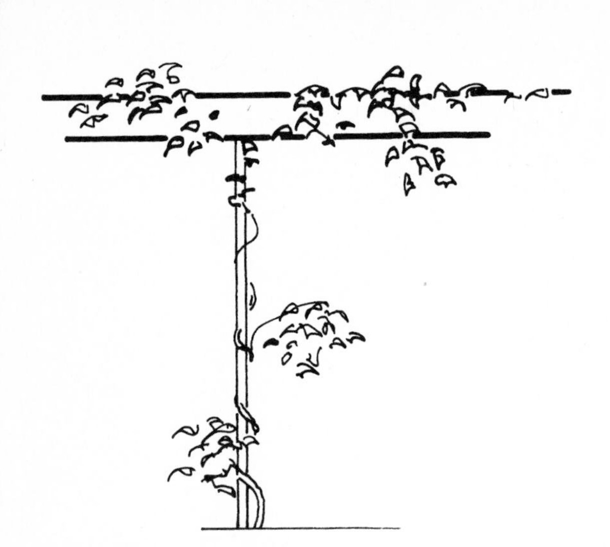

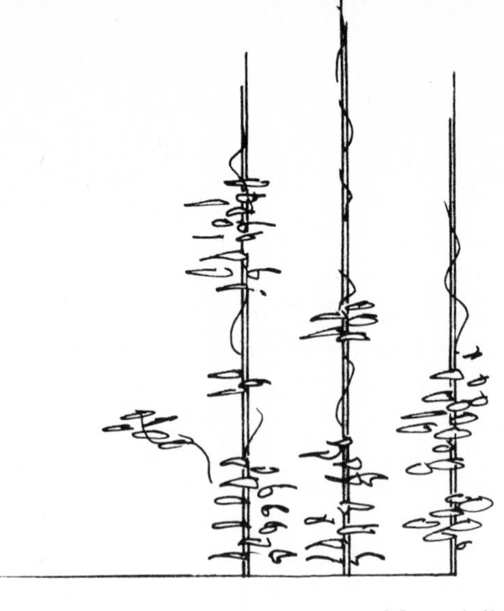

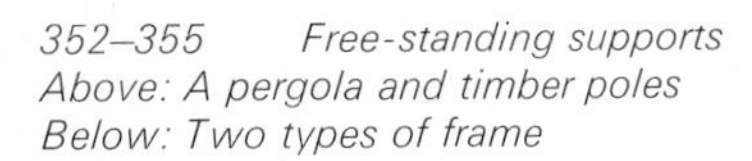

352–355 Free-standing supports
Above: A pergola and timber poles
Below: Two types of frame

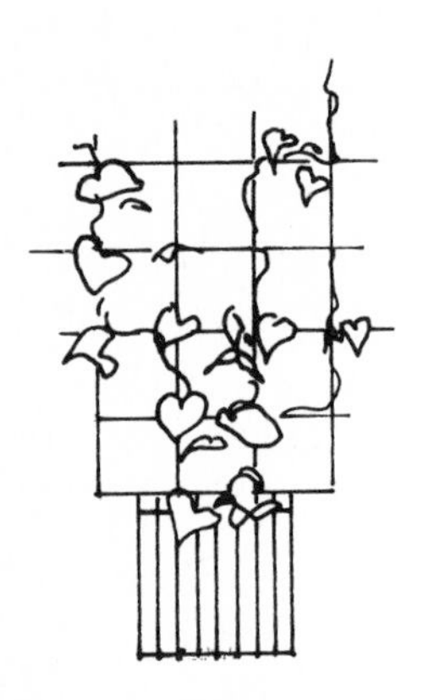

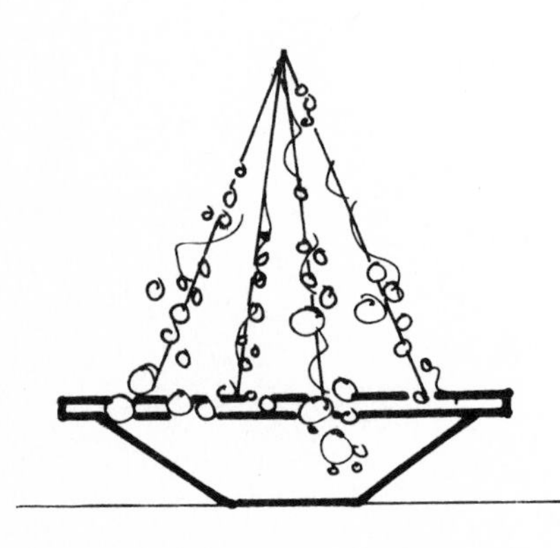

The construction of the wall is important. Most 'climbers' are very happy with a plain brick or stone wall, and the mortar between the bricks or stones is ideal for inserting vine eyes to support the plant where necessary. It is obviously no use to put a plant with climbing roots against a wall which has to be whitewashed at intervals, unless a frame is made which can be let down quite simply with the plant still on it. The same type of frame is necessary for a twiner or a climber with no attachment system which is growing up a bare wall.

The orientation of the wall is as important as its type of construction. Contrary to general belief, there are quite a number of climbers which will grow on a north-facing wall. Others, which appreciate the warmth of a south wall, need their feet in the shade – clematis, for example.

Plants will not grow against or near a newly creosoted fence. It is very toxic and great care should be taken in its use.

A recurring problem is how to cover a chain-link fence. The twiners and twisters are ideal though, sadly, few are evergreen. It is worth noting, however, that generally speaking a deciduous climber – that is, one which loses its leaves in winter – grows much faster than an evergreen.

Whatever system of support you adopt, let it be as insignificant as possible and make sure the lines of it do not oppose those of the house. Broadly speaking, the support, whatever material it is made of, should be vertical or horizontal; a cobweb of new wires at all angles on a brick wall will look a mess. Wires should generally be flush with the wall and not 2 or 3 in. from it. To achieve this use wire attached to lead-headed nails driven into the wall, rather than vine eyes, which will hold the wire away from it.

Colour

Going hand in hand with the maintenance of some of the structural features of a garden is their improvement. Much garden furniture would be enormously improved by a coat of white paint; this is admittedly an annual job – but then teak, too, needs regular oiling.

Colour introduced generally outside can liven up a garden enormously, but it should always be subservient to flower colour. Tones should therefore be fairly muted and, if adjacent to the house, they should tie in with the colour scheme inside.

Walls finished in browns, ochres and golds, are admirable backgrounds, bringing warmth into a winter garden; they also blend well with summer greens. A wall in one of these colours behind a plant group can provide a basis on which to build a colour composition. Cement paints, in a good range of colours, are now on the market and these last a considerable time without the need for annual re-painting. There are also coloured wood stains available which allow the graining of the wood to show through, and these are most suitable for screens and fencing.

Colour can also be introduced outside by painting corrugated asbestos where it is used for internal screen walling or by the use of coloured Perspex as a screen infill. Plastic-coated wire mesh can also be purchased in different colours: this is useful for all manner of supports and screen infills, as it comes in various gauges.

Whatever colour is used outside, it should not be garish or too strong. Always bear in mind that one is creating an overall picture and that the colours should blend with whatever else is contemplated or is already there.

Pergola structures

Before erecting a pergola or overhead-beam structure, it is as well to remember that it will require a certain amount of

356 Fieldstone or rubble piers support a concrete main beam in this pergola; the other beams are made of stained pine

maintenance, not only in the tending of the structure itself, but in tying the plants it supports and letting them down when painting or staining of the frame becomes due.
A simple, light pergola construction can easily be put together by dowelling a horizontal 2 in. thick beam to a vertical scaffold pole set in concrete; a wire should run along the top of the beam under which plants can be tucked. The vertical can be drilled at various points and ties inserted to hold up the plants, or else wire can be twisted round in corkscrew fashion from top to bottom and the plants put under this. Similar structures can be made entirely of timber – though not rustic – or of timber on brick or stone piers. The scale of the verticals, however, should balance with that of the horizontals.

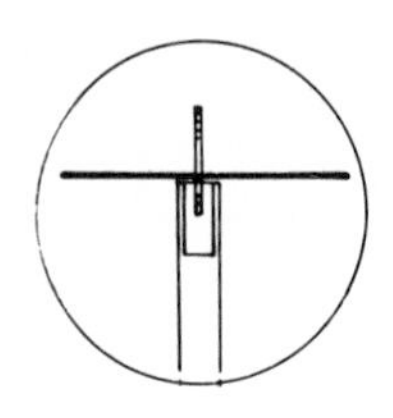

357–359 Pergola construction. A 9×2 in. softwood beam is dowelled at one end to a 2 in. diameter scaffold pole and the other end sits in a metal shoe plugged to the wall of the house. The detail shows the dowelling: a wooden plug in the vertical is joined to the beam with a double-ended screw

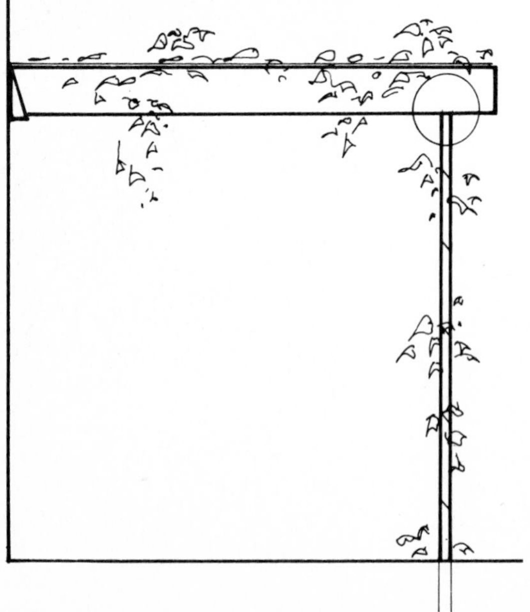

13 SPECIAL FEATURES

WATER

Water has always been an important element in garden layout, in different periods of history, in different climates and on differing social scales (see Chapter 1). The way in which it was contained, and whether it was still or moving, depended on its use in its particular setting.

It is from this starting point – that of use, not imitation – that one should work when deciding whether and how to include water in a design.

Water can be used with or without plants, it can be still like a mirror, it can move slowly as in a stream, or it can move quickly, catching the sun and falling from a height as in a waterfall or fountain. The shape of the area of water will to some extent be determined by its function but in any form it will invariably become a focal point.

One has to decide, in terms of the garden design, whether the water should be formal – though not necessarily regular – or informal, raised or at ground level. The possibilities are limitless, and perhaps the best way to arrive at a positive solution is to discuss first some of the negative aspects.

Water used outside in any way needs regular maintenance. The removal of algae – plants and fish will help here, though they also need attention – unblocking fountain jets, scrubbing the inside of a bowl: all need doing fairly regularly.

Accessible water of any depth at ground level should be avoided where young children are likely to play, as it has a compulsion about it which will always draw children. Dreadful stories are told of children drowning in an inch of water – though this is probably an exaggeration; they can just as easily drown in a puddle, the bath or the washing-up bowl. Water raised up in some sort of container to the shoulder level of a small child presents much less of a hazard but can still be played with, and boats can still be sailed on it.

Water in a paved area is usually better raised as well. The automatic reaction when at close quarters is to touch and to look into it, and this can be made easier if there is a containing wall to sit on. Small areas of still water at ground level are seldom successful, since they tend to look mean, and a reasonable expanse is necessary to get reflections.

360, 361 Below: Still water used as a mirror – a pool by Sylvia Crowe Bottom: A formal pool at ground level by Gustav Lüttge. Note the water laps the bottom of the concrete overhang

One of the major drawbacks is the chill effect that water can have in winter, especially on rainy days, and obviously the larger the area the more this will be emphasized. Furthermore, a design which relies on the contrast of a horizontal sheet of water with the vertical line of irises or bulrushes will fail in winter when these die down: it is for this reason that the effect of a natural pond sometimes fails. To counteract this there is often a tendency to pretty up the pond with little bridges, cobbles and statuary.

Where a fountain is contemplated, the effect of the wind blowing the water about should be taken into account. Ideally all the water should fall into the pool – if it doesn't, the fountain jet should be adjusted.

362, 363 Top: An interesting fountain detail in Switzerland
Above: Interconnecting water basins by Sylvia Crowe at the Cement and Concrete Association show garden. The contrast between the horizontal emphasis of the water and the vertical lines of the building is softened by a superb Rheum

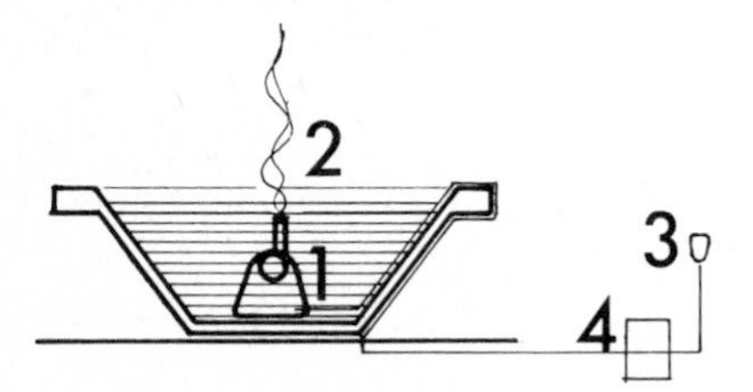

364 A simple fountain in a precast concrete container. The self-circulating pump runs off mains electricity

1 *inlet*
2 *fountain*
3 *mains supply (200/250 volts A/C)*
4 *isolating transformer with safeguard barrier*

365 A terrace and raised pool by Gustav Lüttge

366 *Above: A pool worked into the basic design of a terrace with a timber bench seat beyond*

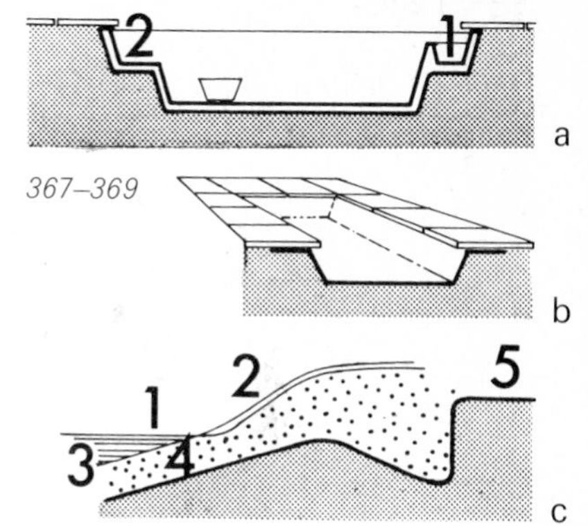

367–369

a: Section of a concrete pool with shelves for marginal plants. Note that the water comes to the underside of the paved surround which overlaps the pool sides by a few inches

1 *shelf for marginal planting*
2 *shelf for plants in containers*

b: A small pool made with plastic sheeting. In this case it is even more important to use the overhang to cast shadow on the vertical sides of the pool

c: Plastic sheeting used in a larger pool. Detail of soft edging

1 *water level*
2 *slope of 1 in 5*
3 *slope of 3 in 5*
4 *gravel fill (12 in. deep)*
5 *plastic sheeting*

Formal water

When used in conjunction with paving, the pool must fit into the pattern and be considered as just another element in the plan; it should not be allowed to overwhelm the overall design. A common error is to use too large a pool. It is worth hunting for small containers. They often come with fountains, and, when grouped with plants, become a pleasant 'incident' only and not the *tour de force* of the area. Hollowed-out rocks, or simple tubs in the Japanese tradition, can also be used.

Running water can enliven an area, both visually and by its sound. With a little ingenuity it is possible to create simple 'incidents' using one of the various plant containers on the market and incorporating a self-circulating pump – run off a concealed main led from the house.

The larger type of formal pool can be constructed in reinforced concrete, brick with concrete liner or moulded plastic. Any of these solutions are admirable. When using concrete, however, advice on adequate thickness and waterproofing is essential, since cracking is practically impossible to repair without recourse to the use of plastic sheet.

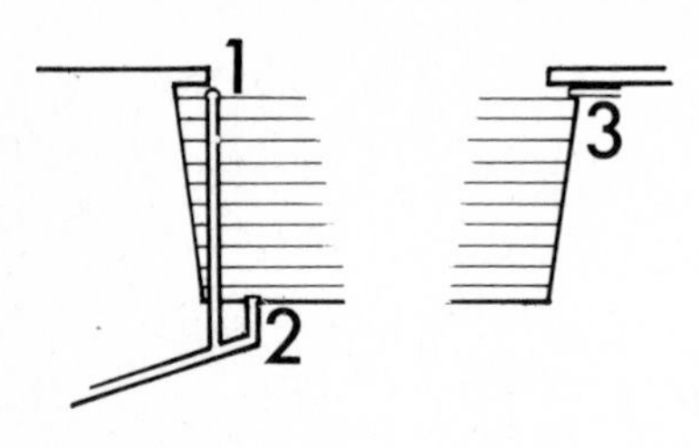

370, 371 Above: Pool section showing inlet feed, overflow and outlet

1 *overflow*
2 *outlet*
3 *inlet*

Below: The sound and movement of falling water have a particular attraction for children

372

Plastic sheeting is available on the market as a liner for simple pools – it even comes with rocks printed on it! After excavating and lining the hole with sand, the sheet is spread and the pool is ready for filling. With small pools, however, the problem of how to disguise the edges never seems to be resolved satisfactorily, and the creases in the sheet never look quite right. Furthermore, there will be no means of draining the pool for cleaning – and a suitable place for siphoning the water away is not always available. On the larger scale where a less formal effect is needed, plastic sheet is a better proposition as it is far easier to disguise the edges with cobbles and planting.

When incorporating a fountain or waterfall in a paved area, a mammoth display should be avoided. Some fountain attachments are like upturned watering-can roses, and produce an effect more suitable for a Victorian park than a domestic garden. It is all too easy to over-design, and complexity of arrangement mars the simple charm of flowing water. One is seeking to provide a pleasant place to live and relax in, not a formal showpiece.

In hotter climates fountains are used more liberally, not only for their sound, but to moisten and cool the atmosphere with their spray, and to catch the sun, since it is only in the sunlight that a fountain really comes to life. It is interesting to note that in the shaded grottoes of the eighteenth- and nineteenth-century gardens running water was used to evoke melancholy!

Natural water

The natural sheet of water should sit into the general garden plan at its lowest point, even more than a formal area or bowl arrangement. In nature water always sits at the bottom of a valley, and, to be convincing, informal water in the garden must seem to do the same. As in the great eighteenth-century park gardens, the surrounding land form should run as cleanly as possible into the water.

A sheet of water can be used for reflection, which is a valuable way of bringing light into a dark corner. If the water is sited close to the house it is often possible to have reflections dancing on the ceilings on a sunny day. Plants disturbing the surface will, however, destroy this effect.

Swimming pools

Developments in constructional techniques and materials in recent years have made the private swimming pool a much more economic proposition.

This is not to say that pools are inexpensive; however, they can be a good investment, for the pleasure they bring, and for the value they add to a property. The more natural a pool can be made to look, the better, and much can be done with low plantings near it and the placing of large stones in the Japanese manner. However, in many climates a pool must be drained in the winter, thereby losing its aesthetic character, so it is often best to position it in a screened area of its own. It is essential that the pool should be sited in a sunny sheltered part of the garden, with adequate provision for changing, sunbathing and drying off beside it, and overhanging trees should be avoided. Provision should also be made for a pump chamber and chlorinating plant and equipment storage. Water and electricity supplies are also necessary.
Specialist advice should be taken on exact positioning and type of pool for your particular situation.

373 Rock shapes used to soften a formal pool at a Swiss house. Note the shuttered concrete wall and cantilevered steps

374–376 Free-shaped swimming pools need not always be kidney-shaped.
Bottom: Swimming pools with paved surround, steps and diving board

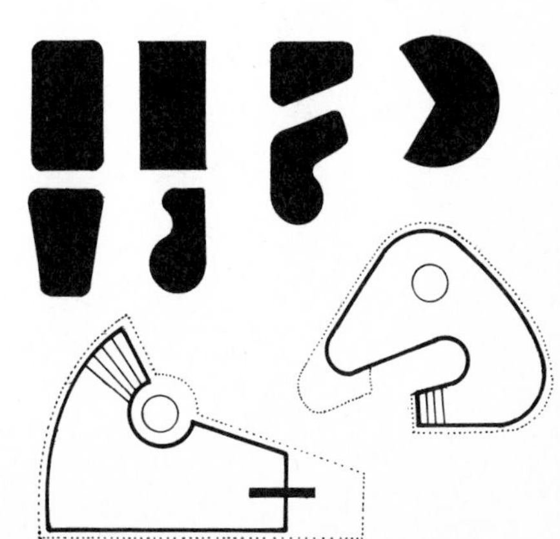

377, 378 *Right: A rockery which is a copy of natural scenery, an exhibit by Gavin Jones Ltd at the Chelsea Flower Show*
Below: A slab or rock worked into the surround of a pool and contrasted with a castor-oil plant to make an incidental point of interest

ROCK GARDENS

A rockery should be a place to grow alpines; a copy of a natural rock outcrop, with a minimum of soil and lying in a well-drained position – but how often is this the case? Almost invariably lumps of rock are scattered on an earth bank and overplanted with lobelia and yellow alyssum. The display is riveting for a fortnight in spring, but a paradise for weeds during the rest of the year. If one wishes to grow alpines, it is a better idea to plant them in a bed of gravel chippings flat on the ground. Add the occasional boulder and strongly-shaped plant as a contrast and the result will be not only far more rewarding, but also much easier to build and maintain.
If you are lucky enough to possess a rock outcrop in your garden, or can afford to have a rockery built with massive stone pieces, the result can be very fine. It should be remembered, however, that in the natural setting there is often more rock than soil visible, that not every plant is different from its neighbour, and that pointed dwarf conifers are definitely not an appropriate part of the scene.

THE SPECIAL GARDEN

If there is to be an area devoted to growing special plants with a short period of interest, such as iris or primula, etc., it should be screened in the same way as a swimming pool, so that it is not too apparent in the off season.

This special type of garden tends to be a hangover from a bygone, more gracious era when the garden was large enough to contain separate areas of specific interest. One can, however, provide other interests in such an exclusive garden, either by designing it in such a way that the particular plant is contained in a strong pattern of box or yew hedging which 'reads' by itself, or by introducing shrubs and herbaceous plants to vary the form and lengthen the period of interest.

THE HERB GARDEN

Some herbs make ideal plants for inclusion in a mixed shrub and herbaceous border because of their good colour or form – red sage (red salvia) – for instance, but there is something evocative of high summer about a special herb area with its warm scents and buzzing bees.

379–381 Left: A simple herb garden with raised beds
Below: Possible patterns for a knot garden of herbs

There are two schools of thought on how herbs should be grown: whether in rigid compartments – making gathering much easier, it has to be admitted – or in a controlled riot, planted as any other part of the garden might be, in mixed groups.

When the compartment school have their way, herbs are usually grown in a small formal area laid out in a traditional pattern of the Knot or Parterre garden, with a strict edging of parsley or thyme, lavender or *Santolina*. Amusing variations could also be designed on slightly less traditional and symmetrical lines.

The small, formally-patterned herb garden is best sited within a paved or gravelled area adjacent to the house, where its

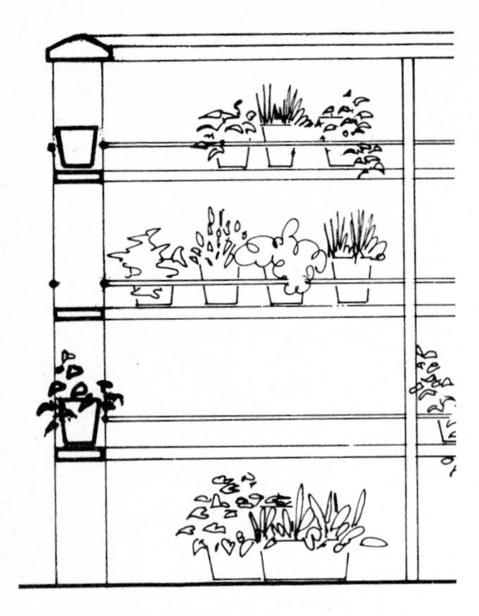

382 Pots of herbs on shelves; geraniums or bulbs could also be incorporated when in flower. This arrangement makes a good screen for a service area

scale can be appreciated, and where it is easily accessible from the kitchen.
It is sometimes suggested that herbs can be grown in pockets in a paved area but, unless the area is to take little use, when the point of it might be questioned anyway, they become both an irritation and a positive hazard.
Herbs can also be grown very successfully in pots, which can be grouped with others containing bulbs or annuals. As a number of herbs are evergreen, they will give some life to the group in winter. Another method is to stand the pots in layers on timber shelves. This makes maintenance and cutting easier for an elderly person and at the same time can provide a screen – round the kitchen door for instance.

Basic herbs

Sow seeds of	sweet basil	parsley
	borage	dill
	burnet	sweet marjoram
	chervil	summer savory
Get roots of	spearmint	lemon balsam
	peppermint	chives (bulblets)
Get plants of	sage	thyme
	bay	rosemary
	lavender	fennel

THE ROSE GARDEN

The cut flower of the bush rose, the hybrid tea (HT) of the garden, is without doubt extremely beautiful. It is the epitome of all that is sweet and pure and most worthwhile cultivating. It is portrayed on birthday cards and calendars and stamped in all colours on headscarves and wallpapers. The sad fact remains, however, that as a growing plant the HT or bush rose is not a pretty thing. The flower heads, exquisite though they are, are too far apart and in a rose garden they appear as a mass of pretty dots with no overall cohesion.
The shrub rose and many of the floribunda roses with their flower-laden, low-hanging branches are much more satisfactory visually and surely also have more of the old-world charm, scent and nostalgia which we seem to treasure and try to re-create in the rose garden.
The colours of many of the shrub roses are less garish and unnatural than those the hybridizers have managed to produce in the HT and floribunda. (The one that starts the flowering season as one colour and ends it as another is a

383 English rose garden by Sylvia Crowe. The floribunda and HT roses are planted in box-edged beds while taller shrub roses and old-fashioned herbaceous shrubs grow between the yew piers. At Oxford

particular horror.) The flowering period of the shrub rose is shorter, unfortunately, although there are some perpetual flowerers available, and it does have decorative hips in the autumn. Its beauty, grace and scent, however, make up a thousandfold for its shorter period of flower.

The design of a rose garden depends on the type of rose one proposes to put in it. Neither the design nor the look of the plants will be improved, however, by subjection to a meticulously worked out geometric pattern of beds in a mown sward. This is municipal horticulture at its worst and has no place in the private garden. From a practical point of view such a pattern works only when seen from the air.

As always in design, simplicity pays off. Regular beds in a paved terrace would seem to be the ideal way of growing roses. One can then tend them whatever the weather, sit near them, and there is no edging to be done. Beds need not always be of the same size or shape, and should not necessarily balance exactly – an element of asymmetry makes for interest. For instance, a large square bed of low-growing roses could be balanced and enhanced by a smaller

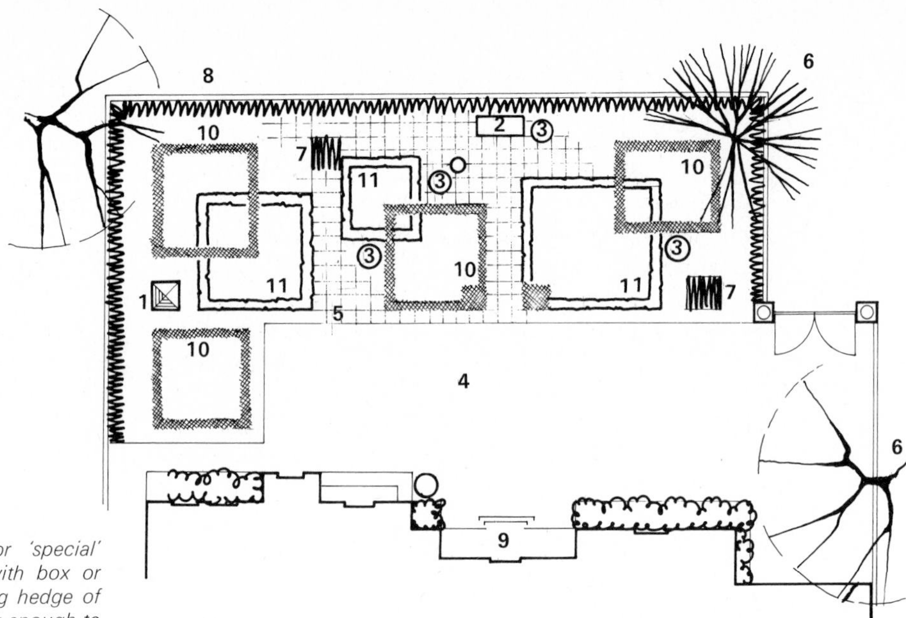

384 Plan for a rose or 'special' garden with beds edged with box or Santolina, *and a surrounding hedge of yew. Such a pattern is strong enough to be interesting in itself when the plants are not in flower*

1 *dovecote*
2 *bench seat*
3 *tubs for bulbs and annuals*
4 *gravel forecourt*
5 *brick paving squares*
6 *existing tree*
7 *clumps of clipped yew*
8 *yew hedge*
9 *front door*
10 *box hedge*
11 Santolina *hedge*

one next to it planted with a taller variety. It is generally best to keep one type and colour of rose to one bed, as the spotty effect of the average rose garden is only increased by mingling flowers of different colours in the same bed.

One of the drawbacks of the formal rose garden is its forlorn look in winter, with beds of seemingly lifeless twigs rising from the bare earth. An underplanting or edging of lavender, box or *Santolina* helps to get rid of this aridity, and a pretty pattern or simple Knot garden could be designed by using one or more types of edging. If the beds are occasionally punctuated with some upright rosemary, yew, *Choisya*, or some other locally available evergreen of a different colour and scale, it helps to break the regularity of the pattern.

There is no reason why floribunda roses should not be worked into the herbaceous or shrub border as well; in fact they look very much better grown this way than in formal beds. Shrub roses most definitely lend themselves to this treatment; some species are particularly vigorous and look wonderful spraying out from among other shrubs.

Perhaps the idea of a special garden given over to a particular plant is a thing of the past. In earlier days, if the garden was not at its best, one didn't go into it. Few of us can afford such luxury now.

THE VEGETABLE GARDEN

The vegetable garden is very much part of the overall scheme of many gardens. Yet too often it is relegated, with no hard

access provided, to the corner furthest from the house and screened off by a decaying rustic pergola.
The obvious position for vegetables is one near the kitchen door, with a hard path leading to it. If the area is then screened with hedging, areas of planting, or wing hedges, it can double up as a place to hang washing, have a compost heap, or burn the rubbish as well.
With some thought, however, it should be possible to grow vegetables without having to hide them completely. After all, the use of vegetable leaves in flower arrangements presumably argues an acceptance of their beauty – why should this not apply also in the garden? Certainly the beauty and range of the shades of green in some of the allotments and vegetable areas on the Continent has to be seen to be believed.
Some of the old formal vegetable areas in walled gardens were most attractive, because planting areas were contained in box hedges, rows of espalier fruit trees and nut walks.
The introduction of herbs – many of which are evergreen and flowering – into the vegetable area will break it up and give interest in the winter. Gourds in summer will provide a brilliant splash of colour, while soft fruit and fruit trees of varying heights, standard, half-standard or bush, can also add interest and productivity.
Smaller raised beds can add interest to the area and make maintenance and picking easier for those unable to bend, though they are not suitable for machine cultivation.

385 A raised bed, made of in situ *concrete, for salad vegetables or herbs*

386 A French vegetable garden with gravel paths, box-edged beds and trained fruit trees (by Vilmorin-Andrieux)

PLAY AREAS

If there are children in the family, the chances are that the whole garden will be a play area. An area can be assigned to them, but keeping them to it will be another matter.

It is not possible to go into all the aspects of children's play and what is required, but one or two broad generalizations can be made.

Children revel in chaos of their own making – or rather what seems chaos to us – and have a love of invention, so one tries to cater for this in one part of the garden in the fond hope of deterring them from rampaging too often into the rest of it. Large play equipment, swings, slides, play houses, and all the paraphernalia for adventure play can be sited in the children's area. A climbing frame or good shaped log, suitably placed, can be an attractive feature, not only for play but from a visual point of view as well, and steps, changes of level and slight contoured mounds are also enjoyable dual-purpose features.

Areas taking heavy wear should be left with rough grass, or could be laid with granite setts or slabs through which grass will grow, but not wear down.

A good-sized area of dry paving is necessary for most ages, and for younger children a hard track or path for tricycles is a good idea – for bicycles, too, if the area permits.

A sand-pit is always appreciated by younger children, and the larger the better. The pit should be designed so that as little sand as possible spills out of it but, as half the joy of sand is making pies with it, some form of table should be provided, slightly raised above sand level. Coarse sand should be used, as opposed to builder's fine sand. The pit should obviously drain as quickly as possible after rain (see detail) and, in an urban area, should have a light frame to go over it at night to keep out cats.

387, 388 Sand-pits
Top: A simple variety using a manhole section
Above: A portable sand-pit by Ursula Seleger Hansen

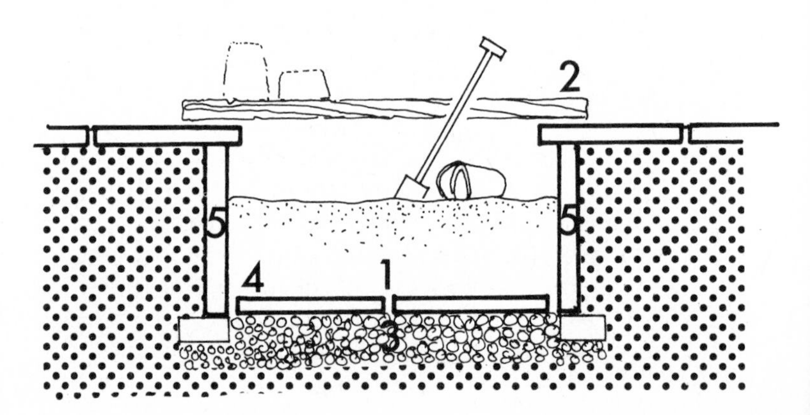

389 Section of a sunken sand-pit

1. *sharp sand, 12 in. deep*
2. *plank over the pit to act as a table*
3. *a 6 in. ash base for good drainage*
4. *bottom made of precast concrete slabs laid in open joints (to assist drainage)*
5. *precast slab or $4\frac{1}{2}$ in. brick walls*

390 Above: A tree house

A simpler form of removable sand-pit can be made by filling a large tyre – preferably a tractor tyre – with sand, and making a table with a plank across the rim.

On no account have a pool or paddling place too close to the sand-pit (though the children would love it) or the sand and water will change places and a sticky mess will develop in both. A very shallow pool, perhaps only an inch or two deep, with a cobbled base would be appreciated and enjoyed like a puddle for splashing in and cycling through.

Both these features may be incorporated in a terrace area, where they can be quite attractive, and supervision from the house is possible.

14 GARDEN FURNISHINGS

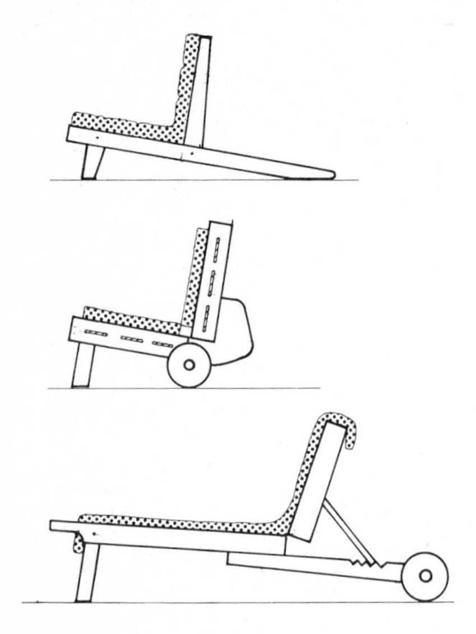

391–393 *Top: A simple wooden chair for relaxing in. The cushion is removable*
Centre: A chair with a wheel. When the cushion is removed, the back folds over the seat
Bottom: An adjustable sun-bathing couch with removable mattress. The back lets down, and the whole thing can be wheeled away and up-ended like a barrow for storage

394, 395 *Below: A do-it-yourself cedar chair*
Right: The matelas

The terrace, patio, garden, or what you will should be a place for relaxation; a place where the old can snooze in the shade, Mum can sew, Dad can read and the children can play. Many of these activities call for chairs.

CHAIRS

What type of chair is wanted for outside use?
For eating outside one needs a chair that can be drawn up to a table and yet is comfortable enough to relax in after the meal. For snoozing, sewing, reading etc. one needs a chair with an adjustable headrest that one can sit deeply into or lie comfortably upon, like the *matelas* of the Mediterranean beaches.
In either case the chair should look deep, comfortable and inviting; it should be light enough to move easily, yet solid enough to be steady and to withstand the elements; it should be so designed that it is ready for use when a cushion is added (which can be taken indoors when it rains) and the design, whether delicate or massive, should suit the site and make a sculptural point of interest when the chair is not in use.
The teak bench and deck chair and the white metal seat are all intended for sitting in, but they are either too hard, too

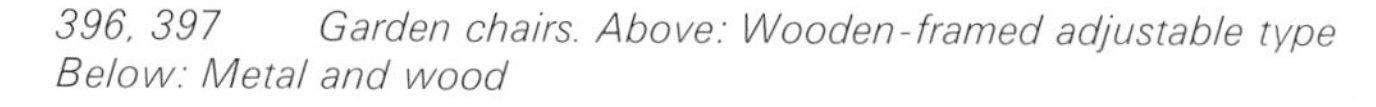

396, 397 Garden chairs. Above: Wooden-framed adjustable type
Below: Metal and wood

398–400 Top: Painted aluminium
Centre: Tubular metal
Below: Fibreglass

precarious, or too awkward to negotiate to permit relaxation, and the gaudy, plastic-seated aluminium chair is fit only for picnics on the by-pass.

Timber, whether painted or naturally finished, seems to be the most suitable constructional material for most garden furniture. It is produced, however, in a variety of other materials as well. Rush and basketware are most comfortable, but cannot be left outside indefinitely. Metal furniture is available in various forms, either modern or traditional in character, and heavy or light according to the metal used. If painted, this needs always to be in pristine condition or it can look very shabby and uninviting, and cushions will usually be necessary to soften the chair both physically and visually. Manufacturers in general have not yet seen the

401

402

403

404 Below: A concrete block for use as a bench or table

potential of fibreglass and the acrylic materials for garden seating. Their flexibility and durability would surely make them ideal for garden furniture.

BUILT-IN FURNITURE

Visually, bench-type seating fits into the garden area very well, and seating built into the site, either in a warm corner or on top of a low retaining wall, should be used more often. It can also be used to strengthen the lines of the garden design, or be combined with an adjacent barbecue corner to provide a definite use. A table and bench seating built as one unit is available on the market, and this is an ideal solution for children, who can use it for painting and reading.

UPHOLSTERY

Upholstery for garden furniture is a matter of personal taste. However, in hot climates the brighter colours and stronger patterns usually look better than they do in cooler ones where they often produce too garish an effect.

BARBECUE

One of the gifts of the twentieth century is the barbecue, and all the models available seem to function on the same lines, varying only in the amount of food that can be prepared at any one time. Hibachi stoves from Japan have also become very popular.

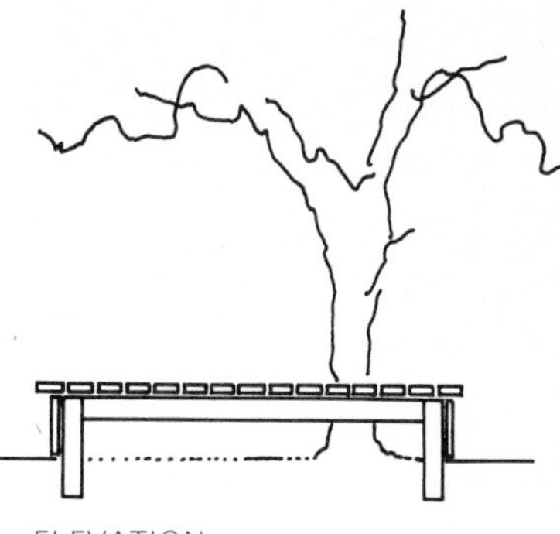

ELEVATION

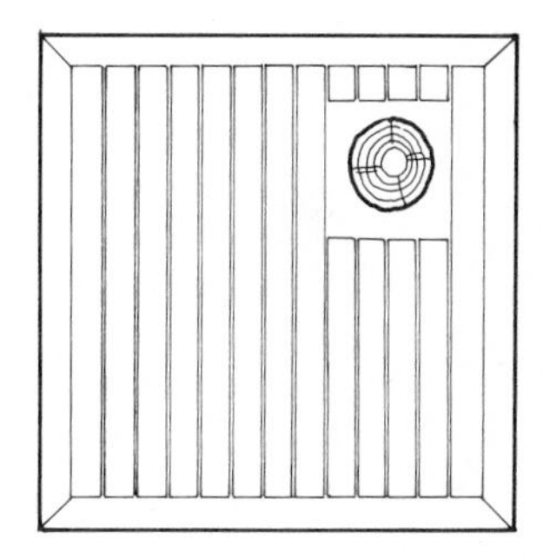

PLAN

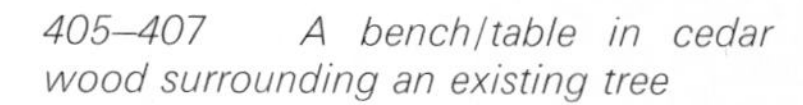

405–407 A bench/table in cedar wood surrounding an existing tree

408, 409 Below left: A bench designed by Sylvia Crowe
Below: Benches of all shapes and sizes

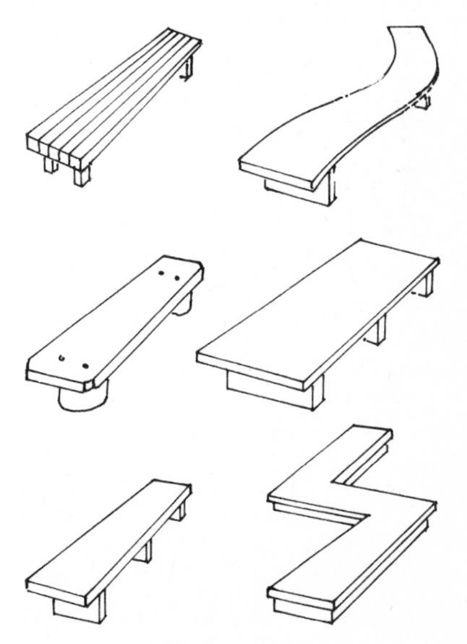

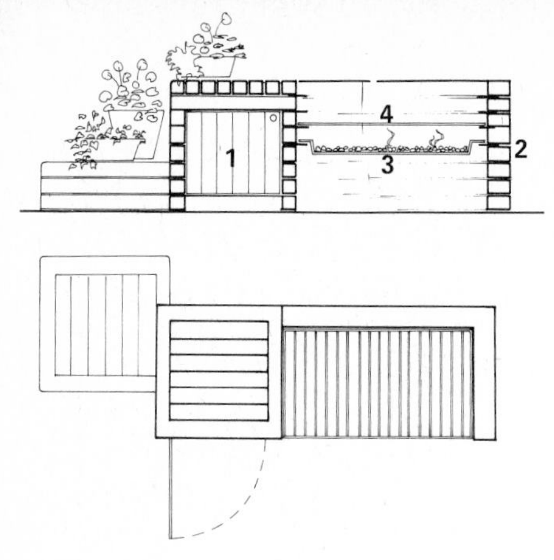

410, 411 A brick barbecue

1 *charcoal storage cupboard with brick work top above*
2 *wall surround of $4\frac{1}{2}$ in. brick*
3 *adjustable charcoal tray*
4 *cooking grid*

412 An outside fireplace

Barbecues have tended to get themselves a bad name, as rain or insects usually seem to disturb parties around them, but when built in a sheltered part of the garden and restricted to family use at weekends and on summer evenings, they are invaluable and extend the use of the garden considerably.

If built *in situ* of brickwork, with a metal grid over the charcoal brazier (a footscraper is ideal), the barbecue can be adapted quite simply to form an open fire when necessary. When building it, allow plenty of bench space for preparing and serving the food and provide cupboards for charcoal and logs.

Groups of pots for bulbs and annuals can disguise the barbecue in winter and early spring, so that it can in fact provide quite an interesting feature out of season. It can also be used to burn paper napkins and other trash.

LIGHTING

If the garden has been designed as an extension of the house, it seems a pity that the effect should vanish when darkness falls.

Lighting can be used to illuminate and dramatize plant material, or, by the use of good-looking fittings on a terrace, to provide a source of interest in itself. Both ways provide a feature to be seen from inside. (The effect of illuminating a garden under snow, for instance, is magical.) It is also important for lighting paths, walks, steps and general outside living areas in both summer and winter.

The level of illumination required in the garden is often overestimated when lighting fitments are being selected – the end result being a blaze of light more suitable for the sea front than a domestic outside room. Lighting outside should generally be subtle and underplayed and should be varied by the use of the occasional coloured lamp.

413

414 Ranch house and terrace at night (Andrew Young)

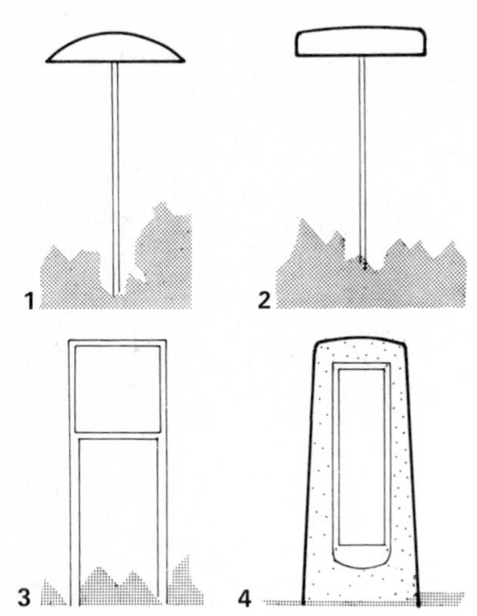

415–423 Outside light fittings. 1, 2, *mushroom-shaped lights;* 3, *permanent fitting mounted on a low frame;* 4, *bollard with inset light;* 5, *miniature flood and spotlight fittings, for emphasis and directional use;* 6, *a louvred fitting which reflects the light downwards – this can be mounted on a post or on the wall;* 7, *a simple, wall-mounted bracket-lantern;* 8, 9, *movable fittings with earth spikes and cable connection case*

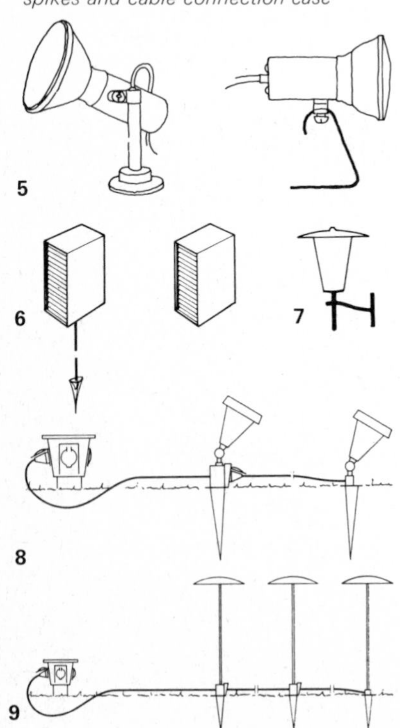

Where a tree, a group of plants, or a stretch of still water is to be illuminated, the source of light and its design are not important, since the viewer is interested in the object being lit rather than the means of lighting it. In fact the lights themselves should not be seen – although the manufacturers would tell us otherwise – and a bulb in an old tin can, as long as it is electrically sound and waterproof will quite often do the job admirably.

The light source should always be set low, so that the tree or shrub is silhouetted against the sky, and positioned so that the viewer never looks into it or walks through its beam.

Lights should be arranged on the spot, moving them around until the right effect is achieved and all cables and wires should either be buried (run in a piece of polythene hose) or hidden. If they are not buried, the lighting can be moved to illuminate particular plants when in flower.

Where the light is to become a decorative feature in itself, like a Chinese lantern, it should be positioned, like lamps indoors, below eye-level. Out of doors there is something particularly ghostly about a source of light shining down from a height.

On a large scale, fluorescent tubes are more successful sources of coloured light than incandescent lamps with colour filters, and they also use less electricity. Green can be used for lighting shrubs and tree foliage, pink to make a feature of copper foliage or deep red floral colour, and gold for highlighting tree trunks. Statuary or structural features should not need coloured lighting.

Where lighting serves a practical purpose, such as illuminating paths and steps, the tendency is again to position it too high, making one bright light do the job three or four lower, dimmer ones could and should do far more attractively. There is a fairly wide range of lighting fitments on the market for just this job.

It can sometimes be an advantage to install a permanent ring main round the area to which temporary installations and surface cables can be connected. Unless you are considerably more than an amateur electrician, help should be sought from someone who is familiar with wiring. In all cases cables must terminate in waterproof boxes and all light fittings and switches must be weatherproof and child-proof. All fittings should be properly earthed.

URNS, POTS AND TUBS

These items can be used either as statuary (a fine urn) or to serve a utilitarian purpose (a mere container to hold plants). An individual container can only rarely fulfil both functions, although a good collection of plants overflowing a simply shaped pot can sometimes be not only utilitarian but also give the effect of statuary. The rule should, therefore, be to have either a decorated pot standing by itself as an aesthetic object, or a simply shaped pot well planted. If one tries to have both, the planting will inevitably hide half the ornamentation anyway.

Planting of pots

In the so-called 'maintenance-free' garden, actual planting can be reduced to small groups of plants in pots which need only autumn and spring replacement.

Pots can either be arranged formally, when the plants in them should be formal also, or be bursting with colour and grouped at random. Strong splashes of colour are better placed in the foreground of the arrangement.

It is invariably wise to plant only one type and colour of flowering plant per pot or tub. The area to be filled is so small that variations of colour in the same pot create a messy effect and the point of the group is lost. If more colours are wanted have another pot as a contrast.

424–426 Top: An interesting collection of pots (A. du Gard Pasley)
Centre: Pottery used as sculpture and complemented by good planting
Below: Ornamental terracotta pots grouped on a terrace (Gordon Patterson)

427

428 *Ordinary terracotta pots and an old copper boiling urn*

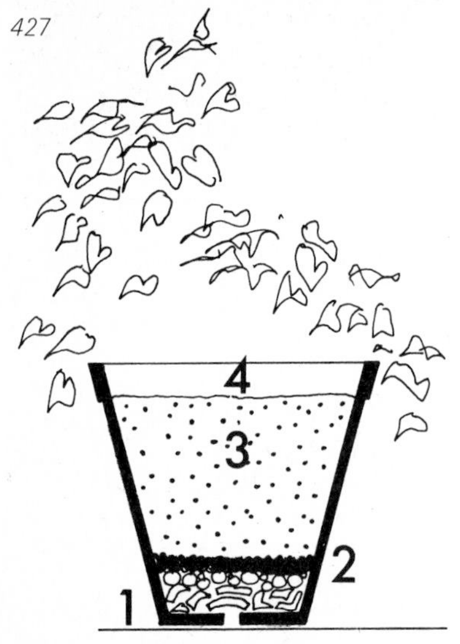

429, 430 *Above: Planting a pot*

1, layer of crocks, one piece covering drainage hole; 2, ash or upturned turf; 3, soil or compost; 4, space for watering

Below: The pot is incidental!

The occasional ivy or strikingly shaped plant (such as yucca) or even an evergreen shrub in a tub with annuals or bulbs planted round it will give the group some interest out of the flowering season.

For spring colour, single tulips and hyacinths are particularly admirable. The taller summer annuals and geraniums produce interest throughout the rest of the year.

The geranium is not to be despised, as it thrives with little attention, flowering even more profusely when ill-watered. Many different colours of geraniums can be used in different containers to provide a splendid contrast.

When selecting shrubs to plant in pots in a sunny position, choose those specimens which thrive with little moisture and full sun.

It goes without saying that all pots or tubs should have adequate drainage material and suitably large holes in the base for surplus water to run off. A layer of broken pots or crocks should go into the bottom with coarse ash on top; if the container is deep enough an upturned turf can be placed over this before filling in with a good vegetable topsoil or a suitable compost. Firm the soil down well before planting so that its level comes a little way below the top of the pot, in order to allow moisture to collect there when the plant is watered.

Urns, pots and tubs come in a variety of materials and shapes to suit all pockets and all tastes, from the most traditional to the very modern. The type used will depend on the variety of plant and the situation involved.

Terracotta

The ordinary red earthenware pot, which comes in all sizes, is made of this. Its simplicity and warm colour make it suitable for most positions.

Terracotta pots do tend to need more water than pots made of non-porous materials, but on the other hand, the plants in them tend to be more vigorous, as terracotta allows the roots to breathe better – an essential factor in plant growth.

Terracotta pots and urns from Italy are available with exterior decoration on them. They are most handsome, either as objects of interest in themselves, or when planted with shrubs. In Italy they are used to hold citrus.

431–433 Top: Sectional concrete pots in a garden by Sylvia Crowe

Above: Concrete drainpipe sections sunk into the ground at different levels

Below: Standard shapes of concrete container

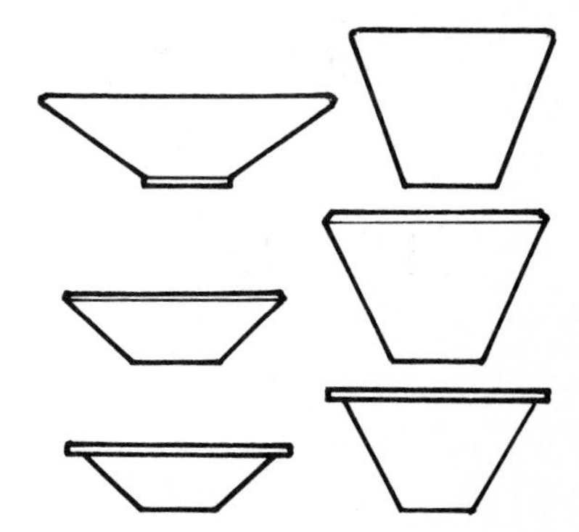

Concrete containers

The thickness of concrete, and proportionate bulk of this type of pot, make it a big and heavy item, more suitable for the town centre than domestic outside room. This type of pot has been so misplaced and misplanted in new housing developments that it has become a cliché. Well planted and sited, however, it can look very well, and it is one of the largest standard containers in most garden centres.

Concrete containers come in varying forms and finishes, but their simplicity of shape can be ruined by too pronounced a surface texture. The shapes available include conical, tubular, hexagonal, rectangular and curved. There are also varieties which can be built up to the desired height with sectional rings. Some of the shallower bowls, however, do not contain enough earth at the edges to encourage plant growth, and it is therefore difficult to get plants to flop over the sides.

Many of the larger pots for municipal work have a fine-gauge wire container sitting inside the bowl, which facilitates plant removal and allows flowering specimens, which have been brought on elsewhere, to be dropped in as replacements.

434 Asbestos containers

Asbestos

The use of this material in the garden is not sufficiently exploited – perhaps because of fears about its effects. It is both strong and durable, can be moulded into beautiful shapes, and its lightness makes it most suitable for roof-garden use.

There are various circular and conical planting bowls on the market which can be painted to give a more attractive finish, and ornamental jars in fine, simple, statuesque shapes are also available.

435

436, 437 Top: Fibreglass containers
Above: Tubs made of fibreglass/cement composition

Fibreglass

Like asbestos, this is a material which could be used much more in the garden. At the moment it is used mainly in the manufacture of reproductions of wooden or metal tubs and urns – the prices being not much different from those of the originals! It could be moulded in beautiful clear colours and smooth, flowing, organic lines to make statuary or containers.

One firm produces simple white containers with a broad turnover lip which, because of their lightness, are ideal for roof gardens.

China

China is not a frostproof material, and this limits the use in the garden of some of the very beautiful pots available; they are, however, admirable for the conservatory or sunroom. This is not a cheap material to use.

Composition

A mixture of glass fibre and cement has produced a light but durable material for garden use. Inexpensive pots are manufactured in various simple shapes ideally suited to the modern home. The finish is either white or natural, but the material is easily painted.

Metal

When metal containers are used in conjunction with plants, care has to be taken to treat them, usually with a bitumastic paint, so that the toxic effects of metallic salts do not injure the plants. There is a tendency in hot weather for the temperature to rise more in metal containers than in those made of other materials, and this leads to rapid drying out. Zinc, aluminium or painted galvanized iron are the metals most often employed and their use is now principally confined to special designs, or to linings for window boxes and wooden tubs.

Stone

Available only in traditional forms, stone containers are very heavy and are most suitable for permanent planting or sink gardens. The types of stone used vary in different localities.

Wood

Wooden tubs or half-barrels (which are becoming scarce) are hard to beat for groupings on a paved area. They come in varying shapes and sizes and can either be left in their natural finish or else varnished or painted. Timber used in their construction includes Burma teak, iroko and oak.

If they are not lined with metal – which will extend their life considerably – check that no toxic liquids were stored in the barrels before they descended to garden use, and if the barrels are to be painted, use non-toxic paint or stain.

Tubs may need to be moved out of the way when more room is needed – for table tennis or a party, for instance and in this case it is simple to make a small trolley to fit under the bottom of the tub. It is also useful to have a reserve tub which can be wheeled in to freshen up a flagging arrangement.

438, 439 Above: A well-planted wooden tub
Below: A wooden Versailles tub with metal bands

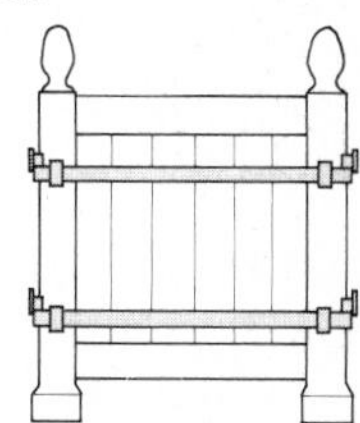

SCULPTURE AND STATUARY

In modern times the first use of sculpture in the garden occurred during the Italian Renaissance. Pieces were easily found in the ruins of ancient Rome, and in fact some of the earliest of these gardens were virtually outdoor museums for the owners to show off their treasures. Placed in front of a dark yew hedge, a statue looked most imposing and provided a focal point of interest in a country where it was difficult to achieve such effects with floral colour.

440

Statuary was used again in French gardens, where the scale of building was enormous, and where raised walks with walls and balustrades provided vantage points from which to look down on to the tortured shapes of the box *broiderie* pattern. In these surroundings, statuary was the natural ornamentation for the walls and walks.

In England, Kent, and later Brown, used sculptural effects in their parkland designs, making a point of interest in an otherwise rather monotonous view by siting an obelisk or temple in an Elysian landscape of smooth greensward, with a background of trees.

441 A fibreglass reproduction of an antique bust

442, 443 Above: A fibreglass wall plaque
Below: A simple sculptural incident

Statues in the classical form were not widely used in England for the next hundred years or so – they were often rather inadequately clothed! Sculptural features were employed, however, in the shape of ornate garden seats and garden houses, often made of iron; and rustic woodwork was also popular. The Edwardian garden tended to carry on this tradition, and the trappings became more and more rustic and sentimental, with wishing wells, rustic arches, and so on. In America the story has been much the same.

Garden ornamentation has not really developed since, and gnomes, storks, shy virgins and painted 'bunnies' still find a place, unfortunately, in the suburban garden.

The short-lived use of modern concrete sculpture in association with the *avant-garde* houses of the 1920s and 1930s seemed to die prematurely although the simple forms were a beautiful foil to the stark architecture and the greenery against which they were set.

Ornamentation should be integrated with the design of the garden, and the accents it provides should not look as if they were applied as an afterthought. Since the garden should, above all else, be a place of peace and relaxation, visually as well as physically, both the scale and the colour of the ornamentation should fit the character of the setting.

Until gardens are designed to reflect and cater for twentieth-century living, however, their ornamentation is bound to be as backward as their design. Many of the ornaments on the market today are, in fact, of eighteenth-century origin – either genuine articles or inferior copies – and far too large in scale for the average modern garden layout. The massiveness of decorative wrought ironwork was beautiful in its original grandiose setting but does not reduce successfully to the scale of suburban ornament. In the same way much of the Victorian or eighteenth-century ornamentation is too detailed for use in a modern garden, where rival influences of tree and shrub shape, flower colour and paving treatments detract from statuesque detail.

Of the traditional materials, bronze, although bright when newly cast, darkens upon contact with the elements and therefore needs a light-coloured background. Marble and stone both mellow outside and harmonize beautifully with surrounding greenery. Lead becomes a soft warm grey, going silver by moonlight, and lends itself to special arrangements and positions. The use of any of these materials has to be considered in relation to the environment involved. (Marble and brick, for instance, do not complement each other, except in special cases.)

444 A classical marble statue

The virile elementary shapes which are produced today in iron, steel or concrete look very well when grouped with plants of contrasting colour or shape.
The high price of modern sculpture does, however, limit its use on a domestic scale, although it is now accepted as an external feature. There is, however, a certain antipathy to modern sculpture, even among those who can afford it. This arises not only because the sculpture is not understood, but also because the sculptor today does not go out to get his market. Few pieces are shown in conjunction with plants or paving, and galleries exhibit in stark surroundings. Until

445 Below: An open-air sculpture exhibition by a lake

446 A Victorian romantic plant-grouping round a statue

447 A flock of fibreglass sheep by Nicholas Munro reminiscent of the deer and cattle in eighteenth-century parks

448 The disappearing gardener

the buyer can see the potential of a piece, he will not put up the money to purchase it.

The possibilities of new materials for garden decoration are unlimited and as yet unexplored; concrete, plastic materials and fibreglass are examples. Pieces of metal left over after a part had been cut out, groupings of springs, dribbles of brightly coloured plastics, piles of glass chippings are all very suitable in the garden for a very modest outlay.

The garden which meanders aimlessly with no focal point of interest is a bore, and a correctly sited object can relieve this tedium and give something for the eye to rest on. In a small area, it can become the focal point of the whole layout and, if it is made of a more or less similar material, can provide a vital link with the house.

The attraction of statuary must be its shape and its positioning in relation to the things around it, and not necessarily the actual subject of the piece: few of us know the story of a mythical god anyway. For the very old and the very young, the tactile quality of an object is important. Sound is another element which can be considered: the play of water or the tinkle of Chinese bells. Much modern sculpture combines all these qualities – and if the piece can be given a functional part to play so much the better.

On a more modest scale, one can incorporate a well-shaped log or tree root, or a grouping of rocks and boulders which, while being decorative, can be used to sit or play on.

Ornamentation does not necessarily have to be free-standing, though it is usually thought of in these terms. A relief or an interesting arrangement of bricks in a wall will serve the purpose. The decorative wall panel is, however, rather more than an ornament, though its effect can be ornamental when contrasted with the right plants.

Garden ornaments today are slowly getting away from the classical influence. The feature needed in our modern gardens has to be on a smaller scale to fit its smaller site. What it is made of, or what its subject-matter may be is unimportant; the primary considerations are that it please its owner and that in its final situation, grouped with the right plants against the right background, it give pleasure the whole year round, making a focal and culminating point in the outside room.

BIBLIOGRAPHY

The author admits to taking much technical information from:

Beazeley, Elizabeth. *Design and Detail of the Space between Buildings*. London 1960
Weddle, A. E. (ed.). *Techniques of Landscape Architecture*. London 1967
both of which he recommends to students of landscape design.

Other books consulted are listed below.

BASIC DESIGN

Brodatz, Phil. *Textures, a photographic Album for Artists and Designers*. New York 1966
Feininger, Andreas. *Form in Nature and Life*. London 1966
Grillo, Paul Jacques. *What is Design?* Chicago 1961
de Sausmarez, Maurice. *Basic Design, the Dynamics of Visual Form*. London 1964

LANDSCAPE DESIGN

Allen of Hurtwood, Lady. *Planning for Play*. London 1968
Chadwick, George F. *The Park and the Town*. London 1966
Colvin, Brenda. *Land and Landscape*. London 1948
Crowe, Sylvia. *Garden Design*. London 1958
The Landscape of Power. London 1958
The Landscape of Roads. London 1960
Jellicoe, G. A. *Studies in Landscape Design*. London 1960
Sitwell, Sir George. *On the Making of Gardens* (1909). London and New York 1951
Sorenson, C. T. *The Origin of Garden Art*. Copenhagen 1963
Tunnard, Christopher. *Gardens in the Modern Landscape*. London 1938

HISTORY OF LANDSCAPE DESIGN

Blomfield, Reginald, and Thomas, F. Inigo. *The Formal Garden in England*. London 1936
Clifford, Derek. *A History of Garden Design*. London 1962
Fox, Helen M. *André Le Nôtre, Garden Architect to Kings*. London 1963
Massingham, Betty. *Miss Jekyll, Portrait of a Great Gardener*. London 1966
Masson, Georgina. *Italian Gardens*. London 1961
Mitford, Nancy. *The Sun King*. London 1966
Robinson, W. *The Wild Garden*. London 1870
Shepherd, J. C., and Jellicoe, G. A. *Italian Gardens of the Renaissance*. London 1953
Stroud, Dorothy. *Capability Brown*. London 1957
Humphrey Repton. London 1962
Wilber, Donald N. *Persian Gardens and Garden Pavilions*. Rutland, Vt./Tokyo 1962

GARDEN DESIGN

Allen of Hurtwood, Lady, and Jellicoe, Susan. *The New Small Garden*. London 1956
Bardi, P. M. *The Tropical Gardens of Burle Marx*. London 1964
Baumann, Ernst. *New Gardens*. Zurich 1955
Church, Thomas D. *Gardens are for People, How to Plan for Outdoor Living*. New York 1955
Jellicoe, Susan and Geoffrey. *Modern Private Gardens*. London 1968
Kassler, Elizabeth B. *Modern Gardens and the Landscape*. New York 1964
Roper, Lanning. *Successful Town Gardening*. London 1957

TREES, SHRUBS AND CONIFERS FOR SCREENING PURPOSES

*Bambusa
Betula (birch)
*Cedrus deodara
Cotoneaster cornubia
*Cotoneaster lactea
*Cotoneaster watereri
*Cupressocyparis leylandii
Kalmia latifolia (mountain laurel)
*Ligustrum (privet)
*Picea abies (spruce)
*Pinus sylvestris
Populus nigra italica
Prunus avium grandiflora (cherry)
*Prunus laurocerasus (laurel)
*Pseudotsuga douglasii (Douglas fir)
*Rhododendron
Rosa rugosa
Sorbus (rowan or mountain ash)
Sorbus aucuparia
*Thuja (arbor vitae)

**Evergreen*

TREES AND SHRUBS THAT WILL GROW IN TOWN GARDENS

Acer platanoides (maple)
Ailanthus glandulosa
Arbutus unedo
Aucuba japonica
Berberis, deciduous variety
Bergenia
Betula
Buddleia davidii varieties
Catalpa
Chaenomeles (Japanese quince)
Cornus (dogwood)
Cotoneaster
Crataegus (hawthorn)
Cytisus scoparius varieties (Scotch broom)
Daphne mezereum
Deutzia
Euonymus
Fatsia (castor-oil plant)
Forsythia
Hedera (ivy)
Hibiscus
Hosta (plantain lily)
Ilex (holly)
Jasminum
Laburnum
Ligustrum
Mahonia aquifolium
Malus (apple)
Pernettya
Philadelphus (mock orange)
Prunus (cherry)
Prunus laurocerasus (laurel)
Pyracantha
Sorbus (mountain ash)
Spiraea
Symphoricarpus (snowberry)
Syringa (lilac)
Veronica
Viburnum
Vinca
Weigela

TREES, SHRUBS AND CLIMBING PLANTS SUITABLE FOR CHALK AND LIMESTONE SOILS

Aralia
Arbutus unedo
Aucuba
Beech
Berberis
Birch
Box
Buddleia
Carpentaria californica
Carpinus (hornbeam)
Cedrus atlantica
Cedrus atlantica glauca
Cercis (redbud)
Chaenomeles (flowering quince)
Choisya (Mexican orange blossom)
Cistus (rock rose)
Clematis
Cornus alba varieties
Corokia
Cotoneaster
Crataegus (hawthorn)
Cupressocyparis leylandii
Cupressus macrocarpa (Monterrey Cypress)
Cytisus (broom)
Davidia involucrata (dove tree)
Deutzia
Elaeagnus
Erica carnea (heath)
Erica darleyensis
Erica mediterranea
Escallonia
Euonymus
Forsythia
Fuchsia
Genista
Hedera (ivy)
Helleborus (Christmas and Lenten rose)
Hibiscus
Hoheria
Hydrangea hortensis (not blue)
Hydrangea villosa
Hypericum
(St John's wort)
Juniperus
Kerria
Laburnum
Ligustrum
Lonicera (honeysuckle)
Magnolia kobus and wilsonii
Malus (apple)
Metasequoia
Philadelphus
Pinus
Polygonum (Fleece flower)
Potentilla
Prunus (all forms)
Pyracantha (firethorn)
Pyrus (pear)
Quercus (oak)
Rhus typhina (Staghorn sumac)
Ribes (currant)
Rose
(also some shrubs & species)
Rubus (blackberries and raspberries)
Skimmia
Spartium
Syringa
Tamarix
Taxus (yew)
Thuja (arbor vitae)
Ulex (gorse)
Veronica
Viburnum
Vinca
Vitis
Weigela

PLANTS FOR DRY, SUNNY POSITIONS

Berberis
Buddleia
Caryopteris
Ceratostigma (plumbago)
Choisya
Clerodendron
Convolvulus
Crataegus prunifolia
Cytisus scoparius varieties
Fuchsia (hardy varieties)
Genista
Hibiscus
Lavandula
Olearia (tree aster)
Perovskia
Potentilla
Prunus (some)
Rhus cotinus (sumac)
Rose species (various)
Rosmarinus (rosemary)
Senecio
Spartium (Spanish or weavers broom)
Tamarix
Ulex (gorse)
Veronica
Vinca

SHRUBS WHICH PREFER OR TOLERATE SHADE

Arundinaria (bamboo)
Aucuba
Berberis
Camellia
Cassiope
Chaenomeles (flowering quince)
Choisya
Clethra (sweet pepper bush)
Cornus alba elegantissima
Cotoneaster
Daphne
Euonymus
Fatsia
Fothergilla
Fuchsia
Gaultheria
Hydrangea
Hypericum
Kalmia latifolia (mountain laurel)
Leucothoe
Mahonia
Pieris
Pyracantha
Rhododendron nudiflorum (pinxter-flower)
Skimmia

PLANTS FOR SHADY WALLS

Camellia
Chaenomeles (flowering quince)
Clematis montana
Cotoneaster horizontalis
Euonymus radicans
Hydrangea petiolaris (climbing hydrangea)
Jasminum nudiflorum (winter jasmine)
Pyracantha
Roses (some)
Schizophragma integrifolia

SHRUBS WHICH PREFER SANDY SOIL

*Amelanchier (shadbush)
Atriplex (saltbush)
Buddleia
*Calluna (heather)
Caryopteris
Cistus
*Cytisus
*Daboecia
*Embothrium
*Enkianthus
*Erica (heath)
Escallonia
*Eucalyptus
*Genista
Gleditschia
Hippophaë
*Hydrangea
*Kalmia
Lavandula
*Ledum
*Leucothoe
Myrica pensylvanica (bayberry)
Olearia
*Pernettya
Philadelphus
Phlomis
*Pieris
Potentilla
Rhus
Rosmarinus
Santolina
Spartium
*Vaccinium (blueberry)
Conifers

These plants need a lime-free soil

PLANTS SUITABLE FOR COASTAL AREAS

Ampelopsis
Arbutus unedo (strawberry tree)
Berberis
Buddleia
Caryopteris
Ceanothus, deciduous varieties
Chaenomeles
Choisya
Cistus
Cornus
Cotoneaster
Cupressocyparis leylandii
*Cupressus macrocarpa
Cytisus
Deutzia
Elaeagnus
*Escallonia
*Euonymus
Fagus (Beech)
Fatsia
Forsythia
*Fuchsia
Hedera
*Hippophaë
*Hydrangea
Hypericum
Kerria
Laburnum
Lavandula vera (Lavender)
Ligustrum
Lonicera nitida
*Olearia haastii (tree aster)
Osmanthus
Pernettya
Philadelphus
Pinus radiata
Pinus sylvestris
Potentilla
Prunus laurocerasus (cherry laurel)
Prunus pissardii
Pyracantha
Rhus
Rosa rubiginosa (sweet briar)
Rosa rugosa – and other strong growing roses
Salix (willow)
Skimmia
Sorbus (mountain ash)
Spiraea
Symphoricarpos (snowberry)
*Tamarix
Veronica
Viburnum opulus (snowball)
Weigela

Suitable for the sea front

PLANTS WHICH ASSIST IN INDICATING SOIL CONDITIONS

Plant	Soil
Sphagnum moss	Wet, acid, peaty soil
Heather and ling (Erica and Calluna spp.)	Dry, acid soil
Rushes and reeds (Juncus and Carex spp.)	Wet, poor soil
Common stinging nettle (Urtica dioica)	Potentially fertile soil
Chickweed (Stellaria media)	Potentially fertile soil
Canterbury bell (Campanula glomerata)	Chalky or limy soil
Thistle (Carduus spp.)	Waste ground
Sheep's sorrel (Rumex acetosella)	Poor, light, dry, acid soil
Foxglove (Digitalis purpurea)	Dry, sandy or gravelly soil
Hoary plantain (Plantago media)	Dry, hard, stony, alkaline soil
Barren or wild strawberry (Potentilla sterilis or Fragaria vesca)	Dry, stony, barren soil
Common furze or gorse (Ulex europaeus)	Poor, infertile soil
Heath bedstraw (Galium saxatile)	Dry, light, acid soil
Silverweed (Potentilla anserina)	Damp places (profuse on clay)

INDEX

Numbers in italic refer to illustrations

PHOTOGRAPH CREDITS

All photographs other than those credited are by the author.

Aerofilms Limited 62; Morley Baer 20; Leonardo Bezzola 6, 62; Ernst Braun 24; Brenda Colvin 9; J. E. Downward 165; Max Duprain 281, 414; Paul E. Genereux 30, 110; Reinhard Grebe 192; Helmut Hahn 61, 70, 75, 271; Stephen Harrison 58, 59; Aenne Heise 51, 275, 276; Mattie Edwards Hewitt 120; Humex Limited 345; Walter Klein 52; Ann-Marie Lagercrantz 13, 166; La Maison Française 375, 378; Lepeschkin 16; Monica Lehmann 18, 194; Thomas Lüttge 361, 365; Michael Manser 54; F. Maurer 269; Sigrid Neubert 268; Adrienne and Peter Oldale 147, 176, 177, 193, 214–16, 219; Old Sturbridge Village 17; Maynard L. Parker 231; Roche 165; Foto Salchow Köln 49; Dolf Schnebli 60; Josef A. Seleger 231, 346, 388; John Stoddart 113; Syndication International 12, 14, 15, 159; Taylor and Green 25, 272, 273, 274; Albert Winkler 24